SEE NO SHARIA

'COUNTERING VIOLENT EXTREMISM' AND THE DISARMING OF AMERICA'S FIRST LINE OF DEFENSE

By Frank J. Gaffney, Jr. and Clare M. Lopez

CIVILIZATION JIHAD READER SERIES
Volume 9

CENTER FOR SECURITY POLICY PRESS

Copyright © 2016

ISBN-13: 978-1530234332
ISBN-10: 1530234336

See No Sharia: 'Countering Violent Extremism' and the Disarming of America's First Line of Defense is published in the United States by the Center for Security Policy Press, a division of the Center for Security Policy.

February 24, 2016

THE CENTER FOR SECURITY POLICY
1901 Pennsylvania Avenue, Suite 201 Washington, DC 20006
Phone: (202) 835-9077 | Email: info@securefreedom.org
For more information, please see securefreedom.org

Book design by Adam Savit
Cover design by Alex VanNess

"Well may the boldest fear and the wisest tremble when incurring responsibilities on which may depend our country's peace and prosperity."

-President James K. Polk,[1] 1845 Inaugural Address

TABLE OF CONTENTS

TABLE OF CONTENTS 5
EXECUTIVE SUMMARY 9
KEY FINDINGS 19
PROLOGUE 25
INTRODUCTION 29
CHAPTER 1: HOLY LAND FOUNDATION CASE 33
   A Successful Prosecution 37
   A Follow-on Prosecution Stillborn 38
   What Happened to the Follow-on Prosecutions? 40
   The Next Battle: Legitimating *Zakat* 42
   A Duty Unfulfilled, a Nation Betrayed 43
CHAPTER 2: THE JIHADISTS' CAMPAIGN TO
   SUPPRESS FREE SPEECH 45
   'Islamophobia' 46
   Prohibiting 'Defamation' of Islam 47
   The OIC's 'Ten-Year Program of Action' 49
   Enlisting the United Nations 51
   UN Human Rights Council Resolution 16/18 and the
      Istanbul Process 53
   Concluding Observations 56
CHAPTER 3: THE FBI AS A CASE STUDY OF AMERICA'S
   UNRAVELING COUNTER-TERRORISM POLICY 57
   The Muslim Brotherhood 'Inside the Wire' 58
   The Bureau's Transformation 61
   Legitimating the Brotherhood 62
   Changing the FBI's Lexicon 64
   Censoring the FBI Training Program 66
   Punishing Those Who 'Offend' Muslims 67
   Diverting the Bureau's Attention 68

CHAPTER 4: SUBMISSION AT THE DEPARTMENT OF HOMELAND SECURITY 71
- Opening Up to the Muslim Brotherhood 73
- Skewing the DHS Lexicon 73
- The DHS under Obama 76
- Organizing for Countering Violent Extremism 76
- The CVE Working Group 77
- Penetrating the Countering Violent Extremism Working Group 79
- Illustrative CVE Working Group Recommendations 82

CHAPTER 5: THE DEPARTMENT OF DEFENSE SUBMITS TO C.V.E. 85
- Rules of Engagement 86
- Culture Cards 87
- The Islamic State 88

CHAPTER 6: SUBMISSION WITHIN OTHER PARTS OF THE U.S. GOVERNMENT 91
- The White House 92
- The State Department 94
- The Intelligence Community 95
- The Department of Justice 96
- The Treasury Department 97
- The Inevitable Endpoint of a See-No-Shariah Policy Approach: The Great Purge 99

CHAPTER 7: THE GREAT PURGE 101
- 'See-No-Shariah' 102
- A Concerted Offensive to Blind Our First Lines of Defense 104
- FBI Rocked by More Incoming Fire 105
- Red (and Green) Letter Day: October 19, 2011 108
- If You See Something, *Don't* Say Anything 115
- Attorney General Eric Holder Supports the Great Purge 118
- The Muslim-American Community: 'Nothing to See Here Folks, Move Along' 119
- Purging the Trainers 120
- The FBI and the Purge 122
- Justice Department Purge Guidelines 125
- The FBI Capitulates 126
- Conclusion 127

CHAPTER 8: AFTER THE PURGE: HARD LESSONS UNLEARNED 131
- Egypt and the Muslim Brotherhood 132
- 'We, the People' 134

    Clarity About the Brotherhood 135
    The Justice Department Leaves Open the Door to
        Shariah Blasphemy Restrictions 136
    CVE's "Bitter Harvest": Benghazi and the Boston Marathon 138

CHAPTER 9: THE WHITE HOUSE SUMMIT ON COUNTERING VIOLENT EXTREMISM 143
    Setting the Stage for a CVE Summit 144
    Early Indications that Islamists Don't Like CVE 145
    Plunging Ahead with a White House CVE Summit 146
    The Islamic Supremacists Push Back 148
    What 'Model' Programs? 150
    The Summit Goes Bust 152
    Taking Both Paths – A Dual Tactical Approach 155
    Groupthink-Imposed Willful Blindness at the Summit 157
    After the Summit 158
    A New 'Model Community' for CVE: New York City? 160

CHAPTER 10: CONGRESS AND COUNTERING VIOLENT EXTREMISM 163
    The Unhappy Story of the 'National Security Five' 164
    The 114th Congress and CVE 165

CHAPTER 11: CVE'S DEVASTATING IMPACT ON OUR FIRST LINES OF DEFENSE 171
    Extending the Welcome Mat for Top Jihadists 172
    Meetings as Submission 173
    Enabling Material Support for Terrorism 174
    Admitting Unvettable Syrian Refugees 176
    The Destruction of Our First Lines of Defense 178

EPILOGUE 183
    More of the 'See-No-Sharia' 184
    Pandering to the Islamic Supremacists 184
    Dissembling About Inconvenient Facts 186
    A Whistleblower Reveals the Damage Being Done by CVE 188
    Disappearing the Dots 190
    The White House Doubles Down on CVE 191
    The Islamists Next Gambit on Capitol Hill 192
    'Global Engagement' or Unilateral Disarmament in the
        War of Ideas 193
    There Goes New York 195
    Conclusion - Where Do We Go From Here? 197

ACTION RECOMMENDATIONS 199
    USG: Executive Branch 200
    USG: Legislative Branch 201
    USG: Judicial Branch 202

U.S. Society: Academia 202
U.S. Society: Law Enforcement 203
U.S. Society: Media 203
U.S. Society: Workplace 204
APPENDIX I: HIGHLIGHTS OF THE HOLY LAND FOUNDATION CHRONOLOGY 205
APPENDIX II: OTHER SPECIALLY DESIGNATED GLOBAL TERRORIST ORGANIZATIONS LINKED TO HAMAS 211
APPENDIX III: DEPARTMENT OF JUSTICE LETTER TO REP. SUE MYRICK REGARDING CAIR'S TIES TO HAMAS .. 213
APPENDIX IV: TIMELINE OF MUSLIM BROTHERHOOD FRONTS' INVOLVEMENT IN CVE POLICYMAKING 215

EXECUTIVE SUMMARY

Words matter. And in the present phase of what we call "The War for the Free World," it is of the utmost importance to the national and homeland security that the United States' first lines of defense be free to use the correct words to: name and define the enemy; describe accurately its threat doctrine; and develop and implement an effective strategic plan of action for victory.

This book traces the course of one of the most successful influence operations in American history: the Muslim Brotherhood's penetration and increasing success at subordinating our security to its jihadist agenda. That agenda is designed to prevent us, first, from properly understanding our foes and thereafter, incrementally to dismantle our ability to resist them and their Global Jihad Movement.

CHAPTER ONE: THE WATERSHED HOLY LAND FOUNDATION CASE

America's largest and most significant prosecution of funding for terrorism, *U.S. v Holy Land Foundation*, is a useful prism through which to view the challenge the country faces from Islamic supremacists. The U.S. government's prosecution of this shariah-adherent Texas-based charity demonstrated conclusively that what we face in the global jihad movement are enemies who are assiduously pursuing our destruction. The trial also showed that the jihadists are employing various techniques, from the pre-violent to the violent, to accomplish that goal.

The government's deliberate and intentional neglect of the evidence, indictments and 108 guilty verdicts against American Muslim Brotherhood front groups for support of Hamas terrorism in the Holy Land Foundation trial will ultimately be seen as evidence, indictments and guilty verdicts against the Obama administration, itself. After the trial's conclusion, anyone who remained knowingly involved with these groups should be considered a willing accessory to the subversive activities of the Brotherhood's network in America.

At the very moment in history when they could have, and should have, acted decisively to protect both our homeland and the supremacy of our Constitution, those elected and appointed to safeguard of our security and unalienable rights chose to abdicate their responsibilities. In so doing, they have – knowingly or unknowingly – subordinated *the supreme law of the land* to a foreign one (i.e., shariah) and its agents. They have submitted to insidious and potentially mortal threats to our freedoms, cynically disguised in the red, white and blue trappings of "Civil Rights and Civil Liberties."

Many times, history has shown us that those who sacrifice their integrity for a false sense of security will inevitably lose both. The Holy Land Foundation trial provided the trajectory of a fundamental betrayal of trust – suppression of free speech – which has left our first lines of defense severely handicapped, if not actually incapable of performing their vital missions.

CHAPTER TWO: THE JIHADISTS' CAMPAIGN TO SUPPRESS FREE SPEECH

In order to understand what has happened to U.S. counter-terrorism policy over the past fifteen years, it is essential to understand some of the external forces that have been operating since before 9/11. The purpose of these forces has been to define what non-Muslims can know, say and do about the threat posed by global jihadists as a means of securing our defeat. They have had dramatic successes with regard to each of these targets.

An early focus of the Islamic supremacists' efforts has been inventing and popularizing the term "Islamophobia," which was quickly assimilated into the global vernacular. Additionally, the Istanbul Process – with its roots in UN Human Rights Council Resolution 16/18 – marks the zenith to date of the Global Jihad Movement's international campaign to secure the non-Muslim world's submission to shariah, starting with the adoption worldwide of what amount to its blasphemy restrictions.

Throughout this campaign, critics have expressed grave concern that the so-called "defamation of religion" gambit was not only contrary to international law, but also to the U.S. Constitution's guarantee of freedom of expression. They have noted that its embrace by Western governments opens the door to the actual *suppression* of free speech via hate-speech legislation and the prosecution of those deemed to have transgressed such laws. In addition, the adoption of such restrictions by the media, publishers and social media platforms will have the practical effect of silencing those who are, nonetheless, willing to challenge the jihadists.

The Obama administration has simply disregarded such concerns, choosing instead to align itself with and otherwise submit to the demands of the OIC to criminalize Islamophobia and/or defamation of religion. This behavior fits a larger, and now well-established, pattern of accommodating Islamic supremacists – even to the point of allowing them to participate directly in the development and implementation of policy towards "terrorism," "violent extremism" and other euphemisms for the *real* present danger: the global jihad.

CHAPTER THREE: THE FBI AS A CASE STUDY OF ISLAMIST INFLUENCE OPERATIONS AND AMERICA'S UNRAVELING COUNTER-TERRORISM POLICY

Using the Federal Bureau of Investigation as a prime example, it is evident in this analysis and those that will follow concerning other elements of our first lines of defense that we have been grievously disarmed as a result of: assiduous influence operations by Islamic supremacists; the help they receive from allies on the Left; and official policies that enable, or at least accommodate, such initiatives.

As a result, the nation's premier law enforcement agency has favored confused euphemisms over clear language as the basis for its approach. For example, the FBI's 2008 "Counterterrorism Analytical Lexicon," identifies the threat of:

> "[A]ny ideology that encourages, endorses, condones, justifies, or supports the commission of a violent act or crime against the United States, its government, citizens, or allies in order to achieve political, social, or economic changes, or against individuals or groups who hold contrary opinions..."

This stands in stark contrast to the explicit 2002 testimony by then-Executive Assistant Director of the FBI Counterintelligence Division, Dale Watson. Rather than obfuscate the threat, Watson defined it clearly as, "The radical international jihad movement, formalized terrorist organizations, and state sponsors of international terrorism." Comparing these two conflicting statements charts an ominous trajectory of willful blindness and official submission to Islamic supremacists that, unfortunately, is not unique to the FBI. Indeed, this dynamic is evident throughout the other U.S. government agencies responsible for our national and homeland security.

CHAPTER FOUR: SUBMISSION AT THE DEPARTMENT OF HOMELAND SECURITY

On July 27, 2005, a key moment arrived in the U.S. government's official embrace of the Islamists' preferred euphemism, "Countering Violent Extremism." NPR host Steve Inskeep was among the first in the media to announce that Obama administration and military officials seem to be shifting their public vocabulary from the "Global War On Terrorism" to the "Global Struggle Against Violent Extremism" (G-SAVE).

The evidence of United States ambassadors, presidential administrations, and high-ranking officials in the U.S. government attending meetings with known Muslim Brotherhood members, shows the beginnings of submission to the countering violent extremism thought-process and vernacular. The creation of several campaigns, memos and internal working groups, displays the Department of Homeland Security's high level of involvement in furthering the CVE agenda.

Many of these individuals and/or the Islamic organizations they represent have been engaged in years-long adversarial relationships with the USG over its counter-terrorism and law enforcement policies. What is important to understand is that often, they were aided and abetted in such struggles by DHS.

Real damage is being done by allowing American-based Muslim Brotherhood front groups "inside the wire" of government policymaking. It adds insult to serious injury that organizations that share with our enemies a commitment to Islamic supremacism are able to obtain protective cover through their involvement with the CVE apparatus.

CHAPTER FIVE: THE DEPARTMENT OF DEFENSE SUBMITS TO CVE

At the tip of the spear of our first lines of defense are the United States armed forces. They have borne the brunt of the heavy lifting in what was once known as the Global War on Terror. And they have been terribly served, as has the nation they strive to protect, by the serial accommodations made by our leaders under both parties to Islamic supremacism.

During the George W. Bush administration, the U.S. military was hamstrung by efforts to win the "hearts and minds" of Muslim populations with which we were at war. Successive civilian and military leaders at the Pentagon have drunk the Kool Aid of political correctness, acquiesced to White House directions reflecting the demands of our enemies, foreign and domestic, and, in the process, needlessly exposed our men and women in uniform to peril and defeat.

During the Obama administration, the U.S. Department of Defense (DOD) began modifying its "Rules of Engagement" in Iraq and Afghanistan to accommodate the sensibilities of Muslims in the countries where the USG was trying to introduce democracy.

The bottom line for our men and women in uniform, and for the rest of us, must be: If fighting a war by the proxy of public relations (a.k.a. CVE) has not worked with the Taliban, al Qaeda or ISIS – or, for that matter with Boko Haram, Hamas, Iran, al Shabaab, al Nusra or other Islamic supremacists, then why on earth should we expect the CVE approach to work any better here in America?

CHAPTER SIX: SUBMISSION WITHIN OTHER PARTS OF THE U.S. GOVERNMENT

It is beyond the scope of this short book to document comprehensively the extent to which the U.S. government writ large has been penetrated and subverted by the influence operations of Islamic supremacists, profoundly compromising the nation's first lines of defense. A few examples from other relevant executive branch agencies will hopefully suffice to round out the foregoing, more detailed examinations of the conduct in this regard of the FBI and the Departments of Homeland Security and Defense.

Needless to say, in the absence of policy direction from the Commander-in-Chief and his immediate senior subordinates in the Executive Mansion and National Security Council, it seems unlikely that those elsewhere in the national and homeland security agencies would have willingly followed the trajectory of accommodation and submission to the Muslim Brotherhood.

This saga accelerated dramatically with the "Great Purge," when CT training designed to equip our first lines of defense – especially the FBI, intelligence community and Departments of Defense and Homeland Security – that was deemed "offensive" (or even *possibly* offensive) to Muslims was summarily eliminated.

CHAPTER SEVEN: THE GREAT PURGE

As with similar events throughout history, the "Great Purge" that was inflicted upon America's front lines of defense against the Global Jihadist Movement in 2011-2012 quickly turned into a feeding frenzy. It began with the FBI and the rest of the relevant agencies trying to accommodate the demands of "outreach partners" in the American Muslim community for heightened sensitivity to their feelings. But it wound up sucking those agencies into a vortex of political warfare waged by Islamists and the radical leftists who support and enable them, a true "Red-Green axis" that is determined to shut down their missions under the pretext of respecting "Civil Rights and Civil Liberties" (CRCL).

During this period, virtually the entire U.S. government turned away from counter-terrorism threat analysis and responses rooted in facts – and towards a so-called civil rights-based approach known as Countering Violent Extremism. If the power of American's civil rights and civil liberties were really being used to *protect* our freedoms as our Founding Fathers intended, CRCL would serve as an impenetrable shield against even the faintest hint of shariah in America. As a sure proof of this commitment, we would not see our borders shattered, but rather protected, with members of the law enforcement community serving as watchmen, instead of serving as targets themselves.

Sadly, what we see today is just the opposite: CRCL is being used by the Obama administration as a sledgehammer, to pound our first lines of defense into submission on the anvil of Countering Violent Extremism. In addition, many lessons can be learned from Egypt's experience with the Muslim Brotherhood before, during and after the revolution that was egged on by American policymakers.

CHAPTER EIGHT: AFTER THE PURGE: HARD LESSONS UNLEARNED

On February 10, 2011, Director of National Intelligence James Clapper appeared in open session before the House Intelligence Committee and made his evidently scripted, and certainly malfeasant, remarks about the Muslim Brotherhood's supposedly "secular" and benign nature. He was accompanied on that occasion by FBI Director Mueller, who mildly dissented from that preposterous characterization.

The government's Countering Violent Extremism approach has created – and continues to impose – formidable disincentives for law enforcement and counter-terror specialists to conduct the necessary research, and/or adequately to question individuals seeking entry into America (whether a U.S. citizen, legal permanent resident or foreign national). In turn, these deficiencies prevent us from protecting our country as effectively as official oaths require.

Far from considering in the wake of the disasters of the Great Purge and the debacles that followed – and, to varying degrees, flowed from it – a much-needed and serious course-correction, the Obama administration has doubled down on its commitment to the disastrous CVE/CRCL approach. This attitude was particularly evident in the February 2015 White House "Summit To Counter Violent Extremism."

CHAPTER NINE: THE WHITE HOUSE SUMMIT ON COUNTERING VIOLENT EXTREMISM

It is beyond the scope of this monograph to report on the proceedings of the entire, three-day White House Countering Violent Extremism Summit in February 2015. We will, however, explore the extent to which this event illuminated the Muslim Brotherhood's deep penetration of the Obama administration and the impunity with which the USG's Islamist interlocutors have responded to their perception that America is *submitting* to them. This has emboldened efforts to complete the CVE effort by repeating at the state and local level what has been accomplished at the federal level.

Tragically, it is not hard to see where such accommodations to the Islamists will take the organization that has superbly performed the immensely difficult task of protecting the top jihadist target in America – New York City. Thanks to a recently imposed settlement of litigation brought against it by a coalition of hard left and Islamist organizations (the Red-Green axis), the New York Police Department will have to labor under the kind of crippling constraints in terms of situational awareness and law enforcement capabilities that have rendered the nation's other front lines of defense so ill-equipped to counter the threat posed by Islamic supremacism.

CHAPTER TEN: CONGRESS AND COUNTERING VIOLENT EXTREMISM

Given all that has been written to this point about the Obama administration's abdication of its responsibility in the face of the threat of Islamic supremacism in America, one might be forgiven for assuming the United States Congress – particularly one led in both houses by the opposition party – would be holding the administration accountable for the damage it is doing to our first lines of defense. Unfortunately, you would be wrong.

In 2012, five members of Congress wrote letters to the inspectors general of four federal departments and the Office of the Director of National Intelligence requesting information on the involvement of Muslim Brotherhood front groups in those agencies. The vicious, bipartisan response to this legitimate inquiry for information made it clear to every lawmaker: Taking on the Islamists could be hazardous to one's future in Congress.

In 2015, the chairman of the House Homeland Security Committee, Rep. Michael McCaul, introduced H.R. 2899, the "Countering Violent Extremism Act of 2015", which would create a new agency within DHS tasked to develop strategies and data concerning "violent extremism" within the government. The practical effect would be to institutionalize the Obama administration's seriously defective CVE policy and associated programs.

CHAPTER ELEVEN: CVE'S DEVASTATING IMPACT ON OUR FIRST LINES OF DEFENSE

No study of the Obama administration's embrace of the Countering Violent Extremism approach to counter-terrorism would be complete without an assessment of its impact – and that of other, derivative policies and initiatives – on the mission and morale of federal law enforcement officers and other professionals manning our first lines of defense.

As with the message sent to legislators via the Red-Green and even Republican attacks on Rep. Michele Bachmann et.al., the Lieutenant Colonel Matthew Dooley affair – in which, as an instructor at the National Defense University, Dooley faced punishment and public shaming over his teaching of an approved curriculum because it addressed issues of Islamic doctrine – served notice on our men and women in uniform, and those in the other agencies that make up our Nation's first lines of defense, more broadly: You deviate from the party-line on the "see-no-shariah" CVE approach to homeland and national security at your peril.

The cumulative effect of the Countering Violent Extremism policies and programs has not only been to cripple those we rely upon to protect us. It has actually emboldened those against whom such protection is needed now more than ever. And it has left our nation and its people far more vulnerable, at home and abroad.

KEY FINDINGS

- In the years since 9/11, Muslim Brotherhood operatives have gained access to the top levels of U.S. national security leadership under presidencies of both parties.

- The peril associated with such access is evident from the fact that – as established in the nation's largest terrorism financing trial, *U.S. v. Holy Land Foundation* – the mission of the Muslim Brotherhood in North America is "destroying…Western civilization from within."

- One ominous symptom of the influence operations that have been enabled by the government's penetration by such enemies has been the removal from the official lexicon of all references to the role played by Islamic doctrine, law and scripture in inspiring jihad (holy war) against this country.

- The cumulative, subversive effect of Muslim Brotherhood and other Islamist influence operations has become increasingly acute over the course of the Obama presidency. Literally from that administration's inception until the present day, the U.S. government has deliberately engaged in "Muslim outreach" to Islamic supremacist individuals and organizations known to be tied to the Brotherhood. In some cases, such individuals have been enlisted as advisors and appointees on sensitive matters of national security. This has, in effect, allowed the enemy "inside the wire" – a vantage point from which they have intensively advanced policies, initiatives and programs intended to cripple the U.S. ability to defend against the Global Jihad Movement (GJM).

- An evidence-driven strategy needed to identify, confront and defeat the GJM has been replaced by one dictated by priorities dubbed "Civil Rights/Civil Liberties" (CRCL), "Engagement and Dialogue" and "community outreach." The practical effect of the latter has been to obscure and protect Islamic supremacists in our midst. These CRCL priorities have also been extended to foreign nationals, and into the arena of foreign policy.

- The U.S. government's approved catch-all label for this mutated approach to national and homeland security strategy is "Countering Violent Extremism" (CVE), which was demonstrably adopted under the influence of Muslim Brotherhood-associated "community leaders." Here, too, a number of these operatives have been tapped as advisors or implementers of CVE initiatives within federal and/or state and local agencies.

- The Countering Violent Extremism approach has had the practical effect of rationalizing the diversion of official attention and energies from confronting Islamic supremacism and its jihad. Instead, much official scrutiny is now applied to groups said to be equally, if not actually *more*, threatening than the jihadists. According to CVE, the latter include: "Constitutionalists," veterans, Tea Party activists, anti-abortionists and gun-owners.

- Muslim Brotherhood front groups routinely collude with radical leftist organizations such as the American Civil Liberties Union (ACLU) and the Southern Poverty Law Center (SPLC). Prime targets for this sort of "Red-Green" axis are U.S. national security policies and capabilities and the constitutional freedoms – especially the guaranteed right to free expression – they are supposed to safeguard. Their lash-up with leftist allies has afforded Islamic supremacists even greater access to, influence over and cooperation from the Obama administration in subverting the nation's first lines of defense against all enemies, foreign and domestic.

- Thanks in part to such influence operations, the Obama administration has engaged in an intensifying campaign to stifle free speech that "defames" Islam or "offends" its adherents. This campaign aligns closely with, and has helped advance, that of the Organization of Islamic Cooperation (OIC), whose so-called "10-Year Program of Action" aimed at prohibiting and punishing criticism of Islamic figures, doctrine or practices world-wide has been institutionalized by the UN Human Rights Council in its Resolution 16/18. The OIC's 10-year plan portentously marked its tenth anniversary in December 2015.

- At the insistence of the Red-Green axis, a "Great Purge" was instituted by the Obama administration in 2011-2012. This devastating influence operation allowed Islamic supremacists and as-yet-unidentified "subject matter experts" to purge government trainers, training materials and other information deemed "offensive to Muslims" from the training curricula of every major security-related agency in the U.S. government, including the Intelligence Community and Pentagon.

- The practical effect of the Great Purge has been to deny personnel in our first lines of defense an accurate understanding of, jihad, the Caliphate or the Global Islamic Movement. Harsh treatment of those who deviate from what might be called a "see-no-shariah" party-line has established that doing so is now a career-ending offense. The message has not been lost on those charged with our national and homeland security.

- CVE and the Great Purge – further impelled by incessant criticism and specious legal action (a.k.a. "lawfare") from Muslim Brotherhood-linked individuals and organizations and their leftist allies – has also drastically altered commonsense rules that used to govern FBI and local law enforcement terror investigations. Now, for example, "probable cause" evidentiary practices have been trumped by Civil Rights and Civil Liberties concerns, resulting in handicapped or prematurely terminated inquiries and cases. Public safety and the common defense are poorly served, but the Islamic supremacist agenda inexorably advances.

- A recent example of this extending to local law enforcement has been the New York Police Department acquiescing to the demands of a coalition of hard left and Islamist organizations to purge a professional and important analytical counterterrorism product known as the *Radicalization in the West* report, and to put an end to surveillance and investigations of mosques with known and suspected terror ties.

- The Islamic supremacist campaign to curtail Americans' First Amendment right to free speech reached Capitol Hill with the introduction in December 2015 of House Resolution 569. This proposed bill uses language about "violence, bigotry and hateful rhetoric towards Muslims" that is alarmingly reminiscent of OIC and UN Human Rights Council efforts to prohibit and punish "defamation of religion." In practice, such restrictions – which map to shariah blasphemy codes – are meant to protect exclusively the civil rights and civil liberties *of Muslims*.

- The forcible imposition of the CVE narrative by the U.S. government actually costs lives. The crippling "rules of engagement" it has spawned exact a price in blood from our military. And the FBI and local law enforcement officers face an impossible task at home insofar as CVE strips them of the ability to recognize and act on essential "indicators and warnings" at the ideological stage of jihad – i.e., *before* a violent attack occurs, such as those at Ft. Hood, Texas, Boston, Massachusetts, Chattanooga, Tennessee and San Bernardino, California.

PROLOGUE

On January 13, 1944,[2] a group of senior aides to then-Treasury Secretary Henry Morgenthau, Jr.[3] released *A Report on the Acquiescence of the FDR Government in the Murder of the Jews.* Their investigations uncovered a pattern of attempts by the U.S. State Department to obstruct rescue opportunities and block the flow of information about the Holocaust to the United States. Noting that the Jewish refugee issue had become "a boiling pot on [Capitol] Hill," the opening sentences of the report stated:

> One of the greatest crimes in history, the slaughter of the Jewish people in Europe, is continuing unabated. This Government has for a long time maintained that its policy is to work out programs to serve those Jews of Europe who could be saved. I am convinced on the basis of the information which is available to me that certain officials in our State Department, which is charged with carrying out this policy, have been guilty not only of gross procrastination and willful failure to act, but even of willful attempts to prevent action from being taken to rescue Jews from Hitler.

The same "gross procrastination and willful failure to act," along with overt and "willful attempts to prevent action from being taken," has been the Obama administration's standard operating procedure vis-à-vis what is officially known as Countering Violent Extremism (CVE), the doctrine through which it views what was once considered the Global War on Terror. And, as in 1944, the increasing threat of violent jihad attacks here in America has the potential to become another "boiling pot on Capitol Hill" – and, increasingly, a crisis of confidence in our government on the part of the American people.

Like the conclusions of the Morgenthau team's report on the Holocaust, the bottom line of this monograph about can be summed up in two words: They knew.

Who are "they"? What is it they "knew"?

"They" are the elected- and non-elected representatives within the executive, judicial and legislative branches of the U.S. Government, who have been entrusted by the American people with the solemn and sworn duty to support and defend the Constitution of the United States against all enemies, foreign and domestic. This was an indispensable obligation before September 11, 2001, but it became an absolute imperative after 9/11.

To be sure, we had, as a nation wrestled with the threat of domestic terrorism before 9/11. Two events in 1993 – one a matter of intense public scrutiny at the time, the other which remained a state secret for another fifteen years – illustrated the two poles between which U.S. counterterrorism policy veered in the decade before jihadists flew commercial jetliners into the World Trade Center and the Pentagon.

As Andrew C. McCarthy has discussed in *Willful Blindness: A Memoir of the Jihad*,[4] the U.S. government responded to the first jihadist attack on the World Trade Center with the successful prosecution of the Blind Sheik, Omar Abdel Rahman, and his co-conspirators.

That same year, other Islamic supremacists associated with the Muslim Brotherhood's Palestine Committee[5] were monitored by the FBI in a clandestine meeting in Philadelphia with representatives of the Brotherhood's Palestinian franchise, Hamas.[6]

In its course, they agreed to set up a front group[7] known as the Council on American Islamic Relations (CAIR)[8] to raise funds for Hamas and conduct political warfare on its behalf. The government allowed them to execute their plan and, as we shall discuss, has actually actively engaged with CAIR's founders and others associated with that organization.

This monograph is written with the hope that we as a Nation will have the wherewithal to recover, and to avoid similar gross lapses in judgment in the years ahead.

                                        Frank J. Gaffney, Jr.
                                        Clare M. Lopez

                                        15 February 2016

INTRODUCTION

In March 2003, Tom Ridge, the first Secretary of the Department of Homeland Security Secretary, wrote that his new agency was "Dedicated to preventing terrorist attacks within the United States, reducing America's vulnerability to terrorism, and minimizing the damage from potential attacks and natural disasters."

This monograph is intended to explain both how and why those in the front lines of defense of our country have been gravely handicapped in fulfilling these essential goals.

The explanation must start with the campaign that Islamic supremacists launched years before 9/11 to blind the Free World and those sworn to defend it. This campaign has had remarkable success. These include the widespread adoption of the concept of "Islamophobia" (first conjured by Islamic supremacists and their friends on the left in the early 1990s)[9] and the various achievements of the Organization of Islamic Cooperation's (OIC)[10] "program of action." This program, which is explicitly aimed at criminalizing the "**defamation**[11] of Islam," began gaining momentum within the United Nations in 1998,[12] and continues in earnest to this day.

The following pages provide a review of the evolution of the U.S. government's official "counter-terrorism" policy over the past two decades.

In particular, this monograph traces the metamorphosis of this policy – which early in the George W. Bush presidency was guided by an objective, facts-based law enforcement approach, but by the latter days of that administration had morphed into a subjective, policy-driven approach defined by imperatives defined by what has become known as "Civil Rights and Civil Liberties (CRCL)[13]."[i] This cancerous approach has metastasized under the Obama administration.

We will start with a discussion of what was at one time the preeminent Muslim charity in the United States – the Holy Land Foundation (HLF)[14] – and how it came to be designated and prosecuted as a terrorist organization for materially supporting Hamas. That Palestinian franchise of the Muslim Brotherhood had itself been designated as a terrorist organization in 1995.

During the early post-9/11 phase, President Bush issued on September 24, 2001[15] an Executive Order entitled "Blocking Property and Prohibiting Transactions With Persons Who Commit, Threaten to Commit, or Support Terrorism." This directive gave rise to *Operation Green Quest*, which was unveiled[16] by then-Assistant Attorney General Michael Chertoff, who headed the U.S. Department of Justice (DOJ) Criminal Division. It was authorized to "closely examine underground financial systems, illicit charities and corrupt financial institutions."

Regrettably, this successful[17] Operation was shut down at the end of June 2003[18] for various reasons, including a lack of coordination and other conflicts[19] between U.S. Immigration and Customs Enforcement (ICE)[20] and the FBI in on-going terrorism financing cases. It was also vehemently opposed by[21] influential leaders of MB front groups[22] in the Washington, D.C. area –including those with ties to individuals who were subjects of the investigation.[ii]

Another early indication of the ominous trajectory U.S. counter-terrorism policy would take during the Bush years came on December 12, 2002[23] when Secretary of State Colin Powell announced the creation of the U.S.-Middle East Partnership Initiative (MEPI).[24] This was a program designed, in his words:

> ...to be a "continuation, and a deepening, of our longstanding commitment to working with all peoples of the Middle East to improve their daily lives and to help them face the future with hope." In light of the continuing war against terrorism, the reconstruction of Iraq, and increased violence in Israel and the West Bank and Gaza Strip, MEPI emphasizes what some analysts call the softer[25] elements of U.S. foreign policy: foreign aid, trade, education, and democratization. MEPI is a key component in the Bush administration's policy of promoting democracy in the Middle East.[iii]

By 2005-2006, federal agencies were engaged in behind-the-scenes cooperation with some of the very same individuals and organizations they had been investigating just a year or two earlier in connection with the Holy Land Foundation case and/or Operation Green Quest.

As we shall see, this carefully coordinated program of quiet cooperation resulted in the promulgation in 2008[26] of the *Words Matter* memo, which includes one of the first uses of the phrase "Violent Extremist" in an official USG document.

[ii] A published report describes the role Muslim Brotherhood leaders may have played in terminating Operation Green Quest: "Just two weeks after the Customs task force raided the Saudi-backed groups in northern Virginia, two leading Muslim activists with ties to the groups were allowed to meet with Paul O'Neill, then the secretary of the Treasury Department (which, at the time, controlled Customs) to complain about the conduct of the raids. The meeting was arranged by Grover Norquist, the influential Republican activist; Norquist is also the founder and former chair of the Islamic Institute, a conservative Muslim outreach group in which both of the men who met with O'Neill are officers and which has received funding from some of the raided individuals and groups, including Abdurahman Alamoudi." See: http://www.islamdaily.org/en/charities/2237.charity-cases-why-has-the-bush-administration-fail.htm). For more on Grover Norquist's role in enabling Muslim Brotherhood influence operations, see: *Agent of Influence: Grover Norquist and the Assault on the Right* (http://www.amazon.com/Agent-Influence-Norquist-Security-Archival/dp/0985029218).

[iii] MEPI remains active to this day. For a review of recent MEPI publications and fact sheets, see MEPI's publication page located at the Department of State website.

Coincidentally, the Holy Land Foundation trial concluded in November 2008[27] at approximately the same moment in as the publication of the *Words Matter* memo, with the jury returning 108 guilty verdicts against five of the HLF's Islamic supremacists [28] charged with material support of Hamas.

Again, these two events show us the growing contrast between a law enforcement-based counter-terrorism approach and a CRCL-based one.

As we shall also see, matters have become dramatically worse during the presidency of Barack Obama. Thanks to the expanded influence of Muslim Brotherhood operatives and other influential Islamic supremacists, the U.S. government's official counter-terrorism policy has now mutated into something called Countering Violent Extremism (CVE).[29]

We will explore: the insidious nature of this CVE program; how it is being practiced and exacerbated through what is known [30] as "engagement" [31] and "dialogue" [32] (E&D) with "American Muslim communities" [iv]; the detrimental impact it is having in both domestic and foreign policy arenas; and suggestions for how this disastrous situation can be corrected.

This narrative will detail the conduct of various federal agencies that make up our nation's first line of defense as we amass evidence of the failure of U.S. policy-makers to come to grips with the true nature of the global jihadist threat we face – and to develop and implement effective countermeasures to it. Inevitably, there will be some duplication in this documentation and overlapping chronologies. We ask the reader's indulgence as we try to provide a reasonably complete, yet accessible, depiction of the crisis we face at the moment.

[iv] For additional background on these partnerships in the name of E&D, see Judicial Watch's report on then-Attorney General Eric Holder's 2010 meeting with American Muslim "community leaders"]."

CHAPTER 1: HOLY LAND FOUNDATION CASE

America's largest and most significant prosecution of funding for terrorism, *US v Holy Land Foundation*, is a useful prism through which to view the challenge the country faces from Islamic supremacists. The U.S. government's prosecution of this shariah-adherent Texas-based charity demonstrated conclusively that what we face in the global jihad movement are enemies who are assiduously pursuing our destruction.

The 2007-2008 Holy Land Foundation trial also showed that the jihadists are employing various techniques, from the pre-violent to the violent, to accomplish that goal. It marked a watershed in terms of federal efforts to stop them, as it authoritatively exposed their ambitions, revealed the extent of the conspiracy to achieve the destruction "of Western civilization from within" and the infrastructure then in place in America for that purpose.

The trajectory of this case—from the investigations that led to its inception; to the successful prosecution of five co-conspirators; the naming of hundreds more *unindicted* co-conspirators; and, finally, to both the failure to prosecute any of the latter, and the collaboration with many of them in the shaping and the undermining of U.S. policy towards the global jihad—exemplifies the mortal struggle we are in. It also illustrates brilliantly why we are losing.[v]

A look at what has befallen our nation's front lines of defense and why we are losing must necessarily begin with the run-up to the prosecution of this shariah-adherent charity, insights from the trial itself and what has, or has not, been done since.

In December 2001, within months of 9/11, the U.S. Treasury Department designated a Texas-based Muslim charity doing business as the Holy Land Foundation for Relief and Development (HLF) as a terrorist organization. According to the government, HLF had, "provided millions of dollars of material and logistical support to another designated terrorist organization, Hamas." For its part, Hamas had first been designated as a terrorist organization by President Bill Clinton on January 23, 1995 [33] via Executive Order 12947, "Prohibiting Transactions With Terrorists Who Threaten To Disrupt the Middle East Peace Process."[vi]

The Holy Land Foundation was said to have moved money to Hamas through direct fund transfers to "offices in the West Bank and Gaza that are affiliated with Hamas and transfers of funds to Islamic charity committees ('Zakat

---

[v] For a more in-depth analysis of the Holy Land Foundation case and its significance, see Andrew C. McCarthy's *The Grand Jihad: How Islam and the Left Sabotage America.*
[vi] Hamas was designated again on October 8, 1997, this time as a Foreign Terrorist Organization (FTO) by the U.S. State Department, Bureau of Counterterrorism.

committees') and other charitable organizations that are part of Hamas or controlled by Hamas members."³⁴

Treasury also announced that Mousa Mohamed Abu Marzook, a political leader of Hamas – who was himself identified by the U.S. government as a Specially Designated Terrorist in 1995 – had "named HLF as the primary fund-raising entity for Hamas in the United States. HLF funds were used by Hamas to support schools that served Hamas ends by encouraging children to become suicide bombers and to recruit suicide bombers by offering support to their families."³⁵

In July 2004, the Holy Land Foundation and five of its principals were indicted and charged with providing material support to a designated terrorist organization, Hamas. This prosecution would prove to be the largest terrorism-financing trial in U.S. history.

On May 29, 2007,³⁶ an enormously revealing document was filed in preparation for the Holy Land Foundation trial in U.S. district court in Dallas, Texas. Entitled *Government's Trial Brief*, it provided an enormous amount of information about the activities of Hamas and its affiliated enablers (e.g., the Council on American Islamic Relations, the Islamic Society of North America and the North American Islamic Trust) here in America.

Among its highlights were the following:

> **Page 13-14:** During the [October 2-3, 1993]³⁷ meeting [in Philadelphia], the participants [of the Palestine Committee of the Muslim Brotherhood in North America and Canada]³⁸ openly discussed the problems that the Oslo Accords³⁹ posed for achieving their objectives. The U.S was fertile ground for fundraising and propaganda, offering the essential Constitutional protections which afforded the freedom to operate. Since the United States had publicly positioned itself behind the peace process, the attendees were concerned that *disclosure of their true purpose would threaten their established infrastructure* by aligning them with what they knew was a terrorist organization.
>
> Attendees were admonished not to mention "Hamas," but rather to refer to it as "*Samah*," which is Hamas spelled backwards. Attendees questioned how they could continue their quest to defeat the [Oslo] peace process without being viewed as "terrorists." They discussed their concern that the peace process would attract Palestinian support and further complicate their ultimate goal of creating an Islamic state throughout Israel. They agreed that they must operate under an ostensible banner of apolitical humanitarian exercise in order to continue supporting Hamas' vital social recruitment effort. [Emphasis added.]
>
> **Page 16:** In the years following the adoption of new anti-terrorism laws⁴⁰ [in the 1990s], the defendants continued providing support to the same

organizations and institutions that they supported prior to the legislation; however, much more of the defendant HLF's money was being diverted to its own offices and/or representatives located throughout the West Bank and Gaza.

Page 23-24: The (ISA)[vii] witness, who has studied in depth the international Hamas social infrastructure, will testify about Hamas' world-wide support structure, which the witness will describe as a closed community of institutions and organizations dedicated to supporting Hamas. The witness will further describe the relationship between this closed community of *Zakat*[viii] committees and the international closed community, and how that relationship defines their activities. As part of his testimony the witness will describe the characteristics common to the international network of funds supporting Hamas, including the use of "overseas speakers" and the support for martyrs and prisoners. The witness will identify specific overseas speakers enlisted by the defendant HLF to raise funds, and their relationship to Hamas and other terrorist organizations, as well as identify particular individuals whose families were supported by the HLF.

The government also introduced into evidence what amounts to a kind of "Rosetta Stone" for understanding the strategy and goals of the Muslim Brotherhood in America: a secret document, written by a top Brotherhood operative named Mohamed Akram, laying bare his organization's first thirty years of subversive "civilization jihad" in America and its capabilities and strategy for "destroying Western civilization from within."[ix]

As it turns out, a leitmotif of the Holy Land Foundation prosecution – and point of the concerted efforts subsequently made, both by Islamists and by government officials, to suppress its insights – would be precisely, as the *Government's Trial Brief* put it "that disclosure of [the Islamists'] true purpose would threaten their established infrastructure."[41]

By 2006-2007, the vast North American Muslim Brotherhood-Hamas network had gone into crisis-management mode. They realized that, if the U.S. government could actually take down their preeminent *Zakat* charity, and somehow managed to saw off a good-sized limb from the MB-Hamas tree, then they might even be able to chop the whole thing down.

So, like chameleons, the Brotherhood fronts professed to make a fundamental transformation from Green (the color of Islam)[42] to Red, White and

---

[vii] Israel Security Agency, sometimes known as the Shin Bet.
[viii] For a detailed look at Zakat and it's role in financing jihad terrorism, see, Shariah Finance Watch, "How Zakat Funds Jihad," August 28,
[ix] See *The Explanatory Memorandum on the General Strategic Goal of the Group in North America* (https://www.centerforsecuritypolicy.org/2013/05/25/an-explanatory-memorandum-from-the-archives-of-the-muslim-brotherhood-in-america/).

Blue; they wrapped themselves in the flag of America's constitutional civil rights and civil liberties.

It is important to note that the tactical shift to "operate under an ostensible banner of [an] apolitical humanitarian exercise" was not just done vis-à-vis financial support of Hamas in the far-away West Bank and Gaza. This shift was also done right here in America, as Brotherhood front groups that were overt supporters of Islamic supremacism under the banner of Hamas were suddenly transformed into enthusiastic supporters of ecumenical interfaith engagement and dialogue.[x]

Once this strategic transformation was complete, these Muslim Brotherhood- and Hamas-linked individuals and organizations soon benefited from being shielded and protected, not only by churches and synagogues, but by successive U.S. administrations, a practice that continues to this very day.

A SUCCESSFUL PROSECUTION

This is all the more extraordinary since, on November 24, 2008[43], the U.S. Department of Justice (DOJ) obtained 108 guilty verdicts for all five defendants in the Holy Land Foundation (HLF) trial[44].

The 108 counts included: 1) conspiracy to provide material support and resources to a foreign terrorist organization [i.e., Hamas], 2) conspiracy to provide funds, goods and services to a specially designated terrorist and 3) conspiracy to commit money laundering.[xi]

In a press release issued after the verdicts were announced, Patrick Rowan[45], the Assistant Attorney General for National Security, stated: "Today's verdicts are important milestones in America's efforts against financiers of terrorism," adding that "This prosecution demonstrates our resolve to ensure that humanitarian relief efforts are not used as a mechanism to disguise and enable support for terrorist groups."

Such resolve would, presumably, have next put in the dock some – if not all – of the large number of individuals and organizations with proven ties to the Muslim Brotherhood network in North America[46] who were identified in the HLF trial as unindicted co-conspirators. Prominent among those listed were three of the most influential Brotherhood front groups in America: the Islamic Society of North America (ISNA)[47]; incorporated July 14, 1981) [48], the Council of American Islamic

---

[x] For an expose of the cynical use made by the civilization jihadists of such "dialogues," see Stephen Coughlin's *Bridge-Building to Nowhere: The Catholic Church's Case Study in Interfaith Delusion* (https://www.centerforsecuritypolicy.org/2015/11/23/e-book-release-bridge-building-to-nowhere/).
[xi] FBI press release, May 27, 2009.

Relations (CAIR);[49] incorporated as a 501(c)(4) on September 14, 1994)[50], and the North American Islamic Trust (NAIT; incorporated in 1973).

In fact, ISNA[51] and NAIT[52] were founded out of America's original Muslim Brotherhood front, the Muslim Students Association (MSA)[53], formed in the 1960s by a small group of influential U.S.-based Brotherhood leaders. A number of these Islamists were also responsible for spawning[54] other MB front groups (e.g., the International Institute of Islamic Thought (IIIT)[55], which was targeted during Operation Green Quest[xii]). NAIT supports and provides services to ISNA, MSA, their affiliates, and other Islamic centers and institutions. It also finances Islamic supremacist mosques in the United States and Canada.

A FOLLOW-ON PROSECUTION STILLBORN

Fortunately for the Muslim Brotherhood, Barack Obama was elected president of the United States twenty days before the Holy Land verdicts were handed down. Although the reported[56] intention of the Dallas U.S. Attorney's office was to prosecute[57] some or all of the unindicted co-conspirators identified in that trial,[xiii] the Obama Justice Department appears to have chosen instead to redefine the nature of the threat, creating an arbitrary and highly subjective distinction between supposedly "non-violent," "moderate," "reform-minded" [58]Islamic groups, and violent radical[59] ones.

Consider, for example, this quote from the National Strategy for Counterterrorism (NSCT) homepage (dated June 29, 2011)[60]. It defines "the threat" as follows:

> This Strategy recognizes there are numerous nations and groups that support terrorism to oppose U.S. interests, including Iran, Syria, Hezbollah and HAMAS, and we will use the full range of our foreign policy tools to protect the United States against these threats. However, the principal focus of this counterterrorism strategy is the network that poses the most direct and

---

[xii] For more on more on the IIIT, see the Center for Security Policy Occasional Paper, "The International Institute of Islamic Thought (IIIT): The Muslim Brotherhood's Think Tank"", http://www.centerforsecuritypolicy.org/2014/07/27/iiit-think-thank/ ",
http://www.centerforsecuritypolicy.org/2014/07/27/iiit-think-thank/
[xiii] One of the lead prosecutors, then-Assistant U.S. Attorney Jim Jacks, has publicly declared that there was no White House pressure to forego prosecution of the unindicted HLF co-conspirators. Rep. Peter King, however, has stood by his assertions to the contrary. See: http://www.politico.com/blogs/under-the-radar/2011/04/us-attorney-no-white-house-role-in-cair-prosecution-decision-035428 See: http://www.politico.com/blogs/under-the-radar/2011/04/us-attorney-no-white-house-role-in-cair-prosecution-decision-035428

significant threat to the United States – Al-Qaeda[61], its affiliates and its adherents.[xiv]

To this day, none of the Holy Land Foundation trial's unindicted co-conspirators have been prosecuted, let alone closed down by the government. In fact, to the contrary, as we shall see in the following pages, a number of them have been embraced by the U.S. government and brought "inside the wire" of its counter-terrorism policymaking processes.

In hindsight, the failure to prosecute [62] the unindicted HLF co-conspirators is but one of a number of decisions that have had profoundly deleterious effects on America's domestic and foreign counter-terrorism policy. Indeed, while much of the blame for the dangerous chaos that is U.S. government's counter-terrorism programs rests with the Obama administration, the truth is that a number of the predicates for such disasters were set during the George W. Bush administration.

Among the latter's astonishing oversights and catastrophic failures[xv] were the successful infiltration and influence operations conducted by Anwar Al-Awlaki[63] and Abdulrahman Alamoudi[64] against the U.S. government. Both of these individuals and were widely promoted as moderates and, thus, enjoyed high-level access to the Bush administration – even as they were the subjects of criminal investigations[65] by federal law enforcement officials for their links to terrorism.

The record shows that known affiliates of both the Council on American Islamic Relations, the Islamic Society of North America and myriad other Islamic supremacist organizations have been allowed by both the Bush and Obama administrations to participate directly – and with disastrous results for U.S. security – in the development and implementation of the U.S. government's evolving approach to countering what the former called "terrorism," and the latter insists on describing as "violent extremism."

As we shall develop in the next chapters, the cumulative effect of these decisions has been to bring us to our current, absurd and dangerous stance in what was once called the War on Terror: The Obama administration remains steadfastly opposed to recognizing the Islamic State[66] as "Islamic," yet it supports the Muslim Brotherhood as a legitimate, "moderate" Islamic partner. In fact, both are Islamic supremacist groups, equally prepared to use violence[67] to advance their *shared* goals.

[xiv] For a large cache of comments and quotations on this subject (as well as CVE), see the *Compilation of Hearings on Islamist Radicalization – Volume I*; the hearings were held on March 10, June 15 and July 27, 2011.

[xv] For a comprehensive treatment of this record, see Stephen Coughlin's *Catastrophic Failure: Blindfolding America in the Face of Jihad*.

Mr. Obama and his subordinates, nonetheless, remain willing to embrace and engage the Muslim Brotherhood, even as they profess a determination to "degrade and ultimately destroy" the Islamic State.

WHAT HAPPENED TO THE FOLLOW-ON PROSECUTIONS?

On April 15, 2011[68], the then-Chairman of the House Homeland Security Committee, Rep. Peter King, wrote Attorney General Eric Holder, stating the following concerns:

> I have been reliably informed that the decision not to seek indictments of the Council on American Islamic Relations (CAIR) and its co-founder Omar Ahmad, the Islamic Society of North America (ISNA), and the North American Islamic Trust (NAIT), was usurped by high-ranking officials at Department of Justice headquarters over the vehement and stated objections of special agents and supervisors of the Federal Bureau of Investigation, as well as the prosecutors at the U.S. Attorney's Office in Dallas, who had investigated and successfully prosecuted the Holy Land Foundation case. Their opposition to this decision raises serious doubt that the decision not to prosecute was a valid exercise of prosecutorial discretion.
>
> According to the State Department, Hamas finances its terrorist activities "through state sponsors of terrorism Iran and Syria, and fundraising networks in the Arabian Peninsula, Europe, the Middle East, [and] the United States." It raises the most serious question for the Justice Department to decline to even attempt to prosecute individuals and organizations, accused by a U.S. Attorney and found by a federal judge, to have a nexus with fundraising for an organization which conducts terror attacks upon civilians.
>
> I believe that in order to maintain the credibility of the Department, there should be full transparency into the Department's decision. Please respond to this letter by April 25, 2011.

The Justice Department failed to respond by April 25, 2011. Indeed, the Obama administration has resolutely stonewalled Congress to this day. Its unresponsiveness became a focus of a confrontation between General Holder and members of the U.S. House Judiciary Committee on June 7, 2012[69].

During his testimony, Mr. Holder displayed all of this administration's malevolent arrogations of National Security authority, its flagrant hubris, and its deliberate, intentional and abject surrender of our most basic Constitutional liberties and freedoms. It was the culminating exhibition of contempt for due process of law in a long train of "abuses and usurpations."

The following are highlights from a published account of Gen. Holder's appearance before the Judiciary Committee:

Representative Louie Gohmert (R-TX) challenged[70] AG Holder to uphold his oath to "justice," adding that "When I hear an Attorney General of the United States come before us and say, somewhat cavalierly, there is a political aspect to this office, it offends me beyond belief. Your job is justice. When we made a request a year ago – here – for the documents that your department has produced to people who were convicted of supporting terrorism. They are terrorists, and we wanted the documents you gave to the terrorists. We are a year later, and we still don't have them."

Mr. Gohmert added that it made no sense that the Attorney General would be more considerate to supporters of terrorism than to members of Congress, then said, "I am asking for the documents your department produced to the terrorist supporters convicted in the HLF Trial. Can we get those documents?"

Mr. Holder then replied: "Well, certainly you can have access to those things that are on the public record and that were used in the trial. I was also a judge, I sat in this [district of] Washington, D.C."

Mr. Gohmert interrupted, asking again, "So, is that a yes or a no that we will get those documents?"

Mr. Holder ignored the question, and never answered whether or not he would provide the documents.

Then, Representative Trent Franks (R-AZ) asked Mr. Holder to provide Congress with the HLF documents, and, again, AG Holder refused to cooperate. Mr. Franks said, "On April 27, 2011[71], members of this committee asked you to give us information surrounding the decision by a justice to forgo prosecution of the unindicted co-conspirators in the Holy Land Foundation case. This is the largest terrorism finance case, of course, in U.S. history. You've refused to comply with this request. You've still not prosecuted, despite there being what many consider to be a mountain of evidence against these jihadist groups, at least one of which now says it is working inside your agency to help advise on the purge of counter-terrorism training materials. Members of this committee and other committees would like to review this evidence, whether it has to be on a classified basis or not."

After Mr. Franks asked Mr. Holder [to] give his word he would provide the documents to Congress, Mr. Holder replied, "It's hard for me to answer that question."

Interrupting, Mr. Franks said "No it's not. It's not hard to answer. It's will you or will you not."

Finally, Mr. Holder responded, saying, "I can certainly take your request and we can check to see what the nature of the evidence is and make a determination about whether it's appropriate for that material to be reviewed. I just don't know."

The subject then turned to the then-ongoing purge of FBI counter-terrorism training material. Just as FBI Director Mueller had done on October 06, 2011[72], Mr. Holder insisted the purge was not motivated by political correctness, but was simply for the removal of inaccurate information. Mr. Holder also confirmed that "outsiders" were coordinating with the USG in the redrafting of CT training materials, and/or the removal of information that was determined to be "simply not true."

Mr. Franks responded, saying "It's been reported that multiple agencies, including the FBI, are now purging counter-terrorism material of information outside groups might fight offensive, including discussion of things as fundamental as that quote, 'Al-Qaeda is a group that endorses violent ideology that should be examined,' unquote. This strikes many as the sacrificing of vital national security...on the altar of political correctness."

When Mr. Franks asked Mr. Holder to reveal who the outside groups were, Mr. Holder refused to directly answer the question. Instead, he said, "This is something that is being run primarily out of the FBI. I mean, to the extent that there are outsiders who are involved that we are trying to interact with – we could perhaps try to get you those names."

Finally, when Mr. Franks asked whether there was a specific [Hamas-linked] jihadist group involved in the purging process, Mr. Holder refused to confirm or deny whether such a group was involved. Instead, he replied, "I don't think that's accurate, but I will relay that request to the FBI."

This travesty has continued for years. On June 13, 2013, the House Judiciary Committee filed another written request for the HLF documents, but it was also ignored. Then, on April 8, 2014, an even more heated exchange over the documents took place between Mr. Gohmert and Mr. Holder.

To date, none of the documents has been released by the Justice Department. Similarly, the names of unidentified "outsiders" who were involved in the purge of training materials remain state secrets withheld from public debate in Congress and the general public.

THE NEXT BATTLE: LEGITIMATING *ZAKAT*

Immediately after the Holy Land Foundation verdicts were announced, Mustafaa Carroll,[73] Director of CAIR-Dallas, warned[74] that the convictions could have a chilling effect for America's already traumatized Muslim community: "Muslims are concerned about how this is going to affect them. By criminalizing charity, it may even have an impact on American charities in general. People are really afraid."

What Mr. Carroll neglected to mention is that, unlike charities associated with any other religion, shariah specifically stipulates[75] that *at least* 1/8 of the proceeds of all Islamic charity (*Zakat*) should be provided for the support of jihad[76] and/or jihad warriors (*Mujahidin*). As would soon became evident[77], however, his concerns (along with those of several other MB/Hamas-linked front groups in America) about infringement of "civil rights and civil liberties" would be given priority attention and favorable consideration by the Obama administration.[xvi]

A DUTY UNFULFILLED, A NATION BETRAYED

The government's deliberate and intentional neglect of the evidence, indictments and 108 guilty verdicts against American Muslim Brotherhood front groups for support of Hamas terrorism in the Holy Land Foundation trial will ultimately be seen as evidence, indictments and guilty verdicts against the Obama administration itself.

The evidence presented at trial was like the flash of a camera, capturing the Muslim Brotherhood at the scene of the crime. From that day forward, anyone who remained knowingly involved with these groups after the HLF verdicts should be considered a willing accessory to the subversive activities of the Brotherhood's network in America.

Instead, at the very moment in history when they could have, and should have, acted decisively to protect both our homeland and the supremacy of our Constitution, those elected and appointed to safeguard of our security and unalienable Rights chose to abdicate their responsibilities. In so doing, they have – knowingly or unknowingly – subordinated *the supreme law of the land* to a foreign one (i.e., shariah) and its agents. They have submitted to an insidious and potentially mortal threat to our freedoms, cynically disguised in the red, white and blue trappings of Civil Rights and Civil Liberties.

Many times has history shown us that those who sacrifice their integrity for a false sense of security will inevitably lose both. The pages that follow will provide ample evidence of a fundamental betrayal of trust made all the more palpable by the Holy Land Foundation trial, one that has left our first lines of defense severely handicapped, if not actually incapable of performing their vital missions.

[xvi] For much more on this subject, see Shariah Finance Watch's article "Islamic Finance 101" and also see discussion below about President Obama's revisions to Terrorism-Related Inadmissibility Grounds.

CHAPTER 2: THE JIHADISTS' CAMPAIGN TO SUPPRESS FREE SPEECH

In order to understand what has happened to U.S. counter-terrorism policy over the past fifteen years, it is essential to understand some of the external forces that have been operating since before 9/11. The purpose of these forces has been to define what non-Muslims can know, say and do about the threat posed by global jihadists as a means of securing our defeat. They have had dramatic successes with regard to each of these targets.

'ISLAMOPHOBIA'

An early focus of the Islamic supremacists' efforts has been inventing and popularizing the term "Islamophobia." It initially emerged into the global vernacular through a self-described British "race equality" think tank called the Runnymede Trust[78]. [In fact, Runnymede Trust is a classic example of the "Red-Green axis" – a non-governmental organization doing business as a charity bringing together multiculturalism-promoting leftists and Islamist supremacists associated with, for example, Islamic Relief UK.]

In 1992, Runnymede set up a commission to consider anti-Semitism in contemporary British society.[xvii] Its 1994 report[79] entitled *A Very Light Sleeper – The Persistence and Dangers of Anti-Semitism*[80], included a recommendation that Runnymede should consider establishing a similar commission to consider *Islamophobia*.

Two years later, the Runnymede Trust established the Commission on British Muslims and Islamophobia[81] and, in February 1997, this panel produced a document entitled *Islamophobia, Its Features And Dangers, A Consultation Paper*[82]. It defined the term Islamophobia as "[the] dread or hatred of Islam and of Muslims. It has existed in Western countries and cultures for several centuries but in the last twenty years has become more explicit, more extreme and more dangerous. It is an ingredient of all sections of the media, and is prevalent in all sections of the society."

In November of 1997, Runnymede published a third report on the subject, entitled *Islamophobia: A Challenge for Us All*[83]. According to the authors[84] of this third paper:

> Building on the findings of a consultation document, this [1997] report takes on board comments and suggestions from a wide range of people and institutions. It provides a fuller explanation of Islamophobia and its consequences throughout society, and sets out recommendations for practical

---

[xvii] It bears emphasizing that the term *Islamophobia* was coined at least 7 years *before* the attacks on September 11, 2001. In other words, Americans and other Free World societies were being slandered as irrationally hostile to Muslims and their faith long before most Westerners were paying any attention to the threat posed by contemporary jihadists.

action by government, teachers, lawyers, journalists and by religious and community leaders," while adding that this report "was the first of its kind to raise awareness of a very real and dangerous phenomenon in the public and political space.

In 1999, the Commission on British Muslims and Islamophobia was re-established, this time ostensibly independently[85] from the Runnymede Trust. On June 2, 2004[86], it published a 100-page report entitled *Islamophobia: Issues, Challenges and Action*. Since then, the Runnymede Trust and/or the Commission has made a cottage industry of publishing polemical studies, articles and editorials[87] on the subjects of Islamophobia[88] and racism. As stated by Runnymede, these studies focus almost exclusively on the "public and political space." They give very little consideration, however, to the powerful animosities between the shariah-based Muslim world and the non-Islamic West.

Nor do these products recognize that, from an Islamic perspective, *any* resistance to the advance of Islam (e.g., Islamophobia) is seen as illegal and provocative, as well as a deliberate, intentional and irrational refusal to accommodate the socio-political needs and/or demands of the global Muslim community (*Ummah*).

In light of this divine mandate, any opposition to the advancement of Islam is regarded as *Fitnah*, i.e., an intolerable (illegal) form of opposition/oppression, both to the entire global Islamic community and to Allah. This is why we have seen a steady year-by-year increase in the number of jihad attacks here in the West, because the Quran specifically authorizes the use of violence whenever *Fitnah* is encountered. These specific *Quranic* authorizations are also why, all other things being equal, we will continue to see more jihad attacks in the months and years ahead.

To have any hope of being effective, U.S. counter-terrorism policy must understand and take into account the deep power and force of this underlying mandate (the *Deen* of Allah, or calling involving faith, authority, law, rule and subjugation) that the shariah-adherent believe must absolutely prevail on the earth by any means necessary, including violence.

PROHIBITING 'DEFAMATION' OF ISLAM

The Islamic supremacists' next step was to try to *prohibit* Islamophobia in the form of expression that "offends" Muslims. On July 4-6, 1997[89], the *First Conference on Islam In America* was held at Indianapolis University. The Conference was jointly sponsored by ISNA, the Association of Muslim Social Scientists (AMSS)[90] and Indianapolis University. During the Conference, Dr. M. Amir Ali, founder of the Institute of Islamic Information and Education (IIIE)[91] in Chicago, presented his study[92] entitled *Islamophobia In America*.[xviii]

For those who insist that the U.S. Constitution and Islamic shariah law are compatible, Dr. Ali had this to say:

> [The] Islamic system (way of life) includes guidelines in the Quran and *Sunnah* [*Hadith*[93] and *Sirat*[94]] about personal life, family life, social life, application of Islamic legal system, economic life and political life. All aspects of Islamic life are interdependent; one will not operate in the absence of the other. If the criminal legal system is imposed before implementing economic system, social system and political system it would not work; it will only promote injustice in the society. An example of this lopsided approach was the implementation of Islamic legal system (*Hudood*[95]) during the rule of General Muhammad Zia-Ul-Haq in Pakistan. This contributes to Islamophobia.
>
> There appears to be a long term, well-planned, well-financed and well-coordinated global strategy to fight Islam world-wide, in general, and in the West, in particular. There are reports of anti-Islam conferences and strategy sessions held to defeat Islam as a *Deen*[96] and to render it as a personal religion of individuals with no reflection of its teachings in family, social, economic and political life of nations, in the West and in the Muslim majority countries.

Precisely who were the Islamophobes then "criticizing" and "defaming" Islam back in 1997 and 1998? In his 1997-1998 study under the heading "Promoters of Islamophobia," Dr. Ali claimed they included the following:

> Islamophobia promoters may be divided into [the following] subgroups, namely, (a) Secular Fundamentalists, (b) Zionist Fundamentalists, and (c) Christian Fundamentalists also known as Born-Again and Evangelical movements, (d) Hindu Fundamentalists, (e) the Slavs, each with its own agenda against Islam.

More specifically, we can find clues as to who are considered guilty of Islamophobia in the 1969 Charter[97] of what was initially called the Organization of Islamic Conference and was subsequently renamed the Organization of Islamic Cooperation (both share the acronym OIC). The OIC's mission was declared to be to:

[xviii] Footnote 1 in *Islamophobia In America* also provided these insights into the sponsorship of these Islamic supremacist conferences: This is the Part I [sic] of the paper that was presented under the title, "Islam In America: Rough Road Ahead, A Survey of Anti-Islam Activities," at the *First Conference on Islam in America*...The Conference was jointly sponsored by [the] Islamic Society of North America (ISNA), Association of Muslim Social Scientists (AMSS) and Indianapolis University. Part II was presented at the *Second Annual Conference on Islam in America*, held at the Hyatt Regency O'Hare Hotel in Chicago, Illinois, July 3-5, 1998. The Conference was jointly organized by the ISNA and AMSS.

> Preserve and promote the lofty Islamic values of peace, compassion, tolerance, equality, justice and human dignity (p.1); work for revitalizing Islam's pioneering role in the world (p.1); enhance and strengthen the bond of unity and solidarity among the Muslim peoples and Member States (p.1); assist Muslim minorities and communities outside the Member States to preserve their dignity, cultural and religious identity (p.2); support and empower the Palestinian people to exercise their right to self determination and establish their sovereign State with *Al-Quds Al-Sharif*[98] [Jerusalem] as its capital (p.3); protect and defend the true image of Islam, to combat defamation of Islam and encourage dialogue among civilizations and religions (p.4); promote and defend unified position on issues of common interest in the international fora (p.4).[xix]

In other words, the United States and other Western nations have been in violation of a major provision of the OIC Charter since at least 1947[99] to the extent that they supported the existence of Israel in the Middle East. Several other provisions were violated by the U.S.-led coalitions in the 1990 Gulf War I (a.k.a. the first Persian Gulf War) and 2003 Gulf War II (a.k.a. the Iraq War). From the OIC's perspective, Islamophobia and defamation are but a part of the West's transgressions, "crimes" and "offenses" against the *Deen* of Islam.

THE OIC'S 'TEN-YEAR PROGRAM OF ACTION'

On December 8, 2005[100], the OIC held its Third Extraordinary Session of the Islamic Summit Conference in Mecca, Saudi Arabia, and published a document entitled *Ten-Year Program of Action to Meet the Challenges Facing the Muslim Ummah in the 21st Century* (TYPOA). The following statement appears up front in this document:

> In the intellectual and political fields, there are major issues, such as establishing the values of moderation and tolerance, combating extremism, violence and terrorism, countering Islamophobia, achieving solidarity and cooperation among Member States, conflict prevention, the question of Palestine, the rights of Muslim minorities and communities, and rejecting unilateral sanctions. All of these are issues which require a renewed commitment to be addressed through effective strategies. In this context, special attention needs to be given to Africa, which is the most affected region, due to poverty, diseases, illiteracy, famine, and debt burden.

In addition, the TYPOA declares[101] that the TYPOA "aims to strengthen Islamic solidarity and project the true image and noble values of Islam" thus enabling the Muslim Ummah to achieve its renaissance."

[xix] For more on the OIC and its efforts to enforce shariah-blasphemy restrictions and otherwise compel global submission to the Islamic supremacist agenda, see *The Organization of Islamic Cooperation's Jihad on Free Speech*, another monograph in the Center for Security Policy's Civilization Jihad Reader Series.

The Ten-Year Program of Action's Section VI also establishes this important qualification to the meaning of the OIC's commitment to "combating extremism, violence and terrorism":

> Emphasize the condemnation of terrorism in all its forms, and reject any justification or rationalization for it, consider it as a global phenomenon that is not connected with any religion, race, color, or country, and distinguish it from the *legitimate resistance to foreign occupation*, which does not sanction the killing of innocent civilians. [Emphasis added.]

The all-important words here are "legitimate resistance to foreign occupation," which reflect the the unbridgeable semantic gap between what the West calls "terrorism" and what Islamic supremacists consider to be "legitimate resistance."

Also, here are two illuminating declarations from Section VII of the Ten-Year Program, entitled "Combating Islamophobia":

> **2.** Affirm the need to counter Islamophobia, through the establishment of an Observatory[102] [see more below] at the OIC General Secretariat to monitor all forms of Islamophobia, issue an annual report thereon, and ensure cooperation with the relevant Governmental and Non-Governmental Organizations (NGO's) in order to counter Islamophobia...
>
> **4.** Initiate a structured and sustained dialogue in order to project the true values of Islam and empower Muslim countries to help in the war against extremism and terrorism.

On May 17, 2007[103] – a year and a half after the Ten-Year Program of Action was unveiled, members of the OIC met in Islamabad, Pakistan, at the 34th Islamic Conference of Foreign Ministers (ICFM). On this occasion, the foreign ministers "expressed[104] grave concern at the rising tide of discrimination and intolerance against Muslims, especially in Europe and North America." They claimed that, "It is something that has assumed xenophobic proportions."

Representatives of the ICFM also termed Islamophobia the "worst form of terrorism" and called for practical steps to counter the deliberate defamation of Islam, as well as any other forms of discrimination and intolerance against Muslims. They declared that: "This campaign of calumny against Muslims resulted in the publication of the blasphemous cartoons depicting Prophet Muhammad in a Danish newspaper and the issuance of the inflammatory statement by Pope Benedict XVI."

Also, the ICFM "deplored the misrepresentation in the Western media of Islam and Muslims in the context of terrorism," adding that 'the linkage of terrorists and extremists with Islam in a generalized manner is unacceptable," and that it is "further inciting negative sentiments and hatred in the West against Muslims."[xx]

The following year, pursuant to the Ten-Year Program of Action, the OIC established the Islamophobia Observatory[105] under the direct supervision of the OIC Secretary General. The Observatory put out its first report on March 13, 2008[106] which stated in part:

> ...Islamophobia will remain a source for concern for the international community in the near future, but...the *reaction of the Muslim world* to the recent publication of cartoon[s] insulting[107] Prophet Mohammad *succeeded in alerting* the international community as to the *dangerousness of this issue*. The report also takes into account the important role played by the media in dealing with Islamophobia and notes that Western media has fuel [sic] this hate of Muslims, [and that] freedom of expression is a basic right, but that it had to come hand-in-hand with responsibility by the party exercising this right. [Emphasis added.]

ENLISTING THE UNITED NATIONS

The first in a series of efforts to institutionalize through the United Nations international prohibition of Islamophobia predated both the 9/11 attacks and the OIC's ten-year program of action. It occurred in 1998[108], when Pakistan, in cooperation with the Organization of Islamic Conference, urged[109] the UN to pass a "Defamation *of Islam*" resolution. It denounced "religious intolerance," but explicitly was focused on just one faith in "condemning the stereotyping, negative profiling and stigmatization of people based on their religion." The Pakistanis and the OIC won majority approval for their resolution in the UN Commission on Human Rights (UNHCR) in Geneva, as well as in the UN General Assembly in New York.

The original 1998 Defamation of Islam draft resolution mirrored the Pakistan Penal Code[110] (adopted in 1860), a.k.a. the Blasphemy Laws[111] (which were also already in force[112] in many other Islamic countries before 1998). In Pakistan, these include the following severe shariah-based prohibitions and penalties:

> § 295 Injuring or defiling places of worship, with intent to insult the religion of any class. Penalty: Up to 2 years imprisonment or fine, or both

> § 295A Deliberate and malicious acts intended to outrage religious feelings of any class by insulting its religion or religious beliefs. Penalty: Up to 10 years imprisonment, or fine, or both

---

[xx] For a link to all 42 of the ICFM Conferences, see the OIC website.

§ 295B Defiling, etc., of Quran. Penalty: Imprisonment for life

§ 295C Use of derogatory remarks, spoken, written, directly or indirectly, etc., defiles Muhammad's name. Penalty: Mandatory Death and fine.

§ 298 Uttering of any word or making any sound or making any gesture or placing of any object in the sight with the deliberate intention of wounding the religious feelings of any person. Penalty: 1 years imprisonment, or fine, or both

§ 298A Use of derogatory remarks etc., in respect of holy personages. Penalty: 3 years imprisonment, or fine, or both.

Under such a penal system, all trials must, in addition, take place in a Muslim court (Court of Session) with a Muslim judge presiding. Moreover, according to shariah law, non-Muslims[113] cannot defend themselves in a Muslim court.

So, in light of the Pakistan Penal Code, a more complete answer to the earlier question – "Who was Islamophobic and who was 'criticizing' Islam back in 1997 and 1998?" – appears to be, simply, the West as a whole (along with any other unfortunate non-Muslim minorities who may be living in Islamic countries).

In 2006, the UN Human Rights Council (UNHRC) was created to replace the discredited and properly reviled UN Commission on Human Rights. With UNHRC approval, a resolution entitled *Combating Defamation of Religions* was submitted that year to the UN General Assembly. It was adopted on December 19, 2006[114] with 111 member countries voting in favor, 54 against and 18 abstentions.

A virtually identical non-binding[115] resolution was adopted by the UN General Assembly on August 29, 2007[116], and for nearly every year thereafter until 2011 (for example, see the April 2004 UN Press Release,[117] the text of UNHRC resolution 7/19[118] of 2008 and the March 2009 UNHRC resolution).[xxi]

In March 25, 2010,[119] the Human Rights Council (UNHRC) adopted yet another resolution introduced by Pakistan[120] on behalf of the OIC, also entitled "Combating Defamation of Religions," with 20 member states voting in favor and 17 against[121]. At the time, the International Freedom of Expression Exchange (IFEX)[122] argued in a joint letter signed by 40 IFEX members that:

> Any decision to combat defamation of religions contradicts the right to freedom of expression," adding that "any resolution on defamation of religions would be counterproductive to its goals of promoting equality and non-discrimination of individuals on the basis of their religion by supporting state practices which discriminate against religious minorities, dissenting

---

[xxi] For a comprehensive archive of all of the UNHRC resolutions on Defamation of Religions, see the UNHCR Refworld website.

voices and non-believers Efforts to codify defamation of religions will have negative long-term effects on freedom of expression.

Nonetheless, the resolution passed.

Pakistan and the OIC have also aggressively pursued measures to amend the original December 21, 1965[123] International Convention for the Elimination of All Forms of Racial Discrimination (ICERD), to include a clause which would criminalize all "insults to religion." Essentially, this effort would constitute an international blasphemy law. The good news is that this initiative has not been approved thus far in the face of strong opposition from free speech advocates and human rights organizations around the world.

UN HUMAN RIGHTS COUNCIL RESOLUTION 16/18 AND THE ISTANBUL PROCESS

The bad news is that, on March 24, 2011[124], the UN Human Rights Council adopted with U.S. support an ostensibly *non-binding* Resolution 16/18.[125] The resolution's formal title was "Combating Intolerance, Negative Stereotyping and Stigmatization of, and Discrimination, Incitement to Violence and Violence Against, Persons Based on Religion or Belief." Its section 5f calls upon UN member states to engage in "Adopting measures to criminalize incitement[126] to imminent violence based on religion or belief." The thrust of this language is distressingly reminiscent of the object of the Pakistani Penal Code[127] discussed above.

On July 15, 2011[128], Secretary of State Hillary Clinton helped kick off what has become known as the "Istanbul Process" with her participation in the inaugural *OIC High-Level Meeting on Combating Religious Intolerance* in Istanbul, Pakistan. In remarks on that occasion, she declared:

> I want to applaud the OIC and the European Union for helping pass Resolution 16/18 at the Human Rights Council. I was complimenting the Secretary General on the OIC team in Geneva. I had a great team there as well. So many of you were part of that effort.
>
> ...Together we have begun to overcome the false divide that pits religious sensitivities against freedom of expression, and we are pursuing a new approach based on concrete steps to fight intolerance wherever it occurs. Under this resolution, the international community is taking a strong stand for freedom of expression and worship, and against discrimination and violence based upon religion or belief.
>
> The Human Rights Council has given us a comprehensive framework [i.e., Resolution 16/18] for addressing this issue on the international level. But at

the same time, we each have to work to do more to promote respect for religious differences in our own countries.

In the US, I will admit, there are people who still feel vulnerable or marginalized as a result of their religious beliefs. And we have seen how the incendiary actions of just a very few people, a handful in a country of nearly 300 million, can create wide ripples of intolerance.

We also understand that, for 235 years, freedom of expression has been a universal right at the core of our democracy. So we are focused on promoting interfaith education and collaboration, enforcing antidiscrimination laws, protecting the rights of all people to worship as they choose, and to use *some old-fashioned techniques of peer pressure*[129] *and shaming*, so that people don't feel that they have the support to do what we abhor.

Five months later, on December 12, 2011[130], the State Department convened UNHCR Resolution 16/18 "stakeholders" in a series of mostly closed-door sessions. In connection with this event, Rizwan Saeed Sheikh[131], Director of Cultural Affairs at the OIC General Secretariat and spokesman for the OIC Secretary General, announced:

> OIC Secretary-General Ekmeleddin Mehmet İhsanoğlu[132] launched a process, known as the Istanbul Process, in July 2011, together with the then-US Secretary of State Hillary Clinton and EU Foreign Policy Chief Catherine Ashton, as well as with leaders of OIC and non-OIC member states, to build consensus on confronting Islamophobia. Similar meetings were held later in Washington and London as part of the Istanbul Process, and now the US, UK, the African Union, the Arab League and the OIC are moving in a circle, subscribing the process and taking it forward to discuss the issue specifically. The OIC is going to hold the next event focusing squarely on the issue of *criminalizing denigration* and deciding on whatever actions need to be taken on the basis of Article 20 of the [December 16, 1966][133] International Covenant on Civil and Political Rights (ICCPR).

Since countries within the OIC already have blasphemy laws in place, it is obvious that the focus of this initiative was on forcing Western nations, including the United States, to submit to such restrictions. It is also obvious that, as Secretary of State, Hillary Clinton willingly engaged via the Istanbul Process in forging – in partnership with the OIC – arrangements that would deny constitutional guarantees of freedom of expression to Americans deemed to be negatively stereotyping Islam and Muslims.

On October 5, 2012[134], the Office of the UN High Commissioner for Human Rights (OHCHR)[135] convened a meeting in Rabat, Morocco that released a document entitled "Rabat Plan of Action on the Prohibition of Advocacy of National, Racial or Religious Hatred That Constitutes Incitement to

Discrimination, Hostility or Violence." Known today as the Rabat Plan of Action, it made, among others, the following notable recommendations:

> Being alert to the danger of discrimination or negative stereotypes of individuals and groups being furthered by the media;
>
> Avoiding unnecessary references to race, religion, gender and other group characteristics that may promote intolerance;
>
> Raising awareness of the harm caused by discrimination and negative stereotyping;
>
> At the same time, international human rights standards on the prohibition of incitement to national, racial or religious hatred still need to be *integrated in domestic legislation and policies* in many parts of the world.[xxii] [Emphasis added.]

The Second Session[136] of the *Istanbul Process*, which opened on December 03, 2012[137], was hosted by the UK and Canada, and took place at the Canada House, London. The Third Session was hosted by the OIC, and took place in Geneva, Switzerland on June 21, 2013[138]. The Fourth Session took place on March 24-25, 2014[139] in Doha, Qatar, and the Fifth Session[140] was held in Jeddah, Saudi Arabia on June 3-4, 2015.

Throughout this time, what is now known as the Organization of Islamic Cooperation has been assiduously promoting the meme that Islamophobia is rampant and victimizing Muslims worldwide. According to OIC spokesman Rizwan Saeed Sheikh[141]:

> The [Islamophobia] Observatory is monitoring Islamophobia on a daily basis and translating it into monthly and annual reports. The OIC is publishing annual reports and so far it has published five reports, the last of which was submitted at the Djibouti session of foreign ministers held in November. The Cairo summit appreciated the role of the OIC Observatory in confronting Islamophobia and asked the Secretary General [142] to put more mechanisms in place to strengthen the Observatory.

Again, it is all about the West. And, notice the cynical use of euphemisms, such as "reaction of the Muslim world" and "dangerousness of this issue," to describe the OIC- and Arab League-orchestrated global riots [143] that caused widespread death [144] and damage to property and businesses, and that have contributed to the abridgement of freedom of expression to this day.

[xxii] As discussed in more detail below, Attorney General Eric Holder took some of the recommendations in the *Rabat Plan of Action* a big step forward on December 8, 2014, when he released a revised and updated Department of Justice (DOJ) document entitled *Guidance for Federal Law Enforcement Agencies Regarding the Use of Race, Ethnicity, Gender, National Origin, Religion, Sexual Orientation or Gender Identity*. These 2014 revised guidelines were derived from the original June 16, 2003 DOJ guidelines entitled *Guidance Regarding the Use of Race by Federal Law Enforcement Agencies*.

Exploring the activities of the Islamophobia Observatory would require an entire book in itself. Suffice it to note that the June 17, 2014[145] *Seventh OIC Observatory Report on Islamophobia* offers a representative jeremiad against: 1)Western attitudes toward Islam, 2) 'Islamophobic' individuals and organizations and 3) the U.S. anti-shariah movement. It also includes favorable references to the Council on American Islamic Relations (CAIR), an unindicted co-conspirator in the Holy Land Foundation trial.[xxiii]

CONCLUDING OBSERVATIONS

The Istanbul Process – with its roots in UN Resolution 16/18[146] – marks the zenith to date of the global jihad movement's international campaign to secure the non-Muslim world's submission to shariah, starting with the adoption worldwide of what amount to its blasphemy restrictions.

Throughout this campaign, critics have expressed grave concern that the so-called "defamation of religion" gambit was not only contrary to international law and the U.S. Constitution's guarantee of freedom of expression. They have noted that its embrace by Western governments opens the door to the actual *suppression* of free speech via hate-speech legislation and the prosecution of those deemed to have transgressed such laws. In addition, the adoption of such restrictions by the media, publishers and social media platforms will have the practical effect of silencing those who are, nonetheless, willing to challenge the jihadists.

As we will see, in the following pages, the Obama administration has simply disregarded such concerns, choosing instead to align itself with and otherwise submit to the demands of the OIC to criminalize Islamophobia and/or defamation of religion (i.e., Islam). This behavior fits a larger, and now well-established, pattern of accommodating Islamic supremacists – even to the point of allowing them to participate directly in the development and implementation of policy towards "terrorism," "violent extremism" and other euphemisms for the *real* present danger: the global jihad.

[xxiii] The nature and role of CAIR are described further in below.

CHAPTER 3: THE FBI AS A CASE STUDY OF AMERICA'S UNRAVELING COUNTER-TERRORISM POLICY

The following chronology of events describes through the microcosm of the Federal Bureau of Investigations – the nation's preeminent law enforcement agency – what has been happening across the U.S. government. As is evident in this analysis and those that will follow concerning other elements of our first lines of defense, we have been grievously disarmed as a result of: assiduous influence operations by Islamic supremacists; the help they receive from allies on the Left; and official policies that enable, or at least accommodate, such initiatives.

This compendium is meant to call attention to the most important of such events but is, nonetheless, a representative sample, rather than all-inclusive.

On February 06, 2002,[147] then-Executive Assistant Director of the FBI Counterintelligence Division (CD)[148] Dale L. Watson testified on the subject of "International Terrorism" before the Senate Select Committee on Intelligence. He told legislators:

> The United States faces a formidable challenge from international terrorists. The September 11 attack and the bombing of the USS Cole in the port of Aden in October 2000, as well as the prevention of an apparent attempt by Richard Reid [149] to destroy a Paris-to-Miami flight in December 2001, underscore the range of threats to U.S. interests posed by international terrorism.
>
> In general terms, the international terrorist threat to U.S. interests can be divided into three categories: 1) the international jihad movement, 2) formalized terrorist organizations, and 3) state sponsors of international terrorism [i.e., Iran]. Each of these categories represents a threat to U.S. interests abroad and in the U.S. The most serious international terrorist threat to U.S. interests today stems from Sunni Islamic extremists, such as Usama Bin Laden and individuals affiliated with his Al-Qaeda organization. Al-Qaeda leaders, including Usama Bin Laden, had been harbored in Afghanistan since 1996 by the extremist Islamic regime of the Taliban.

THE MUSLIM BROTHERHOOD 'INSIDE THE WIRE'

However, just a week later, on February 13, 2002,[150] FBI Director Robert S. Mueller III met with key U.S. leaders of American Arab, Muslim, and Sikh organizations. The meeting "sought to build on earlier discussions of a number of issues, ranging from vigilante attacks and other hate crimes[151], to the value of the continuing assistance from the Arab, Muslim, and Sikh communities in the overall effort to provide greater security for all Americans."

Among the attendees at this meeting were: Nihad Awad[152] (a.k.a. Nehad Hammad)[153]; Executive Director of CAIR, Jason Erb[154], Director of Government Affairs for CAIR; Dr. Nedzi Sacirbey,[155] Acting Director of the American Muslim

Council (AMC);[156] and Dr. Hassan Ibrahim,[157] National Director of the Muslim Public Affairs Council (MPAC).

This meeting occurred just five months after 9/11. In retrospect, it can be seen as one of the earliest deviations from a counter-terrorism approach rooted in sound law enforcement practices to an approach largely dictated by Civil Rights/Civil Liberties considerations. Typically, these are, in turn, dictated by so-called American Muslim "community leaders."

At the time of this 2002 meeting, it was already well-known[158] that at least *some* of such "leaders" were problematic. For example, within the LEO community Nihad Awad was known to have been directly involved in the financial support of Hamas,[159] which had been twice-designated as a terrorist organization, once in January 23, 1995,[160] and again on October 08, 1997[161].[xxiv]

One of the top leaders of the American Muslim Council (AMC)[162] at the time of this 2002 meeting was Abdurahman Alamoudi. He was arrested on September 29, 2003[163] on multiple terrorist-related charges and is currently serving a 17-year sentence in federal prison. CAIR was designated as unindicted co-conspirators[164] for financial support of Hamas in the HLF Trial.

As for MPAC, the organization was founded in 1988[165] as an off-shoot of the Islamic Center of Southern California (ICSC),[166] by brothers Maher and Hassan Hathout, who were well-known, self-declared members of the MB. The Hathout brothers emigrated to the U.S. from Egypt in the early 1970's, where they co-founded the ICSC. Both brothers were heavily influenced by the teachings of Muslim Brotherhood founder Hassan Al-Banna.[167]

As we shall see, the fact that MPAC was founded by two prominent Muslim Brotherhood operatives and is intimately involved with CAIR and other Islamic supremacist organizations has not precluded it from enjoying extraordinary access to, among other federal agencies, the FBI, the Department of Justice, the White House, the State Department and the Department of Homeland Security.[xxv]

On February 28, 2003,[168] FBI Director Robert S. Mueller III held another outreach meeting with representatives [169] of the American-Arab Anti-Discrimination Committee (ADC),[170] the Arab American Institute (AAI),[171] the Sikh Mediawatch and Resource Task Force, the Islamic Institute,[172] AMC and MPAC.[173]

[xxiv] See in this connection at Appendix III a letter sent by the Department of Justice on February 12, 2010 to Representative Sue Myrick providing details of the Department's knowledge about CAIR's ties to the Muslim Brotherhood's Palestinian franchise, Hamas.

[xxv] See, for example, a chronology suggesting the extent of MPAC's influence operations at Appendix IV.

Another virtually identical meeting was convened on July 9, 2004[174] with then-Attorney General John Ashcroft and FBI Director Mueller. During this meeting, Gen. Ashcroft justified his outreach to the assembled organizations on the basis that they might help identify jihadists in our midst:

> Credible reporting indicates that al Qaeda is planning a large-scale attack in America in an effort to disrupt our democratic process. While we currently lack precise knowledge about when, where and how they are planning to attack, we are actively working to gain that knowledge. As part of that effort, we are again reaching out to our partners in the Muslim and Arab-American communities for any information they may have. Their assistance has proven valuable in the past, and we continue to seek their help in this time of enhanced threat.

On January 11, 2006,[175] representatives of American Muslim and American Arab organizations met with the FBI to discuss their concerns about incidents of domestic surveillance. Organized by MPAC, this meeting was also attended by members of CAIR, the Muslim American Society (MAS), Muslim Advocates[176] and the All Dulles Area Muslim Society (ADAMS Center).[177]

The imam at the ADAMS Center is Mohamed Magid.[178] He formerly served as the president of the largest Muslim Brotherhood front, ISNA. Magid, as is documented in the pages that follow, has been an extremely effective influence operator for the Islamic supremacists.

According to MPAC's website:

> The meeting was called in response to recent reports of widespread surveillance and radiation[179] monitoring of more than 100 Muslim American mosques, homes and businesses. Community leaders warned that left unchallenged, the reports may reinforce the misperception that the FBI's relationship with the Muslim American community is predicated upon investigations, arrests and prosecutions.

According to the press release issued after the meeting by MPAC, during the meeting, "FBI Deputy Director John Pistole and Public Affairs head John Miller said they were unable to discuss the domestic surveillance program because of on-going classified investigations, [but] stressed their interest in enhancing dialogue with the Muslim American community. They also said that there is an established pattern of Al-Qaeda exploiting Muslim communities for "cover and concealment."

Mr. Pistole described the Muslim American community as their most important resource for counterterrorism. Importantly, Mr. Miller also pointed to 52 federal hate crimes investigations currently being pursued as evidence of the FBI's commitment to ensuring Civil Liberties and Civil Rights.

THE BUREAU'S TRANSFORMATION

On May 10, 2006,[180] the FBI attempted to accommodate the concerns of the American Islamic community by publishing a study entitled *The Radicalization Process: From Conversion to Jihad*. As stated in the Introduction and Key Judgments sections:

> This assessment provides a working model of the radicalization process for a legal U.S. person who is a convert to Islam, utilizing FBI case examples that illustrate the process. *The Radicalization Process: From Conversion to Jihad* is the first in a series of analytical products dealing with various aspects of the radicalization process. Information contained in this assessment is derived from open and closed FBI investigations, academic literature, and is current as of April 10, 2006.
>
> We assess that the radicalization cycle is generally composed of four steps: 1) pre-radicalization, 2) identification, 3) indoctrination, and 4) action. Each one is distinct, and a radicalized Muslim may never reach the final step.
>
> Radicalized U.S. converts to Islam and their potential to attack the Homeland are growing concerns of the U.S. Intelligence Community (USIC). Conversion to the Islamic faith does not always lead the convert down the path of radicalization. The situations that place converts in a position to be influenced by Islamic extremists appear to be more important than the convert's initial motivations for converting.

If this document was meant to accommodate the Bureau's Muslim Brotherhood interlocutors, it was a dismal failure. A brief jump ahead in this chronology is necessary at this point: Five years after this straightforward law enforcement-based assessment was published, and despite the indisputable increase[181] in jihadist attacks around the world during the intervening period, the FBI's *Radicalization Process* report was still considered intolerably Islamophobic by the U.S. Muslim community.

For example, in an October 5, 2011[182] article entitled *MPAC Co-Signs Letter to FBI Demanding Reformation in Flawed, Anti-Muslim Training*, which was published on the MPAC website, the following demands were made:

> MPAC has signed on to a letter authored by the ACLU[183] [American Civil Liberties Union] requesting the FBI withdraw documents and reports published by the bureau with biased and flawed information about Islam and Muslims. Since the rise of the post-9/11 Islamophobic era, the FBI has explicitly stated numerous times *"strong religious beliefs should never be confused with violent extremism."* However, the ACLU found numerous documents, such as the FBI intelligence assessment *"The Radicalization Process: From Conversion to Jihad"* published in March [sic] 2006 that lists the supposed

"steps" and "indicators" of "homegrown Islamic extremists" as those who practice Islam.

These demands were all met. Another, virtually identical incident involving CAIR and the ACLU et.al. on the one hand and New York City Mayor Bill DeBlasio on the other occurred on September 21, 2015[184] (see the Epilogue).

To resume our narrative: On February 28, 2007, the Muslim Public Affairs Council sponsored another public meeting with FBI Director Robert S. Mueller III and then-DHS Secretary Michael Chertoff "to discuss issues impacting the future of the Muslim American community." A press release[185] issued afterwards by the Muslim Brotherhood's MPAC stated:

> "Access to government is as important as the substance of policies," said MPAC Executive Director Salam Al-Marayati[186] "By engaging consistently and substantively with federal government agencies on issues as varied as counterterrorism and civil rights, we can facilitate access to government services for the Muslim American community, while also fostering security and prosperity for our community and our country."
>
> Al-Marayati addressed: 1) engagement between Secretary Chertoff's department [DHS] and Muslim American leaders, 2) the lingering problems of detention at borders, and 3) the trend of major cases trumpeted by our government as counterterrorism knockouts returning as acquittals after being tried in the justice system....
>
> According to an Associated Press report, nearly all of the terrorism-related statistics on investigations, referrals and cases examined by the OIG were either diminished or inflated. Only two of 26 sets of department data reported between 2001 and 2005 were accurate, the audit found. Most of the cases involve technical immigration lapses in visas, finance violations, and petty crimes.[xxvi]

LEGITIMATING THE BROTHERHOOD

Another sign of the Muslim Brotherhood's success in subverting the FBI occurred on December 4, 2007[187] when Muhammad Ali-Salaam[188] received the FBI Director's Community Leadership Award[189] from the Boston Field Office. According to the press release[190] issued by the Boston chapter of the Muslim American Society – a group that is known as the overt arm of the Muslim Brotherhood in this country:

[xxvi] For a more objective review of all the attempted jihadist attacks in the US from 2001-2013, see *60 Terrorist Plots Since 9/11: Continued Lessons In Domestic Counterterrorism.* For a comprehensive and regularly updated list of the more than 27,375 jihadist attacks around the world since 9/11, see the *List of Terrorist Attacks.*

The Muslim American Society of Boston (MAS Boston) and the Islamic Council of New England [ICNE][191] congratulate Mr. Muhammad Ali-Salaam for receiving the Director's Community Leadership Award from the FBI Boston office. Mr. Ali-Salaam has been a long-time representative of the Muslim community and a founding member of the BRIDGES[192] forum (Building Respect in Diverse Groups to Enhance Sensitivity). BRIDGES is a monthly meeting[193] that gathers representatives of the various Law Enforcement agencies, civil liberties organizations, and various communities and organizations including the Muslim American Society (MAS) and Islamic Council of New England. BRIDGES aims to fulfill the necessary role of establishing necessary communication channels to dispel myths, function efficiently and to remind of the importance of both Law Enforcement's role, and civil rights.

Mr. Ali-Salaam has also worked with the U.S. Department of Justice [in Community Relation Services][194] to deliver lectures and presentations on Islam and Muslims, which have reached thousands of local law enforcement personnel in the past few years. Last month [i.e., November 15, 2007],[195] the Los Angeles Police Department scrapped its controversial plan to map their Muslim communities upon strong rejection from Muslim community leaders and civil rights organizations.

This recent event is an example of the importance of establishing strong and trusted channels of communication between the Muslim community and Law Enforcement. In the post-9/11 climate, Law Enforcement may be tempted to employ means or approaches towards ensuring safety, but which would harm and breach the rights of Muslims in America. It is therefore essential for the Muslim community to be at the table with Law Enforcement to voice their concerns and establish a working partnership based on integrity and transparency.

The Muslim American Society was founded in 1993,[196] after a debate among Muslim Brotherhood members in America about whether the organization should remain underground or take on a public persona. As stated in an article published in the *Harvard International Review* by MB Deputy Chairman Mohammad Mamun El-Hudaibi[197] in the Spring of 1997,[198] entitled "The Principles of the Muslim Brotherhood," the two main goals (pillars) of the MB (and the MAS) from the very beginning was the "introduction of the Islamic shariah as the basis controlling the affairs of state and society [and working] to achieve unification among the Islamic countries and states, mainly among the Arab states, and liberating them from foreign imperialism."

Mr. Al-Salaam – who recently retired[199] after 32 years, first as Assistant and then as Deputy Director of Special Projects at the Boston Redevelopment Authority (BRA) – earned notoriety for his involvement in facilitating the controversial[200] Roxbury mosque project of the Islamic Society of Boston.

The Islamic Society of Boston (a.k.a. MAS-Boston) has long been deeply involved in material support of terrorism, including both Hamas and Al-Qaeda. The ISB's Roxbury shariah-adherent mosque is not only the largest in the Northeast, but the organization has numerous, well-established[201] ties to prominent jihadists as well. For example, now-convicted Al Qaeda financier Abdurahman Alamoudi founded the ISB. On December 3, 2008[202] (just after the HLF Trial verdicts), Americans for Peace and Tolerance[203] revealed that three prominent ISB leaders (Hossam Al-Jabri,[204] Jamal Badawi[205] and Osama Kandil),[206] were closely linked to the Hamas-financing Holy Land Foundation, and to the five defendants in the case. (For more on the ISB's unsavory ties, see available reports from the Clarion Project (2013),[207] The New York Post (2014),[208] Americans for Peace and Tolerance (2015)[209] and the Center for Security Policy (2015).[210])

Despite this pedigree, according to the ISB's website[211], MAS-Boston co-convenes a "monthly forum with FBI, Immigration and Customs Enforcement [ICE], Homeland Security, State and Boston Police, and U.S. and State Attorney Generals' offices to educate officials about the needs and concerns of the Muslim community and discuss with the community law enforcement concerns relating to terrorism and security."

This monthly forum appears to be the same as the BRIDGES meetings, which was once co-chaired by Margo Schlanger,[212] the DHS Civil Rights and Civil Liberties Officer, and Mr. Imad Hamad,[213] the Arab-American Anti-Discrimination Committee Senior National Advisor and Regional Director. [xxvii]

CHANGING THE FBI'S LEXICON

The next defining moment in this series of events that have undermined the FBI's ability to perform its mission vis a vis domestic terrorist threats came with the January 28, 2008[214] release of a policy document entitled, *Federal Bureau Of Investigation Counterterrorism Analytical Lexicon*. This 14-page lexicon refers to "Violent Extremism" twenty-eight times and to "religious" just three times, but does not mention the words "Muslim," "Islam" or "jihad" *even once*.

As per the *Introduction*, the *Lexicon* is:

> Intended to help standardize the terms used in FBI analytical products dealing with counterterrorism. Analysis that labels an individual with any of

---

[xxvii] On November 27, 2013, it was announced that Mr. Hamad would retire from the ADC, following "heavy pressure that had built over the last several months for him to leave. Sexual harassment allegations against Hamad shook ADC on both the national and local level after several women came forward alleging they were sexually harassed by him, while he served as the organization's Michigan director."

these terms is not sufficient predication for any investigative action or technique. Nor can any investigation be conducted solely upon the basis of activities protected by the First Amendment or the lawful exercise of other rights secured by the Constitution or laws of the United States. Before applying a label to an individual or his or her activity, reasonable efforts should have been made to ensure the application of that label to be accurate, complete, timely and relevant.

The *FBI Lexicon* defines "Violent Extremism" as follows:

> [A]ny ideology that encourages, endorses, condones, justifies, or supports the commission of a violent act or crime against the United States, its government, citizens, or allies in order to achieve political, social, or economic changes, or against individuals or groups who hold contrary opinions. Violent extremism differs from "radicalism" in that violent extremists explicitly endorse, encourage, or commit acts of violence or provide material support to those who do. "Radicalism" is a much looser term that does not necessarily indicate acceptance or endorsement of violent methods, and is therefore not preferred. "Extremist" should be coupled with "violent" for purposes of clarity. It should be noted that some "extreme" or "radical" activity – such as spreading propaganda – might be constitutionally protected. An analytical judgment that an individual is a "violent extremist," "extremist," or "radical" is not predication for any investigative action or technique.

Also, this *Lexicon* appears to be one of first official uses (though it was certainly far[215] from the last)[216] of the phrase "Homegrown Violent Extremist,"[217] which is defined thusly:

> A "homegrown violent extremist" is a U.S. person who was once assimilated into, but who has rejected, the cultural values, beliefs, and environment of the U.S. in favor of a violent extremist ideology. He or she is "U.S.-radicalized," and intends to commit terrorism inside the U.S. without direct support or direction from a foreign terrorist organization.

In the real world of law enforcement, these kinds of abstract and subjective definitions of basic concepts are toxic to the career of any federal or civilian law enforcement office who takes his/her Oath of Office[218] seriously (i.e., to "support and defend the Constitution of the United States against all enemies, foreign and domestic").[xxviii]

Non-legal terms like "violent extremist" far surpass the legal definition of mere suspicion[219], making it virtually impossible for law enforcement officers to begin to conduct effective counter-terror investigations. Law enforcement officers are hard pressed to develop effective cases if they are required, from the outset, to

---

[xxviii] For more on this see the discussion of Former Customs and Border Protection Officer Phillip Haney's story in the Epilogue.

meet the strict legal standard of probable cause. This is because it is through the initial investigatory contact, possibly generated due an officer's suspicions about an individual's ideological affiliation, that information is obtained with which to establish probable cause. As we'll see in more detail below, 2008 was only the beginning; things got much worse as the years went on.

As it happens, the release of this FBI *Lexicon* coincided with the January 2008[220] release of perhaps the most important document in the emergence of the government's so-called "Countering Violent Extremism" Policy. Written by the Department of Homeland Security's Office of Civil Rights and Civil Liberties (DHS-CRCL), *Terminology To Define The Terrorists: Recommendations From American Muslims*, is discussed at length in Chapter 4.[xxix]

CENSORING THE FBI TRAINING PROGRAM

On March 18, 2010,[221] a press release was posted on the Allied Media Corp website,[222] a public relations firm that specializes in advocacy for Middle Eastern ethnic groups. "FBI Urges Outreach To Halt Radicalization," included the following comments:

> Brett Hovington, the Chief Public Relations Officer for the FBI's Community Relations unit, testified before the House Committee on Homeland Security, Subcommittee on Intelligence, Information Sharing and Terrorism Risk Assessment, on the need to reach out to frustrated youth. Hovington said numerous accounts of young people leaving the U.S. to engage in "criminal and nefarious activities" were a top concern for law enforcement officials. "If we want to stop future generations of youth from choosing the wrong path and fighting against our country instead of for it, we must commit to increasing our *field-based scientific research* on the violent radicalization of youth."
>
> He said...his travels to the Middle East and England taught him that sociologists, psychologists and community leaders all have a role to play in public discourse. "As we see more instances of individuals in the U.S. being radicalized to commit violent acts, our efforts to build understanding and trust becomes more critical than ever," he added. Al-Qaida claims it is trying to recruit Westerners for terrorist operations as part of an effort to reform its strategies in the face of growing international pressure. Hovington said national and local coordination can influence the way in which terrorism and violent radicalization is deterred.[xxx] [Emphasis added.]

[xxix] For additional background, see the November 10, 2011 DHS document entitled *Domestic Terrorism and Homegrown Violent Extremism Lexicon*.

[xxx] In addition to an emerging civil rights-based CVE Policy, we're now beginning to see the parallel emergence of a secular, academic approach, a.k.a." field-based scientific research," designed to "help prevent frustrated youth who want to engage in criminal and nefarious activities, who may choose the

Then, on August 2, 2010,[223] a "coalition of U.S. Muslim, Sikh, Asian-American, and other civil liberties groups sent an open letter to FBI Director Mueller, seeking an explanation of why a leader of an anti-Islam hate group was recently invited to train state and federal law enforcement officers." According to an August 3, 2010 CAIR press release,[224] the letter included the following statements:

> Robert Spencer, co-founder of the hate group Stop the Islamization of America (SIOA),[225] claimed in a blog post that he "gave two two-hour seminars on the belief-system of Islamic jihadists to the Tidewater Joint Terrorism Task Force." Those attending the training reportedly included FBI agents. In its letter to Mueller, the coalition outlined Spencer's bigoted views on Islam and Muslims, including referring to Islam's Prophet Muhammad as a "con man."

Again, the relentless message from these self-appointed "leaders" of the American Islamic community to law enforcement and other government officials is that Islam and Muslims are being falsely accused of participating in and/or prompting violence. These American Muslims insist that their civil rights are being serially violated in misbegotten and futile efforts to prevent terrorism. (This particular influence operation finally bore fruit on December 8, 2014,[226] when the Department of Justice released new civil rights-based guidelines in a Justice Department document entitled, "Guidance for Federal Law Enforcement Agencies Regarding the Use of Race, Ethnicity, Gender, National Origin, Religion, Sexual Orientation, or Gender Identity." It also benefited directly from another influence operation in 2011-2012 described at length in Chapter 8.)

PUNISHING THOSE WHO 'OFFEND' MUSLIMS

In addition to the reception Islamist influence operators have received in some quarters of the executive branch, they have also benefited from strong support in some offices on Capitol Hill. Over the years, the Senate's second-ranking Democrat, Senator Richard J. Durbin, has been particularly assiduous in pressing for accommodations demanded by assorted Muslim Brotherhood front organizations.[xxxi]

For example, on March 27, 2012,[227] Sen. Durbin sent a letter to FBI Director Mueller, essentially reiterating all of the points that civil rights and Muslim groups had brought forward via various meetings, letters and press releases for the

---

wrong path and begin fighting against our country." While emphasizing psychology and sociology, not a word about the influence of religion (i.e., Islam) is included.

[xxxi] In 2015, Sen. Durbin earned the dubious distinction of being dubbed the leader of the Senate's "Jihad Caucus" for his role in organizing a fourteen-senator letter to President Obama urging him to increase the number of (unvettable) Syrian refugees admitted into the United States to 65,000.

purpose of catalyzing and executing a purge of law enforcement and counter-terror knowledge. As with the ACLU-Brennan letter, Senator Durbin's letter contained very specific demands for the punitive actions against USG law enforcement personnel (see Figure 1).

Figure 1: Excerpts of Sen. Durbin Letter to FBI Director Robert Mueller

> I respectfully request that you take additional steps to address inappropriate FBI training on Islam, including:
>
> - Provide the offending training materials to the Judiciary Committee and unclassified versions of the materials to the American people;
> - At the very least, reassign the individuals responsible for providing inappropriate training;
> - Retrain FBI agents who received inappropriate training;
> - Conduct a review of FBI intelligence analyses of Islam, American Muslims, and Arab Americans; and
> - Produce a detailed training curriculum on Islam which has been reviewed and approved by experts in the field.
>
> I look forward to your prompt response. Thank you for your time and consideration, and thank you for your service to our country.
>
> Sincerely,
>
> Richard J. Durbin
> U.S. Senator

As NPR reported the next day:[228]

> The FBI has completed a review of offensive training material and has purged 876 pages and 392 presentations, according to a briefing provided to lawmakers. The office of Senator Richard Durbin, a Democrat from Illinois, made the briefing public when it sent a letter addressed to Robert Mueller, the director of the FBI. According to the letter, which is dated March 27, 2012[229] the FBI gave the Senator an opportunity to review a "handful" of the material.

DIVERTING THE BUREAU'S ATTENTION

Finally for the present purpose, the FBI's willingness to submit to the American Islamic community's never-ending accusations of Islamophobia and/or demands for unprecedented concessions can be seen in a May 28, 2015[230] report entitled *Militia Extremists Expand Target Sets to Include Muslims*. It includes the following excerpt:

> Militia extremists are expanding their target sets to include Muslims and Islamic religious institutions in the United States. This has resulted in increased violent rhetoric and plotting, and has the potential to lead, over the long term, to additional harassment of or violence against Muslims by domestic extremists. The FBI makes these assessments with high confidence on the basis of a large body of source reporting generated mainly since 2013. This information augments prior FBI analysis that established militia extremists target government personnel and law enforcement officers, perceived threats from abroad, and individuals or institutions that seek to constrain Second Amendment rights.

This stands in stark contrast to the explicit 2002 testimony by Dale Watson that opens this chapter. Rather than obfuscate the threat, Watson defined it clearly as, "1) the radical international jihad movement, 2) formalized terrorist organizations, and 3) state sponsors of international terrorism [i.e., Iran]."

Comparing these two statements charts an ominous trajectory of willful blindness and official submission to Islamic supremacists that, unfortunately, is not unique to the FBI. As the following chapters make clear, this dynamic is evident throughout the other U.S. government agencies responsible for our national and homeland security.

CHAPTER 4: SUBMISSION AT THE DEPARTMENT OF HOMELAND SECURITY

***

"When I use a word," Humpty Dumpty said, in rather a scornful tone, "it means just what I choose it to mean – neither more nor less."

"The question is," said Alice, "whether you can make words mean so many different things."

"The question is," said Humpty Dumpty, "which is to be master, that's all."

- *'Through the Looking Glass' by Lewis Carroll, 1871*

***

On July 27, 2005,[231] a key moment arrived in the U.S. government's official embrace of the Islamists' preferred euphemism, "Countering Violent Extremism." NPR host Steve Inskeep was among the first in the media to announce that Obama administration and military officials seem to be shifting their public vocabulary from the "Global War On Terrorism" to the "Global Struggle Against Violent Extremism" (G-SAVE).[232]

Inskeep's comments were interspersed with, among others, audio clips from a speech then-Joint Chiefs Chairman General Richard Myers had delivered at the National Press Club two days earlier.

> NPR: "The catchphrase 'global war on terrorism' has been widely used since September 11, 2001, but military officials have started backing off those words in favor of new language. General Richard Myers, Chairman of the Joint Chiefs of Staff, did so on Monday at the National Press Club."
>
> Myers: "I think I've objected to the use of the term 'war on terrorism' before, because, one, if you call it a war, then you think of people in uniform as being the solution, and it's more than terrorism. I think it's – *violent extremist* is the real enemy here, and terror is the method they use."
>
> NPR: "In that speech, General Myers said *violent extremism, not terrorism*, was responsible for the recent attacks in London and in Egypt."
>
> Myers: "*Violent extremists* can affect us just by creating fear, which has the impact to change our way of life. We've seen a little of that since 9/11."
>
> NPR: "Over the next few minutes, we're going to hear how the phrase 'global war on terrorism' evolved into variations of a new phrase, '*global struggle against violent extremism*.'" [Emphasis added.]

OPENING UP TO THE MUSLIM BROTHERHOOD

On April 7, 2007,[233] Fox News.com carried an Associated Press report that stated:

> A top U.S. Democratic congressman met a leading member of Egypt's Muslim Brotherhood, an outlawed[234] opposition group, during a recent visit to the country. House Majority Leader Steny Hoyer (D-MD) met with the MB's parliament leader, Mohammed Saad El-Katatni,[235] twice on Thursday – once at the Parliament building, and then at the home of the U.S. Ambassador to Egypt, said Brotherhood spokesman Hamdi Hassan.[236] U.S. Embassy spokesman John Berry[237] would only confirm that Hoyer met with El-Katatni at U.S. Ambassador Francis Ricciardone's[238] home at a reception with other politicians and parliament members.

***

> Jon Alterman,[239] a Mideast specialist at the Center for Strategic and International Studies (CSIS) in Washington, who said that Bush administration officials may have avoided meeting MB members because that could strain relations with the secular Egyptian government, one of the closest U.S. allies in the Middle East, adding that, "There's been a growing sense in Washington over 20 years that *Islamic politics* are here to stay, and the U.S. interest in promoting democracy around the world means we should be engaging with *a growing number of actors*." [Emphasis added.]

The following month, on May 8, 2007,[240] in keeping with the new spirit of engagement with a "growing number of actors" involved in "Islamic politics," DHS Secretary Michael Chertoff[241] met with:

> A group of influential [unnamed] Muslim Americans to discuss ways the Department can work with their communities to protect the country, promote civic engagement and prevent violent radicalization from taking root in the United States. Part of the discussion involved the terminology U.S. government (USG) officials use to describe terrorists who invoke Islamic theology in planning, carrying out and justifying their attacks. Secretary Chertoff requested that these leaders continue to reflect on the words and terms that, in their opinion, DHS and the broader USG should use. Based on this request, Civil Rights and Civil Liberties (CRCL)[242] has consulted with some of the leading [unnamed] U.S.-based scholars and commentators on Islam to discuss the best terminology to use when describing the terrorist threat.

SKEWING THE DHS LEXICON

Partially as a result of the May 8, 2007 meeting, in 2008, the Department of Homeland Security Office of Civil Rights Civil Liberties Office distributed a memo entitled, *Terminology to Define the Terrorists: Recommendations from American Muslims* (a.k.a. the *Words Matter* memo).[243]

While at the time the memorandum was not described as official DHS policy, it would soon become obvious that the recommendations in the *Words Matter* memo were destined to become the *final word* on DHS policy. The Memo's recommendations largely advocated for using a lexicon which obfuscated, rather than revealed, the nature of the enemy against which DHS was supposed to protect the homeland.

Consider just two examples of such policy guidance contained in the *Words Matter* memo:

> **Expert Recommendation 1:** Respond to ideologies that exploit Islam without labeling all terrorist groups as a single enemy.
>
> [T]he cult members arrested in Miami [on June 23, 2006][244] should not be called members of Al-Qaeda; and, while they are both terrorist organizations who threaten global security and stability, Hezbollah and Hamas are distinct in methods, motivations and goals from Al-Qaeda. When possible, the experts recommend that USG terminology should make this clear.

While the memo warns that we should not refer to these "cult members" as members of Al-Qaeda, a June 23, 2006 news report specifically states that these African-American U.S. citizens swore allegiance to Al-Qaeda in the presence of an FBI agent. What is more, Hezbollah and Hamas both threaten "global security and stability," yet DHS personnel were being encouraged to consider them as "distinct" from AQ? Why, exactly? The *Words Matter* memo doesn't answer that question. Instead, it created an information black hole, a powerful, gaping void that remains to this day.

More importantly, from a strategic and tactical perspective, although some of the methods (i.e., the tactics) of Al-Qaeda are different than those of Hezbollah and Hamas, it is a dangerously misleading to suggest that these differences are sufficiently great to overshadow what they have in common, namely a divinely inspired determination to achieve shariah's triumph worldwide. After all, how else does one explain the cooperation between groups like Hezbollah and Al Qaeda?[245]

In fact, in the seven-plus years since the *Words Matter* memo was released, the surpassing importance of this bottom line has been confirmed again and again. A case in point was when the purportedly "moderate" Muslim Brotherhood took over Egypt in 2012[246] using "non-violent" and even democratic political techniques, then promptly switched to a very aggressive imposition of shariah law. All the while, it enjoyed the full support[247] of the Obama administration.

Expert Recommendation 9: "Emphasize the U.S. Government's Openness to Religious and Ethnic Communities":

There is no war against Muslims[248] or Islam in America. In fact, the American government is committed to ensuring justice in our country...There is a good level of engagement between the Federal government and Muslim American communities, and it will continue to increase over the upcoming months and years. Indeed, we have the hope of seeing levels of engagement [E&D] between the USG and Arab and Muslim Americans that have never been reached in the history of this country. For example, leading Arab, Muslim, and South Asian American groups have met multiple times with the 1) Secretary of Homeland Security,[249] 2) the Attorney General[250] [DOJ], 3) the Director of the FBI,[251] 4) the Secretary of the Treasury, and 5) senior officials at the State Department.

A number of meetings were indeed held between leading Arab, Muslim, and South Asian American groups and the major U.S. government's national security agencies during the most active phase of the Holy Land Foundation trial. Yet, as established in federal court, these same groups were providing financial support[252] to Hamas (see Appendix I: Highlights of the Holy Land Foundation Chronology.)

It was not long before the Words Matter memo became the subject of intense – and generally fatuous – media interest. To cite but two illustrative examples: On April 24, 2008,[253] the Associated Press distributed a report entitled "'Jihadist' Booted From Government Lexicon." And on May 30, 2008,[254] a CNN.com article appeared under the headline, "Agency Urges Caution With Terrorist Language."

Fortunately, others understood the true implications of the Words Matter memo. The Investigative Project on Terrorism (IPT) published a critical analysis by Steven Emerson on April 25, 2008,[255] entitled "Dangerous Word Games." It appeared the same day as an analysis headlined, "Federal Agencies Adopt Muslim Brotherhood Position On 'Jihad' and 'Islamic Terrorism.'" And on May 2, 2008,[256] IPT issued a press release entitled "Investigative Project Releases Gov't Memos Curtailing Speech in War on Terror."

Other noteworthy warnings about the Words Matter memo included: a May 4, 2008[257] article entitled "DHS Memo Supports Muslim Brotherhood Influence Over U.S. Counter-Terrorism Language"; a May 29, 2008[258] article headlined "The Great War Against Nothing In Particular"; and a May 31, 2008[259] commentary on the CNN report entitled "'Words Matter': Homeland Security Rolls Out Newspeak Campaign, Cautions Against Use Of Terms Like 'Jihadists,' 'Islamic Terrorists,' 'Islamists' And 'Holy Warriors.'"

THE DHS UNDER OBAMA

Things did not improve with the arrival of the Obama administration's team at the Department of Homeland Security, led by Secretary Janet Napolitano.[260] For example, in one of her first interviews in office, which was published on March 16, 2009[261] by Spiegel Online International, Ms. Napolitano was asked whether Islamist terrorism still posed a threat to America. She replied: "Of course it does. I presume there is always a threat from terrorism. In my [testimony],[262] although I did not use the word 'terrorism,' I referred to 'man-caused' disasters. That is perhaps only a nuance, but it demonstrates that we want to move away from the politics of fear toward a policy of being prepared for all risks that can occur."

It is crucial that we recognize the severe strategic and tactical consequences of our ineffectual response vis-à-vis the influence of Islam in America, specifically as seen from the perspective of the Islamic world.

We may regard such behavior as the application of "nuance" or "diversity sensitivity" or "multiculturalism" or "political correctness." According to the Quran and as explained so clearly in the classic Quranic Concept of War,[263] any failure by infidels to respond directly and decisively to the advancement of Islam is seen by Islamic supremacists as a sign of actionable divine favor. Specifically, such foundational documents make plain that, as Allah helps the believers (the "Best of Nations") [264] advance, while punishing the non-believers (the "perverted transgressors"), the latter inevitably descend into a state of confusion, weakness and vulnerability. Ultimately, the non-believers are compelled to submit to the authority of Islam. And the believers are obliged to redouble their efforts to make the infidels "feel subdued."

ORGANIZING FOR COUNTERING VIOLENT EXTREMISM

According to the official Department of Homeland Security (DHS) website,[265]:

> [Countering Violent Extremism (CVE) is] "neither constrained by international borders[266] nor limited to any single ideology. Groups and individuals inspired by a range of personal, religious, political, or other ideological beliefs promote and use violence. Increasingly sophisticated use of the Internet, social media, and information technology by violent extremists adds an additional layer of complexity.

In addition, "Violent Extremists" are defined by DHS as "individuals who support or commit ideologically-motivated violence to further political goals."

The DHS website goes on to state, "Accordingly, DHS has designed a CVE approach that addresses all forms of violent extremism, regardless of ideology, and that focuses *not* on radical thought or speech, but instead on preventing violent attacks." [Emphasis added.]

To formulate, implement and oversee this "CVE approach," the Department of Homeland Security has a Countering Violent Extremism Working Group (CVEWG).[267] It is led by the CVE Coordinator and includes participation from: the Office for Civil Rights and Civil Liberties (CRCL); Office of Intelligence and Analysis (I&A), Federal Emergency Management Agency (FEMA), National Protection and Programs Directorate (NPPD), Office of Policy, Office of Privacy (PRIV), and the Office of Science and Technology (S&T).

The CVEWG also has members from DHS Components, such as Customs and Border Protection (CBP), Federal Law Enforcement Training Center (FLETC), Office of the General Counsel (OGC), U.S. Immigration and Customs Enforcement (ICE), Office of Operations Coordination and Planning (OPS), Office of Public Affairs (OPA), Transportation Security Administration (TSA), U.S. Citizenship and Immigration Services (USCIS), U.S. Coast Guard (USCG), and the U.S. Secret Service (USSS).

THE CVE WORKING GROUP

The CVEWG has as members, moreover, a number of individuals who do not work for the federal government. They include Muslims whose ties to various entities should be a matter of grave concern to the Department, and the rest of us.

Their selection seems to have been influenced, at least in part, by the fact that, circa 2010, numerous invitation-only meetings and focus groups with "stakeholders" had been convened, the machinery of the "CVE approach" had been put in place, and various "scientific field tests" had been undertaken. Apparently, the Department and its Muslim interlocutors considered the time ripe for "robust" action.

Those who were avid supporters of CVE were gratified to see things begin to move faster and faster. For many within the LEO fraternity who saw the handwriting on the wall and refused to embrace CVE, however, the movement was clearly in the wrong direction.

Of particular concern to law enforcement officers was a controversial January 27-28, 2010[268] "Inaugural Meeting" between self-appointed American Muslim "leaders" and DHS Secretary Napolitano,[269] hosted by DHS-Civil Rights and Civil Liberties.[xxxii] This event was convened to ask representatives of the Muslim, Arab, South Asian and Sikh communities "for their help with membership in the upcoming DHS faith-based information-sharing task force." The idea was to establish with the participation of these communities a Countering Violent Extremism (CVE) Working Group, convened under the authority[270] of the Homeland Security Advisory Council (HSAC).[271]

Held just over a year after the November 2008 HLF verdicts, the DHS-CRCL Inaugural Meeting was the subject of controversy[272] because several of the individuals who attended the two-day, invitation-only conference in Washington, D.C. were known affiliates of The Islamic Society of North America, a Muslim Brotherhood front group named as an unindicted co-conspirator in the HLF trial. Two other groups the Muslim American Society (MAS),[273] and the Muslim Public Affairs Council, also had ties to the Muslim Brotherhood.

It must be remembered that the Islamic Society of North America was founded in 1981[274] at the University of Illinois Urbana-Champaign by members of the Muslim Students Association (MSA).[275] The MSA is not only the first Muslim Brotherhood front group in this country (it was established in January 1963); it is also the precursor to virtually every other Brotherhood entity in America today.

Given ISNA's extraordinary access to and influence with the Obama administration, it may seem difficult to believe that this organization is still listed as an unindicted co-conspirator in the Holy Land Foundation prosecution, in the course of which it was explicitly identified as one of the "individuals/entities who are and/or were members of the U.S. Muslim Brotherhood."

Founded in 1988, The Muslim Public Affairs Council is an offshoot of the shariah-adherent Islamic Center of Southern California. Among MPAC founders were two Egyptian brothers, Maher and Hassan Hathout, who were well-known, self-declared members of the Muslim Brotherhood.[276]

As previously noted, the Muslim American Society was created as the public organization of the U.S. Muslim Brotherhood.

Included among the invitees to the Inaugural Meeting was Hassan Al-Jabri[277] (a.k.a. Hossam AlJabri[278] or Hossam Jabri[279]), former Executive National Director[280] of MAS. He also had been the imam and one of three original leaders of the Islamic Society of Boston (a.k.a. the ISB or MAS-Boston), which has longstanding ties to several other, prominent MB front groups. These include: ISNA, NAIT and IIIT, as well as the Holy Land Foundation. (More on the ISB

[xxxii] The documents related to this Inaugural Meeting became public in July of 2010, but only after a Freedom of Information Act (FOIA) request was filed by Judicial Watch

will be found in Chapter 9, The White House Summit to Counter Violent Extremism.)

Simply put, the Department of Homeland Security's Civil Rights and Civil Liberties staff actively recruited – and, therefore, must have positively vetted – prominent leaders of *at least three* well-known North American affiliates of the international Brotherhood apparatus, clearing them to attend the DHS-CRCL Inaugural Meeting *and to help develop America's counter-terrorism policy*. This is nothing less than malfeasance and dereliction of duty, given that the federal government had established in the Holy Land Foundation trial that the Brotherhood's mission in this country is "destroying Western civilization from within."

Former National Security Council Counter-Terrorism Adviser Richard Clarke gave a sense of the dire implications of such a travesty in testimony before the Senate Banking Committee on October 22, 2003:[281]

> The issue of terrorist financing in the United States [the subject of the HLF Trial] is a fundamental example of the shared infrastructure levered by Hamas, Islamic Jihad and Al-Qaeda, all of which enjoy a significant degree of cooperation and coordination *within our borders*. The common link here is the extremist Muslim Brotherhood – all these organizations are descendants of the membership and ideology of the Muslim Brotherhood. [Emphasis added.]

Once again, let's pause for a moment, and reflect on the opening premise of this monograph: *They knew.*

PENETRATING THE COUNTERING VIOLENT EXTREMISM WORKING GROUP

Given the participants, it should hardly be surprising that the Inaugural Meeting did not go as swimmingly as DHS leadership had hoped. According to a February 4, 2010[282] email from David O'Leary, DHS Office of Legislative Affairs,[283] to David Gersten, Acting Deputy Officer for DHS-CRCL Programs and Compliance,[284]:

> Gordon Lederman of Sen. Lieberman's Staff called me asking about the 2-day HSAC[285] [Homeland Security Advisory Council] meeting last week with American Muslim and Arab groups. He was called by a reporter who told him MPAC, ISNA and MAS "rejected the ideas" of soliciting their help with countering violent extremism and were "angry and indignant."

On February 17, 2010,[286] investigative journalist Richard Pollock reported that DHS Secretary Janet Napolitano and her senior staff had met privately[287] on

January 28-29, 2010 with a group of Muslim, Arab and Sikh organizations, and that among the selected group were three organizations directly associated with Hamas, an outlawed terrorist entity. The article went on to say that Secretary Napolitano briefed them on DHS counter-radicalization and anti-terrorist programs.

Pollock's article also quoted Walid Phares,[288] at the time the Director of the Future Terrorism Project at the Foundation for Defense of Democracies (FDD),[289] who criticized[290] the partnership concept: "Through the so-called 'partnership' between the jihadi-sympathizer networks and U.S. bureaucracies, the U.S. government is invaded by militant groups." He warned that this policy embraced by the Obama administration "is how American national security policy has been influenced" by Muslim groups, who are duping administration officials.

Later in the Spring of 2010,[291] at least two individuals with close affiliations to the "angry and indignant" groups who had participated in the DHS Inaugural Meeting and who had "rejected the ideas" of soliciting their help with CVE, were nonetheless appointed to the Countering Violent Extremism Working Group: Omar Alomari[292] (MAS and several other MB front groups), and Mohamed Magid (ISNA).[293]

Here again, these appointments were made *after* the unindicted co-conspirator list was introduced into evidence in the Holy Land Foundation, and after the five defendants had been convicted. Incredibly, DHS-CRCL did not consider direct affiliation with one or more of the organizations that were known financial supporters of Hamas to be a disqualifier for potential candidates for the CVE Working Group.

A third MB-affiliated member of the Working Group was Mohamed Elibiary,[294] who was closely affiliated[295] with Shukri Abu Baker[296] (one of the five defendants in the HLF Trial), as well as with CAIR, another of the unindicted co-conspirators in the HLF Trial. Elibiary was also appointed to President Obama's Homeland Security Advisory Council on October 18, 2010.[297]

In September 2011, while Elibiary was serving on the HSAC and CVE Working Group, he received the FBI's highest civilian award from Director Mueller in a ceremony held at the Bureau's Training Academy at Quantico, Virginia. While there, he appears to have taken cell-phone photographs of books in the Academy's library. These photos subsequently accompanied one of the articles published by *Wired Magazine*'s Spencer Ackerman that stoked outrage about so-called "offensive" materials from the FBI and other first defenders' training curricula (See Chapter 3: The FBI.)[xxxiii]

A fourth CVE Working Group appointee was Dahlia Mogahed,[298] who was a shariah-adherent member of the 2008 Leadership Group on U.S.-Muslim Engagement. She maintained close relationships[299] with Brotherhood-linked groups CAIR, ISNA, MAS and MPAC after she was appointed on April 6, 2009[300] to the White House Office of Faith-Based and Neighborhood Partnerships.[301]

A fifth member of the Working Group was Nadia Roumani.[302] From the time of her appointment to the Working Group to the present day, she has served as either Director and/or Contributing Fellow at the American Muslim Civic Leadership Institute (AMCLI). Although the AMCLI was not designated as a Brotherhood front group in the Holy Land trial, the list of its alumni is a who's who of individuals affiliated with its unindicted co-conspirators.

Consider the following examples of problematic alumni of the ACMLI National Program[303]: Muneer Awad,[304] Zahra Billoo[305] and Dawud Walid[306] (all with CAIR); Zahir Latheef[307], a 13-year affiliate and former[308] National President of the Muslim Students Association; Edina Lukovic,[309] a professional affiliate of CAIR and MPAC who defended[310] Osama bin Laden as a great *Mujahid* in 1999 while she was a UCLA student; Mostafa Mahboob,[311] a professional affiliate of CAIR and MPAC and former Communications Manager of Islamic Relief USA[312] (designated by the UAE as a terrorist organization on November 15, 2014)[313]; Naba Sharif,[314] Board Member of MPAC-NY; Haris Tarin[315], Director of MPAC-Washington DC;[316] Yusufi Vali,[317] Executive Director of the Islamic Society of Boston Cultural Center (ISBCC[318] also closely affiliated with MAS);[319] and the aforementioned Mohamed Elibiary.

One other AMCLI alumna deserves special mention: Linda Sarsour,[320] a close affiliate of CAIR who currently serves as Director of the Arab American Association of New York (AAANY).[321] She was recognized in 2011[322] by the Obama White House as a "Champion of Change." AAANY is one of the signatories of a remarkable September 21, 2015[323] letter, which is discussed in Chapter 9.

[xxxiii] Elibiary ultimately resigned on September 03, 2014 after a controversy erupted over a number of his Tweets including: "As I've said b4, inevitable that 'Caliphate' returns"; the U.S. is an "Islamic country with an Islamically compliant Constitution"; and that national security "uber hawks camp misread 9/11." A letter from DHS suggests that his resignation was in part an attempt minimize fallout to DHS over Elibiary's alleged role in the "inappropriate disclosure of [unspecified] sensitive law enforcement documents."

Interestingly, on October 10, 2015,[324] Ms. Sarsour addressed[325] the "Justice Or Else!" rally, held in Washington, D.C. to commemorate the 20th anniversary of the so-called "Million Man March." During her speech, she proclaimed:[326]

> We are one, sisters and brothers, and our liberation is bound up together. The same people who justify the massacres of Palestinian people and call it collateral damage, are the same people who justify the murder of young Black men and women. The same people who want to deport millions of undocumented immigrants are the same people who hate Muslims and want to take our right to worship freely in this country. That common enemy sisters and brothers is White Supremacy, let's call it what it is...

Another member of DHS' CVE Working Group was former Los Angeles Deputy Mayor[327] Arif Alikhan, who was appointed as Assistant Secretary for Policy Development by DHS Secretary Napolitano on April 24, 2009.[328] Alikhan is also a close affiliate[329] of MPAC,[330] as well as the Islamic Shura Council[331] of Southern California (ISCSC),[332] yet another adversarial[333] MB "umbrella organization[334] for all of the region's Islamic centers and Islamic organizations, including CAIR-SC, MPAC and Islamic Relief." Like MPAC, the ISCSC was previously led by the Brotherhood's Hathout siblings.[335] The ISCSC has been directly linked[336] to still other individuals and organizations with known ties to Brotherhood fronts, such as ISNA, MAS and MSA.

ILLUSTRATIVE CVE WORKING GROUP RECOMMENDATIONS

Given its makeup, no one should be surprised that the CVE Working Group mostly served to *impede*, rather than enhance, situational awareness about, and the adoption of appropriate actions to counter, the Global Jihad Movement. Several of its internally inconsistent recommendations [337] about "Community Policing" advanced in a briefing to the Homeland Security Advisory Committee in the Spring of 2010 illustrate the point:

- DHS should work closely with the Office of Community-Oriented Policing Services (COPS) at the Department of Justice (DOJ) to better incorporate the concept of community-oriented policing into programmatic and policy efforts associated with homeland security preparedness.

- Communities may be hesitant to enter into relationships with local, state, tribal or federal law enforcement if they perceive that they are viewed as *incubators of violent extremism*.

- Training should seek to instill greater understanding regarding the "us versus them" perspective that many cultures have toward law enforcement and government and enable law enforcement personnel to better understand and address unrest or anger within the community (whether it be ideologically-based or not) in order to prevent violent activities. [Emphasis added.]

In short, many of these individuals and/or the Islamic organizations they represent have been engaged in years-long adversarial relationships[338] with the USG over its counter-terrorism and law enforcement policies.[339] What is important to understand is that often, they were aided and abetted in such struggles by DHS CRCL. A case in point involved the June 11, 2013 *Memorandum and Order Granting In Part And Denying In Part Official-Capacity Defendants' Motion To Dismiss* in which the MB-tied plaintiffs attempted to use their close association with the USG to their advantage. Specifically, they sought to immunize themselves from law enforcement scrutiny.[340]

Ties to the U.S. government were also employed in support of CAIR and MAS after the UAE correctly designated them as terrorist organizations on November 15, 2014.[341]

In short, real damage is being done by allowing American-based Muslim Brotherhood front groups inside the wire of government policymaking. It adds insult to serious injury that organizations that share with our enemies a commitment to Islamic supremacism are able to obtain protective cover through their involvement with the CVE apparatus.

CHAPTER 5: THE DEPARTMENT OF DEFENSE SUBMITS TO C.V.E.

At the tip of the spear of our first lines of defense are the United States armed forces. They have borne the brunt of the heavy lifting in what was once known as the "Global War on Terror." And they have been terribly served, as has the nation they strive to protect, by the serial accommodations made by our leaders under both parties to Islamic supremacism.

During the George W. Bush administration, the U.S. military was hamstrung by efforts to win the "hearts and minds" of Muslim populations with which we were at war. Successive civilian and military leaders at the Pentagon have drunk the Kool Aid of political correctness, acquiesced to White House directions reflecting the demands of our enemies, foreign and domestic, and, in the process, needlessly exposed our men and women in uniform to peril and defeat.

RULES OF ENGAGEMENT

Here too, matters only worsened after President Obama took office in 2009. The U.S. Department of Defense (DOD) began modifying its "Rules of Engagement" (ROE)[342] in Iraq and Afghanistan to accommodate the sensibilities of Muslims in the countries where the USG was trying to introduce democracy.

On September 20, 2009,[343] the Department of Defense released a declassified version of Gen. Stanley A. McChrystal's assessment of the war in Afghanistan. In a section under the headline of "Offensive Information Operations (IO)," the report states:

> Offensive IO must be used to target INS [Insurgent] networks in order to disrupt and degrade their operational effectiveness, while also offering opportunities for lower level insurgent reintegration. ISAF [International Security Assistance Force] should continue to develop and implement a robust and proactive capability to counter hostile information activities and propaganda.
>
> A more forceful and offensive strategic communications approach must be devised whereby INS are exposed continually for their cultural and religious violations, anti-Islamic and indiscriminate use of violence and terror, and by concentrating on their vulnerabilities. These include their causing of the majority of civilian casualties, attacks on education, development projects, and government institutions, and *flagrant contravention of the principles of the Quran*. These vulnerabilities must be expressed in a manner that exploits the cultural and ideological separation of the INS from the vast majority of the Afghan population. [Emphasis added.]

This "Offensive Information Operation" approach is really just a military version of the CVE policy. It is known in the foreign policy arena as "Engagement and Dialogue" (E&D).

As an initial step towards realizing the E&D objectives within his command, Gen. McChrystal wanted[344] to change the goal of public relations efforts in Afghanistan from a "struggle for the 'hearts and minds' of the Afghan population to one of giving them 'trust and confidence in themselves and their government.'" Again, this mirrors the sort of submission inherent in the domestic CVE Policy.

When Gen. McCrystal was cashiered by President Obama, he was replaced by Gen. David Petraeus, who had his own ideas about how to curry favor with native Muslim populations in war zones based on his prior experience with the so-called Counter-Insurgency [COIN] Strategy in Iraq.[xxxiv] On July 8, 2010,[345] an article published in *Stars and Stripes* reported on Gen. Petraeus' revised ROEs:

> Gen. David Petraeus, who became commander of all forces in Afghanistan on Sunday [July 4, 2010], is expected to issue a new tactical directive in a matter of days, according to Col. Rich Gross, the chief legal adviser to International Security Assistance Force in Afghanistan.
>
> Gross said confusion in the field over the existing tactical directive, which seeks to lessen civilian casualties by specifying when force can be used against Taliban insurgents, has resulted in some soldiers feeling as if they are fighting a war with their hands tied. Frustration has been mounting over the stricter tactical directive imposed last year by former ISAF commander Gen. Stanley McChrystal. Parents, politicians and some troops on the ground have been voicing frustration about soldiers being forced to take unnecessary risks because of overly restrictive regulations.

CULTURE CARDS

Additional evidence of the submission in the ROE's could be seen in the September 28, 2011[346] handbook entitled *Culture Cards: Afghanistan and Islamic Culture*, which was written to soften (read, censor) anything perceived as negative towards Islam. The handbook opens with the following statements:

> Military personnel who have a superficial or even distorted picture of a host culture make enemies for the United States. *Each Soldier must be a culturally literate ambassador*, aware and observant of local cultural beliefs, values, behaviors and norms. Why? Understanding local culture allows for better decision making through a better and more holistic picture of the operational environment.
>
> It reduces friction with local nationals.

[xxxiv] For more on the COIN Strategy, its utter futility in addressing Islamist warfare and culture and its disastrous implications for America's military and interests, see Diana West's commentary and analysis at www.DianaWest.net.

It allows better prediction and tracking of second and third order effects, helping avoid unforeseen and unintended consequences.

Leaders who acquire a basic understanding of local history and culture can also recognize and effectively counter the *threat's propaganda, based upon a misrepresentation of history.*

It allows for better operational planning and decision-making.

It can save lives! [Emphasis added.]

The handbook also admonishes military personnel that, "Culture is about how people perceive reality. It may not fit the true facts or history. Soldiers must not let *personal prejudices* cloud their judgment." [Emphasis added.]

There are at least two major flaws in this *Culture Card* approach. First, the threat of Islamic jihad is real and growing; it isn't simply fabricated propaganda, and/or a misrepresentation of history. And, second, the effects of culture and history are not merely byproducts of "how people perceive reality," but of absolute facts that often have severe, even violent historical consequences. These cannot be changed after-the-fact by anyone's personal prejudices.

These flaws were among those discussed in a December 6, 2013[347] *Washington Times* article. It revealed that, instead of reducing the number of attacks in Afghanistan, the misleading ROE guidelines contained in the *Culture Cards* approach actually contributed to a significant increase[348] in the number of fatal attacks in 2009-2010.

THE ISLAMIC STATE

The approach has not improved with the further evolution of the military dimensions of the Global Jihad Movement, notably the emergence of the Islamic State (which the Obama administration insists on calling ISIL). For example, on September 10, 2014,[349] Secretary of State John Kerry declared that, "ISIL claims to be fighting on behalf of Islam but the fact is that *its hateful ideology has nothing to do with Islam.*" He added that, "It is necessary for moderate, reasonable people around the world to repudiate the distortion of Islam that [ISIS] seeks to spread."

The truth is that this exploitation/repudiation narrative did not work out[350] very well in post-Saddam Iraq or Afghanistan, and sadly, it is not working any better at the moment with ISIS. In fact, *from an Islamic perspective*, this approach will *never* work – no matter where in the world it is tried, or what the cultural or political circumstances may be – since non-Muslims do not have the authority to judge Islamic principles. Period.

The bottom line for our men and women in uniform, and for the rest of us, must be: If fighting a war by the proxy of public relations (a.k.a. CVE) has not worked with the Taliban, al Qaeda or ISIS – or, for that matter with Boko Haram, Hamas, Iran, al Shabab, al Nusra or other Islamic supremacists, then why on earth should we expect the CVE approach to work any better here in America?

CHAPTER 6: SUBMISSION WITHIN OTHER PARTS OF THE U.S. GOVERNMENT

It is beyond the scope of this short book to document comprehensively the extent to which the U.S. government writ large has been penetrated and subverted by the influence operations of Islamic supremacists, profoundly compromising the nation's first lines of defense.

A few examples from other relevant executive branch agencies will hopefully suffice to round out the foregoing, more detailed examinations of the conduct in this regard of the FBI and the Departments of Homeland Security and Defense.

THE WHITE HOUSE

In the absence of policy direction from the Commander-in-Chief and his immediate senior subordinates in the Executive Mansion and National Security Council, it seems unlikely that those elsewhere in the national and homeland security agencies would have willingly followed the trajectory of accommodation and submission to the Muslim Brotherhood.

Starting with President George W. Bush's immediate response to the 9/11 attacks – notably, his photo ops. with top Muslim Brotherhood operatives and declarations in their presence that, for example, "Islam is a religion of peace" and "the teachings of the Koran are peace and good" – the door was opened wide to the Islamists' toxic influence operations.

As we have seen, even before President Obama's "New Beginning" speech in Cairo in June 2009, his administration had embraced at the UN Human Rights Council the Organization of Islamic Cooperation's agenda of suppressing freedom of speech.

Then, there was the President's speech at the University of Cairo before an audience that included, at White House insistence, Muslim Brotherhood leaders. Among its many notable passages was this extraordinary expression of personal, as well as official, submission:

> ...I have known Islam on three continents before coming to the region where it was first revealed. That experience guides my conviction that partnership between America and Islam must be based on what Islam is, not what it isn't. And *I consider it part of my responsibility as President of the United States to fight against negative stereotypes of Islam* wherever they appear. [xxxv] [Emphasis added.]

[xxxv] It is worth noting the Islamist pedigrees of two of those credited with helping to shape the President's remarks in Cairo: Rashad Hussain and Dalia Mogahed. Hussain has served as President Obama's Deputy Associate Counsel (2009), Special Envoy to the Organization of Islamic Cooperation (2010), and Special Envoy for Strategic Counterterrorism Communications (2015). Mr. Hussain's extensive

A remarkable sign of submission occurred on December 19, 2011,[351] when Vice President Joseph R. Biden, Jr. made the following comments during an interview with ABC News:

> We are in a position where if Afghanistan ceased and desisted from being a haven for people who do damage and have as a target the United States of America and their allies, that's good enough. That's good enough. We're not there yet. Look, *the Taliban per se is not our enemy*. That's critical. There is not a single statement that the President has ever made in any of our policy assertions that the Taliban is our enemy because it threatens U.S. interests. If, in fact, the Taliban is able to collapse the existing government, which is cooperating with us in keeping the bad guys from being able to do damage to us, then that becomes a problem for us. [Emphasis added.]

This comment helped set the stage for President Obama's subsequent, illegal release[352] in May 2014 of five senior Taliban leaders from the Guantánamo Bay[353] Naval Base detention facility, in exchange for an alleged deserter, Army Sgt. Bowe Bergdahl. This action was essential to a much more important act of submission – the ultimate closure of the Gitmo facility – which he promised to accomplish in his third Executive Order, which he signed on January 22, 2009,[354] just two days after taking office.

Of innumerable other examples that might be cited of submission by Barack Obama to the Islamic supremacists' agenda, one was particularly egregious. In the course of the President's September 25, 2012[355] address to the UN General Assembly, delivered shortly after the murderous attacks of September 11, 2012[356] on U.S. facilities in Benghazi, Libya, he declared: "The future must not belong to those who slander the prophet of Islam." Such a statement was of a piece with the demands for shariah blasphemy restrictions espoused by the likes of al Qaeda's Osama bin Laden, Muslim Brotherhood spiritual leader Yusef al-Qaradawi and the Islamic State's Abu Bakr al-Baghdadi.

Of course, we now *know* that the Obama administration meme that spontaneous mob violence over an Internet video was responsible for the attacks in

---

participation with Muslim Brotherhood-linked organizations are available at www.MuslimBrotherhoodinAmerica.com and the Global Muslim Brotherhood Daily Watch.
Like Hussain, Mogahed has extensive ties to Muslim Brotherhood front groups that are also documented at www.MuslimBrotherhoodinAmerica.com. She has taken credit as a White House advisor for having helped to shape the New Beginning speech's focus on "violent extremism." An interview by her with *Spiegel Online* shortly after the President's remarks in Cairo, reads in part:
Spiegel: "Obama never used the word *terror* in his speech. Instead, he chose to use the term "*violent extremism*" [at least six times]."
Mogahed: "I recommended using that terminology. He framed extremism as a *neutral threat* and didn't connect it with Islam. He mentioned it as a threat that affects Muslims, at least as much as it does the U.S., and he even mentioned that Muslims are the main victims of violent extremism."

Benghazi was a witting, deliberate lie.[xxxvi] The President of the United States, then-Secretary of State Hillary Clinton and National Security Advisor Susan Rice promoted it as a sop to shariah-adherent Muslims with whom they had been working to secure our conformity with that code's expression-crushing blasphemy codes.

THE STATE DEPARTMENT

Again, a comprehensive treatment of the conduct of the Department of State in promoting accommodations to the Saudis, Iranians and other Islamic supremacist nations, to their multinational jihadist cartel – the Organization of Islamic Cooperation, and to their agents of influence inside the United States is beyond our present compass.

Suffice it to say that, going back at least to Secretary of State Colin Powell's tenure, we have seen out of Foggy Bottom a litany of submission to one aspect or another of the Islamist agenda, both in external relations and domestically. For example, in 2007, Secretary of State Condoleeza Rice engineered the resumption of contacts with Egypt's Muslim Brotherhood despite her 2005 commitment not to "engage" with the group. This reversal was justified on the grounds that doing so was "in conformity with a worldwide policy of dealing with political parties that are represented in their national parliaments."[357]

As was discussed previously, Secretary of State Hillary Clinton subsequently championed a full embrace of the Muslim Brotherhood internationally and enabled its influence operations in America, notably by personally intervening to provide a visa for one of its preeminent figures, Tariq Ramadan. She also personally advanced the OIC's effort to enforce U.S. conformity with shariah blasphemy laws via "shaming and peer-pressure."[358]

For his part, as we have seen, Secretary of State John Kerry has repeatedly and mendaciously promoted the central CVE meme that the Islamic State and other jihadists have "nothing to do with Islam." This has served to undermine the credibility, coherence and effectiveness of American foreign policy around the world and helped to enable the civilization jihad at home.

[xxxvi] See Judicial Watch's numerous FOIA'd documents and the Citizen's Commission on Benghazi's interim report.

THE INTELLIGENCE COMMUNITY

On February 10, 2011,[359] the nation's top intelligence officer engaged in one of the most dramatic – and outrageous – examples of official submission to the Countering Violent Extremism narrative. In testimony during a public hearing of the House Intelligence Committee, Director of National Intelligence James Clapper (apparently reading from written guidance) stated:

> The term "Muslim Brotherhood"...is an umbrella term for a variety of movements, in the case of Egypt, a very heterogeneous group, *largely secular*, which has eschewed violence and has decried Al-Qaeda as a perversion of Islam. They have pursued social ends, a betterment of the political order in Egypt, et cetera...In other countries, there are also chapters or franchises of the Muslim Brotherhood, but there is no overarching agenda, particularly in pursuit of violence, at least internationally. [Emphasis added.]

To illustrate his claim about the benign nature of the Muslim Brotherhood, the DNI declared that the organization runs 29 hospitals in Egypt, though "not under the guise of an extremist agenda." He added that they fill a vacuum caused by the absence of government services. But, "It is not necessarily with a view to promoting violence or overthrow of the state."

Later that same day,[360] Jamie Smith, Director of the DNI's Office of Public Affairs, tried to limit the damage caused by Gen. Clapper's outlandish remarks by saying: "To clarify Director Clapper's point – in Egypt the Muslim Brotherhood makes efforts to work through a political system that has been, under Mubarak's rule, one that is largely secular in its orientation – he is well aware that the Muslim Brotherhood is *not* a secular organization."

It is important to acknowledge that Mr. Clapper's misleading testimony about the nature of the Muslim Brotherhood did not simply reflect his own erroneous opinions. Rather, they were derived from a prevailing consensus from within the Intelligence Community that he remains part of to this day.

A few months later, the Intelligence Community engaged in another, portentous act of submission to the Islamists. A conference originally scheduled for CIA headquarters in McLean, Virginia under the co-sponsorship of the CIA Threat Management Unit[361] and the Intelligence Subcommittee of the Metropolitan Washington Council of Governments[362] was scrubbed. In an email explaining why the event was being postponed, CIA Police Officer Lt. Joshua Fielder[363] wrote: "The conference topic is a critical one for domestic law enforcement, and the sponsors – in partnership with DHS – have decided to delay the conference so it can include insights from among other sources, the new [2011][364] *National Strategy for Counterterrorism* in an updated agenda."

This pronouncement obscured what was actually the problem: the "insights" that would have been provided to the conferees from the originally scheduled "sources," which included renowned subject matter experts Stephen Coughlin[365] and Steven Emerson.[366] According to the *Washington Times*,[367] the Department of Homeland Security and the White House had received complaints from Muslim advocacy groups about the views such authorities would express and succeeded in shutting down the conference rather than allowing an intelligence community audience to hear their insights.

Moreover, an unnamed DHS official told *Times* reporter Bill Gertz that, in order to prevent these two CT experts from taking part in future conferences, the Obama administration was "drafting new guidelines designed to prohibit all USG personnel[368] from teaching classes on Islamic history or doctrine." He added that "the new rules would also seek to prohibit the use of federal funds to pay contractors for such training."

"This is a big deal,"[369] former FBI counterintelligence agent David G. Major[370] said of the postponement, adding that if new guidelines are used to block experts like Mr. Coughlin and Mr. Emerson, "we will be in '1984'[371] with 'Newspeak'[372] on our society in total violation of the First Amendment."

The "Great Purge" (the subject of Chapter Seven), took place in the months that followed the cancellation of the intelligence community's conference. It demonstrated conclusively just how consequential was this Islamist effort to penetrate and subvert our first lines of defense.

THE DEPARTMENT OF JUSTICE

An entire monograph could be written about the successful Islamist influence operations run against the Bush and Obama Justice Departments. The foregoing discussion of the Holy Land Foundation case shed light on the support given to Muslim Brotherhood organizations reeling from the convictions of five of their brothers by Attorney General Eric Holder. He was greatly assisted in that effort by his first Assistant Attorney General for Civil Rights (now Secretary of Labor) Thomas Perez.

The leitmotif of their Islamist outreach and enabling can be found in a statement made by General Holder on June 4, 2009,[373] timed to coincide with President Obama's "outreach to the Muslim world" speech[374] in Cairo:

> The President's pledge for *a new beginning* between the United States and the Muslim community takes root here in the Justice Department, where *we*

are committed to using criminal and civil rights laws to protect Muslim Americans.

A top priority of this Justice Department is *a return to robust civil rights enforcement and outreach* in defending religious freedoms and other fundamental rights of all of our fellow citizens in the workplace, in the housing market, in our schools and in the voting booth. There are those who will continue to want to divide by fear – to pit our national security against our civil liberties – but that is a false choice. We have a solemn responsibility to protect our people while we also protect our principles. [Emphasis added.]

What the Attorney General had in mind in terms of "a return to robust civil rights enforcement and outreach" was laid out in a memorandum also issued on June 4, 2009,[375] entitled *Backgrounder on Outreach and Enforcement Methods to Protect American Muslims*. This memo was the first in what became a whole series of documents that mirrored each other in their style of language and content. Such documents include: UN Human Rights Council Resolution 16/18 (2011);[376] Senate Bill 1038 (2013),[377] [4] *DOJ Guidance For Federal Law Enforcement Agencies Regarding The Use Of Race, Ethnicity, Gender, National Origin, Religion, Sexual Orientation or Gender Identity* (2014);[378] and *H. R. 2899* (2015)[379] and H.Res. 569 (2015)[380] discussed in more detail below, in Chapter Eight: CVE and the Congress.

In retrospect, it should have been obvious to everybody what had become quite clear by this point to those of inside the Law Enforcement Officers' "Blue Line": a civil rights-based CVE Policy had completely overshadowed the initial post-9/11 fact-based counter-terrorism policy.[xxxvii] At the Justice Department as elsewhere in the government, this CRCL-dominated approach continued gaining momentum, notwithstanding – and *especially after* – the 108 guilty verdicts in the Holy Land Foundation trial that were returned on November 25, 2008.[381]

THE TREASURY DEPARTMENT

Much could also be said about the role the Treasury Department has played in U.S. counter-terrorism efforts since 9/11. Some of it has been quite good, as Treasury officials have sought creative ways to use financial tools to restrict the cash flows to international jihadist organizations and induce other nations to do the same.

Unfortunately, other parts of the Treasury have enabled practices that are very much at odds with such sensible initiatives. For example, in the aftermath of the government's 2008 $180-plus billion bailout[382] of the American International

---

[xxxvii] The impact these policies had in hampering one such officer, retired CBP officer Phillip Haney, are discussed in the Epilogue.

Group (AIG)[383] – a company that offered shariah-compliant insurance products, the Bush Treasury Department began actively promoting shariah-compliant finance and *Zakat*.

Notably, this was the transparent purpose of an event Treasury co-hosted at its headquarters on November 6, 2008:[384] a seminar for government officials entitled "Islamic Finance 101." The other co-sponsor was the "Islamic Finance Project" at Harvard Law School. The event featured professors associated with the Islamic Finance Project at Harvard Law School.[xxxviii]

The Islamic Finance 101 seminar occurred just two weeks before the HLF trial verdicts confirmed the dangers that at least *some* in the Treasury and Justice Departments understood were posed by *Zakat* and Islamists' materials support of terrorism. According to the official announcement of this event:

> This forum is designed to help inform the policy community about Islamic financial services, which are an increasingly important part of the global financial industry. The Department of the Treasury, working with Harvard University's Islamic Finance Project, will host speakers from academia and industry to share information on the development of Islamic finance, both in the United States and globally.
>
> The primary audience of this seminar is comprised of staff from U.S. banking regulatory agencies, Congress, Department of Treasury and other parts of the Executive Branch. For some in attendance, this may be their first and only opportunity to learn formally about Islamic finance. We expect about 100 people in the audience. The presentations will be short and focused, *directed toward policy makers* rather than academics. [Emphasis added.]

The keynote speech of this event was given by Neel Kashkari. At the time, he was acting as the Interim Assistant Secretary of the Treasury for Financial Stability and Assistant

---

[xxxviii] Harvard is one of a number of prominent American institutions of higher learning that have been beneficiaries of tens of millions of dollars from Prince Alwaleed bin Talal. Bin Talal is a billionaire member of the Saudi royal family whose wealth has been lavishly spent on Islamic supremacist influence operations in this country and elsewhere. Interestingly, the Islamic Finance Project enjoyed the strong support of the Law School's then-Dean, Elena Kagan, now an Associate Justice of the U.S. Supreme Court. In the latter capacity, Ms. Kagan may play an important role in future decisions about the penetration of shariah into America's judicial system. For more on this topic, see other monographs in the Center for Security Policy's Civilization Jihad Reader Series: *Shariah in American Courts: The Expanding Incursion of Islamic Law in the U.S. Legal System* (https://www.centerforsecuritypolicy.org/2015/04/06/shariah-in-american-courts-test/) and *Offensive and Defensive Lawfare: Fighting Civilization Jihad in America's Courts* (https://www.centerforsecuritypolicy.org/2015/10/28/book-release-offensive-and-defensive-lawfare-fighting-civilization-jihad-in-americas-courts/).

Secretary of the Treasury for International Economics and Development – two key positions at that juncture, when the U.S. and global economies and financial sectors were being rocked by the Lehman Brothers' collapse and what flowed from it.[xxxix]

Coming as it did in the midst of the economic and financial meltdowns of the Fall of 2008, an unmistakable message was sent by this event and the prominent role played in it by Secretary Kashkari – who was at the time responsible for doling out the hundreds of billions in Troubled Asset Relief Program (TARP): The Treasury Department was encouraging the "policy community" and the financial institutions it oversees/regulates to view *shariah*-compliant finance positively.

On November 5, 2008,[385] the Center for Security Policy's Christopher Holton commented about the then-impending *Islamic Finance 101* seminar, warning that: "America is losing the financial war on terror because Wall Street is [by opening itself to shariah-compliant finance] embracing a subversive enemy ideology on one hand, and providing corporate life-support to state sponsors of terrorism on the other hand."[xl]

THE INEVITABLE ENDPOINT OF A SEE-NO-SHARIAH POLICY APPROACH: THE GREAT PURGE

The previous pages have described the broad sweep of the U.S. government's systematic abandonment over the past fifteen years of fact-based counter-terrorism, in favor of the so-called Civil Rights-Civil Liberties-dictated Countering Violent Extremism approach.

As we will discuss in the next chapter, this saga accelerated dramatically with the "Great Purge," when CT training designed to equip our first lines of defense – especially the FBI,[386] intelligence community and Departments of Defense and Homeland Security – that was deemed "offensive" (or even *possibly* offensive) to Muslims was summarily eliminated.[387]

[xxxix] Kevin Freeman CFA, a Senior Fellow of the Center for Security Policy, has written a best-selling book, *Secret Weapon: How Economic Terrorism Brought Down the U.S. Stock Market and Why It Can Happen Again*. It reminds us that no less an authority on the subject than George Soros had asserted that Lehman Brothers – and with it the U.S. economy – was subjected to economic warfare in the form of a naked short-selling bear raid. Mr. Freeman's book lays out the considerable evidence that the perpetrators were sovereign wealth funds out of the Middle East. These funds typically are obliged to practice and promote shariah-compliant finance.
[xl] For more of Mr. Holton's analysis, see Shariah Finance Watch.

CHAPTER 7: THE GREAT PURGE

As with similar events throughout history, the "Great Purge" that was waged against America's front lines of defense by the Global Jihad Movement and its enablers in 2011-2012 quickly turned into a feeding frenzy. It began with the FBI and the rest of the relevant agencies trying to accommodate the demands of "outreach partners" in the American Muslim community for heightened sensitivity to their feelings. But it wound up sucking those agencies into a vortex of political warfare waged by Islamists and the radical leftists who support and empower them – – a true "Red-Green axis" that is determined to shut down the authorities' missions under the pretext of respecting "Civil Rights and Civil Liberties."

What follows is a chronological review of some of the major events that occurred during this disastrous time, when virtually the entire U.S. government turned away from counter-terrorism threat analysis and responses *rooted in facts* – and towards a so-called civil rights-based approach known as Countering Violent Extremism.

'SEE-NO-SHARIAH'

As summarized so well by author Diana West in her 2013[388] book, *American Betrayal: The Secret Assault on Our Nation's Character,* our government's ongoing, persistent failures to use available information and facts-based threat analysis were not disconnected, abstract events with no real-world consequences:

> Years of battle – even worse, years of battle-planning – have passed without our leadership having studied, or even having become acquainted with, the principles and historic facts of Islamic war doctrine. Four years into the so-called war on terror, then-Joint Chiefs Chairman Peter Pace even pointed this out in a speech at the National Defense University [at Ft. McNair] on December 1, 2005.[389]

> Notwithstanding Pace's concern, the study and analysis of Islam and jihad remained *de facto* forbidden in policy-making circles inside the Bush White House, which even codified a lexicon in 2008[390] to help government officials discuss Islamic jihad without mentioning "Islam" or "jihad."

> The Obama administration would carry this same see-no-Islam policy to its zealous limit, finally mounting a two-front assault on the few trainers and fact-based training materials that were sometimes (sparingly) used by law enforcement agencies and the military to educate personnel about Islam and jihad.

The Great Purge would hit America's first lines of defense like a tsunami of abject submission in the Fall of 2011. One of the first signs of the impending disaster was The National Counterterrorism Center (NCTC)[391] publication of a study entitled *Behavioral Indicators Offer Insights for Spotting Extremists Mobilizing for Violence.*

This paper was released on July 22, 2011[392] and showed numerous signs of the coming debacle. But, the authors were, at least, still allowed to include terms such as "Islam" and "jihad" on the same page as the word "terrorism." It proved, however, to be one of the last times professionals within the Federal government would attempt to conduct a fact-based trend analysis, while also providing realistic explanations for the continued rise in jihad-related attacks. The opening paragraph read as follows:

> A U.S. Government interagency study of homegrown violent extremists (HVE's) revealed four major mobilizing patterns shared by a majority of HVE cases between 2008 and 2010, providing officials with an emerging picture of distinct behaviors often associated with an individual mobilizing for violence. These four patterns – 1) links to known extremists, 2) ideological commitment to extremism, 3) international travel, and 4) pursuit of weapons and associated training – repeatedly appeared in the case studies, reinforcing initial assessments of potential trends. Awareness of the patterns can help combat the recent rise in these cases, while providing a data-driven tool for assessing potential changes in the HVE threat to the Homeland.

One of the reasons why such analyses would no longer emerge from the nation's "first lines of defense" turned up on the "Danger Room" blog at *Wired Magazine*'s website on July 27, 2011.[393] Entitled "FBI 'Islam 101' Guide Depicted Muslims as 7th-Century Simpletons," it was a prime example of the Red-Green axis at work, with the author a radical leftist named Spencer Ackerman advancing the cause of Islamic supremacists at the expense of the nation and its security. The article included a link to a 62-slide PowerPoint reportedly used in training Bureau personnel.

The FBI's initial response to the "Islam 101" article read in part:

> The FBI new agent population at Quantico is exposed to a diverse curriculum in many specific areas, including Islam and Muslim culture. The presentation in question was a rudimentary version used for a limited time that has since been replaced. It was a small part of a larger segment of training that also included material produced by the Combating Terrorism Center (CTC)[394] at West Point.

On September 14, 2011,[395] Ackerman struck again. This time posting at *Wired*'s blog a post entitled, "FBI Teaches Agents: 'Mainstream' Muslims Are 'Violent, Radical.'" It attacked an FBI agent named William Gawthrop[396] for the contents of a Power Point presentation he used in a training session on an August 24, 2011.

The response to this expose confirmed a grave problem that had become obvious by this point in 2011 to inside observers who once enjoyed wide latitude to develop comprehensive counter-terrorism cases: There were very few Federal, state or local law enforcement officers who were given the professional mentoring, time, resources *and leeway* to do the hard work necessary to put a solid counter-terrorism case together. Unfortunately, it is much worse today than it was back then.

A CONCERTED OFFENSIVE TO BLIND OUR FIRST LINES OF DEFENSE

Within twenty-four hours of Ackerman's latest salvo, the Islamic supremacists launched a concerted offensive. On September 15, 2011,[397] a letter signed by Farhana Khera,[398] the president and executive director of Muslim Advocates,[399] was sent to Cynthia Schnedar,[400] Acting Inspector General in the U.S. Department of Justice (DOJ). The letter included the following grievances:

> We are writing to request that you launch an immediate investigation into the Federal Bureau of Investigation (FBI) use of grossly inaccurate, inflammatory and highly offensive counterterrorism training materials about Muslims and Islam used to train its agents and other law enforcement.
>
> These materials malign and disparage an entire faith community and their religious practice, in flagrant violation of the Department of Justice's (DOJ) mandate to "ensure fair and impartial administration of justice for all Americans" and our country's fundamental values of religious freedom and pluralism.
>
> As reported yesterday in *Wired Magazine*, the FBI is conducting counterterrorism training using materials that include woefully misinformed statements about Islam and bigoted stereotypes about Muslims. The training materials were developed by an analyst employed by the FBI and presumably reviewed and vetted by the FBI. The gravity of this issue and the need for an investigation into the FBI's training of its agents and other law enforcement is long overdue.

For its part, the FBI began a headlong retreat. That same day,[401] FBI spokesman Christopher Allen held a press conference and announced that policy changes "had been underway to better ensure that all training is consistent with FBI standards." He added that, "The training materials in question were delivered as Stage Two training to counterterrorism-designated agents," and that "this training was largely derived from a variety of open source publications and includes the opinion of the analyst that developed the lesson block."

The implication that information derived from "open sources" is somehow less instructive or otherwise valuable than classified information is absurd. After all, the ideology and motivations for the terrorist attacks we see almost every day are posted on mass-media platforms such as Twitter and Facebook, not to mention the innumerable numbers of blogs, websites, videos and books that are openly disseminated by jihadist groups all over the world. Also, given the fact that these same jihadists openly state that their goals are based on historic Islamic doctrines, it remains perfectly reasonable – indeed, *absolutely necessary* – to have counter-terror specialists in America study these concepts.[xli]

A seasoned law enforcement officer, Robert McFadden, who had retired from the Navy Criminal Investigative Service (NCIS),[402] also critiqued the FBI's defense: "Teaching counterterrorism operatives about obscure aspects of Islam without context, without objectivity, and without covering other non-religious drivers of dangerous behavior is no way to stop actual terrorists."

FBI ROCKED BY MORE INCOMING FIRE

As discussed in Chapters 3 and 4, in September 2011, an Islamic supremacist named Mohamed Elibiary, who was serving at the time on the Homeland Security Advisory Council and its Countering Violent Extremism Working Group, received the FBI's highest civilian award from Director Mueller in a ceremony held at the Bureau's Training Academy at Quantico, Virginia. He appears to have taken advantage of this foolishly conferred honor to perform reconnaissance to support the demands made earlier by his fellow Islamists aimed at eliminating from the FBI training curriculum materials "offensive" to Muslims. Within days of the ceremony, further screeds inveighing against the Bureau, its trainers and pedagogy were published at *Wired* Magazine by Ackerman, including one with cell-phone photographs taken of books in the Academy's library.

Shortly thereafter, the Red-Green axis – in this case, a coalition of progressive. left-wing and Muslim Brotherhood-linked organizations that included CAIR, ISNA, MSA and MPAC – wrote a joint letter to FBI Director Mueller. The letter, dated October 4, 2011,[403] demanded the purging of training materials they deemed offensive. It read in part:

[xli] As discussed in another context previously, the May 28, 2015 FBI threat assessment entitled *Militia Extremists Expand Target Sets To Include Muslims* includes the following caveat about open source information: The information in this bulletin is drawn from FBI and open sources of varying reliability. The FBI has medium to high confidence in FBI source information, which includes confidential sources and contacts with varying levels of access, corroboration, and reliability. The FBI has low-to-high confidence in open source information drawn from Internet news articles, video, and Weblogs. Much of the open source information reflects opinion or information borrowed without attribution and is therefore of questionable reliability. It is, however, used here to show the type of information that is available to extremists and influential in affirming their beliefs.

> The undersigned civil and human rights groups write to express our deep concern regarding recently-publicized FBI training materials that manifest anti-Muslim bias and factual inaccuracies. We appreciate that the FBI now recognizes the need for a comprehensive review of its counterterrorism training materials referencing religion and culture. We especially applaud the FBI's unequivocal statement that, "*Strong religious beliefs should never be confused with violent extremism.*" [Emphasis added.]
>
> This statement, however, conflicts with assertions contained in previously published FBI intelligence products. We urge you to expand your comprehensive review of training materials to include intelligence products that contain similarly erroneous and biased information, to withdraw them where necessary, and to issue new guidance clearly stating that religious practices and political advocacy are protected activities under the First Amendment, and are not indicators of future violence.

The next day, MPAC piled on, posting a press release on its homepage entitled "MPAC Co-Signs Letter to FBI Demanding Reformation in Flawed, Anti-Muslim Training." It included this passage:

> MPAC has signed on to a letter authored by the ACLU[404] requesting the FBI withdraw documents and reports published by the bureau with biased and flawed information about Islam and Muslims. Since *the rise of the post-9/11 Islamophobic era*, the FBI has explicitly stated numerous times "strong religious beliefs should never be confused with violent extremism."
>
> However, the ACLU found numerous documents, such as the FBI intelligence assessment[405] "The Radicalization Process: From Conversion to Jihad" published in March 2006 that lists the supposed "steps" and "indicators" of "homegrown Islamic extremists" as those who practice Islam. In the letter, several organizations asked the FBI to conduct a comprehensive review of intelligence and "issue new guidance clearly stating that religious practices and political advocacy are protected activities under the First Amendment, and are not indicators of future violence."[xlii] [Emphasis added.]

It was, presumably, "no accident" that all this Red-Green agitation occurred in the immediate run-up to open-session testimony by the FBI Director before the House Intelligence Committee scheduled for October 6, 2011.[406] Predictably, Director Mueller was obliged to talk about the Bureau's counter-terrorism pedagogy. An account of his appearance by the *Washington Times* ran under the headline "Islam Content Spurs FBI Review of Anti-Terror Training":

> FBI Director Robert S. Mueller III told a congressional hearing on Thursday [October 6, 2011] that the Bureau is conducting a review of training

---

[xlii] DOJ Attorney General Eric Holder essentially fulfilled this request, when on December 8, 2014, he authorized the release of *Guidance For Federal Law Enforcement Agencies Regarding The Use Of Race, Ethnicity, Gender, National Origin, Religion, Sexual Orientation, Or Gender Identity*.

programs after disclosure of materials that equated devout Muslims with a greater propensity for violent extremism. Mr. Mueller said that one part of the training program disclosed in a press account was "inappropriate and offensive," but that the session was a "one-off" and not likely to be repeated. "We have undertaken a review from top to bottom of our counterterrorism training," Mr. Mueller said. "I think these are isolated incidents, and in the course of that review, *we've had outreach to academicians and others* to assist us in reviewing the materials and assuring that that *offensive content does not appear.*"

The comments came in response to questions from Janice D. Schakowsky (D-IL), during a hearing before the House Permanent Select Committee on Intelligence, about leaked training materials from an FBI training session at its institute in Quantico, VA, in March. The materials...stated of Muslims that "the more religious they get, the more violent they are. And, I understand that there's been training [sessions] where the Prophet Muhammad has actually been called a cult leader and [where] the Islamic practice of giving to charity [has been described as] no more than, quote, 'a funding mechanism for combat.'"

The exchange prompted charges that Mr. Mueller was knuckling under to political correctness aimed at muzzling critics of Islam. [Emphasis added.]

Let us recall that all this was going on *less than three years* after the Holy Land Foundation verdicts had laid bare: the nature of the "civilization jihad" being conducted by the Muslim Brotherhood inside the United States; its object – "destroying Western civilization from within" – narratives and operations; and the identities of 300-plus individuals and organizations engaged in that form of *pre-violent jihad*. Several of the groups that had signed the October 4th letter to Director Mueller were among those listed as HLF unindicted co-conspirators.

Nonetheless, the Great Purge was the order of the day. In deference to the demands of Islamists (unindicted HLF co-conspirators and otherwise), a desperate effort was made by the USG not to give offense. Accordingly, very little, *if any*, consideration was given to whether the content of the so-called "offensive training material" was *actually correct*, or not.

Instead, the entire process had devolved into an exercise of *submission* to ever-escalating coercion from various Muslim Brotherhood front groups. Still more outrageous is the fact that several of them had already been proven in federal court to have provided material support to a designated terrorist organization, Hamas.

On October 14, 2011, Assistant Secretary of Defense[407] Jose Mayorga brought the Pentagon into the Great Purge, issuing a memorandum entitled "Request for Joint Staff Cooperation," which stated in part:[408]

Recent media attention on the FBI's CVE training and DOD lectures led the National Security Staff (NSS)[409][xliii] to request Department and Agencies to provide their screening process for CVE trainers and speakers. Request the Joint Staff task the COCOMS's, Services, National Guard Bureau and Components to determine the current processes used to vet CVE trainers.

In addition, the vetting of curriculum development for cultural awareness pre-deployment training for Iraq and Afghanistan should be included.

Please provide the current process of vetting CVE trainers by October 31, 2011.

RED (AND GREEN) LETTER DAY: OCTOBER 19, 2011

Four more developments warrant special mention in this timeline chronicling the submission of our first lines of defense to the Muslim Brotherhood and its allies "Civil Rights and Civil Liberties" gambit. Amazingly, *all of them took place on October 19, 2011* – smack dab in the middle of two milestones of the CVE transformation: First, the July 15, 2011[410] inaugural speech by Secretary of State Hillary Clinton at the OIC-sponsored "High-Level Meeting on Combating Religious Intolerance" held in Istanbul, Turkey and, second, the series of closed-door meetings on the Istanbul Process on Islamophobia,[411] which were hosted by the U.S. Department of State in Washington, D.C. on December 12, 2011.[412]

AGITATION IN THE MEDIA

The first noteworthy October 19, 2011[413] development for the CVE agenda was the publication of an op.ed. in the *Los Angeles Times* by one of the most insidious political warfare operatives among the new generation of Muslim Brotherhood-tied Islamic supremacists: Muslim Public Affairs Council president Salam Al-Marayati. It was entitled, "The Wrong Way To Fight Terrorism." Highlights included the following assertions *and threats*:

> Law enforcement and intelligence agencies' continued use of anti-Muslim training materials could lead to the collapse of a critical partnership with the Muslim American community. A disturbing string of training material used by the FBI and a U.S. Attorney's office came to light beginning in late July that reveals a deep anti-Muslim sentiment within the U.S. government.

[xliii] After a 2009 policy review, the Homeland Security Council – at the time headed by John Brennan, who was both the White House Counterterrorism and Homeland Security Adviser *and* the NSC Deputy National Security Adviser for Counterterrorism, was formally merged with the NSC, to become the National Security Staff (NSS). However, on February 10, 2014, after Brennan had been moved to head up the Central Intelligence Agency, the entire process was reversed via executive order.

If this matter is not *immediately addressed*, it will undermine the relationship between law enforcement and the Muslim American community – another example of the ineptitude and/or apathy undermining bridges built with care over decades. It is not enough to just call it a "very valid concern," as FBI Director Robert Mueller told a congressional committee this month.

The training material in question provided to FBI agents at the academy in Quantico, VA – as first reported by Wired magazine's *Danger Room* blog – contained bigoted and inflammatory views on Muslims, including claims that "devout" Muslims are more prone toward violence, that Islam aims to "transform a country's culture into 7th century Arabian ways," that Islamic charitable giving is a "funding mechanism for combat" and that the prophet Muhammad was a "violent cult leader."

Attorney General Eric H. Holder Jr. and FBI Director Mueller, take some leadership on this matter, or the partnership we've built to counter violent extremism will forever be handicapped. The question you have to answer is simple: *Are we on the same team, or not?* [Emphasis added.]

DOJ ON THE ISLAMISTS' TEAM

The day's second coup for the Red-Green axis was a "conference[414] hosted by the Justice Department's Civil Rights Division on discrimination in the post-Sept. 11 era."[xliv] It featured audience participation and speeches by a number of the leftist and Islamist groups that had signed the October 4, 2011[415] ACLU/MPAC letter. Andrew C. McCarthy,[416] the former Chief Assistant U.S. Attorney in the Southern District of New York who successfully prosecuted the co-conspirators in the 1993 World Trade Center bombing, aptly described the meeting as one that "showcased the expanding alliance between American progressives and Islamists."

McCarthy might have added that it also showcased the expanding alliance between the Red-Green axis and the Obama administration. Among the featured speakers were a number of present and former top DOJ officials, including the Department's Number 2, then-Deputy Attorney General James Cole. He used the occasion to declare: "We must reject any suggestion that every Muslim is a terrorist or that every terrorist is a Muslim," He added, "As we have seen time and again – from Oklahoma City to the recent attacks in Oslo, Norway – no religion or ethnicity has a monopoly on terror."[xlv]

The conference's host was then-Assistant Attorney General for the Civil Rights Division (later Secretary of Labor) Tom Perez.[417] One might say it marked a new zenith for the Obama administration's embrace – literally – of the Muslim

---

[xliv] http://talkingpointsmemo.com/muckraker/advocates-give-government-mixed-review-on-combatting-post-9-11-backlash
[xlv] *Ibid.*

Brotherhood since, at an event at George Washington University, Perez bounded onto stage to *hug* Mohamed Magid. Magid is the imam of the Capital region's largest shariah-adherent mosque complex, the ADAMS Center. At the time, he was also the president of the nation's largest Muslim Brotherhood front organization, the Islamic Society of North America.

According to journalist Neil Munro,[418] at this meeting, "Islamist advocates lobbied the DOJ for: 1) cutbacks in anti-terror funding; 2)_changes in agents' training manuals; 3) additional curbs on investigators; and 4) a legal declaration that U.S. citizens' criticism of Islam constitutes racial discrimination [i.e., a potential federal crime]." Munro also reported:

> Perez did not promise to meet any of the demands made by the Islamists, but he repeatedly promised extensive consultations and flattered the attendees, while speaking in a style that blended the cadences of an academic lecturer and a rural preacher. "There will be times where we have honest differences of opinion, but if we don't talk and don't actively listen and if we don't reflect and recalibrate where necessary, then we won't be doing our job, and you have our continuing commitment to that end," Perez declared.

The leitmotif of this Justice Department-sponsored program was the denunciation by participants, both inside and outside of government, of the FBI's training curricula and trainers.

According to the leftist media outlet *Talking Points Memo*, Perez declared, "The Attorney General is equally upset, the Deputy Attorney General is upset, the FBI Director is upset,[419] and we're upset because we have accomplished so much," Perez said."[xlvi]

Talking Points Memo[420] also reported:

> Attorney General Eric Holder is "firmly committed" to nixing anti-Muslim material from law enforcement training, former U.S. Attorney for the District of Oregon, Dwight C. Holton said Wednesday. Holton, who was U.S. Attorney when the FBI arrested the so-called Christmas tree bomber,[421] said that he spoke specifically with Holder about the "egregiously false" training that took place at the FBI's training headquarters at Quantico and at a U.S. Attorney's office in Pennsylvania, which was first reported on by Wired.[422]
>
> "I want to be perfectly clear about this: training materials that portray *Islam as a religion of violence or with a tendency towards violence are wrong*, they are offensive, and they are contrary to everything that this president, this attorney general and Department of Justice stands for," Holton said. "They will not be tolerated." *The training materials*, Holton said, *"pose a significant*

[xlvi] See the account of this meeting by http://talkingpointsmemo.com/muckraker/doj-official-holder-firmly-committed-to-eliminating-anti-muslim-training.

threat to national security, because they play into the false narrative propagated by terrorists that the United States is at war with Islam."

Holton said that he spoke about the issue with Holder directly when he was out in Oregon. "He is firmly committed to making sure that this is over. Now the reality is it is going to take a bit to go back and figure out what trainings have happened in the past that we need to go back and fix – we're a big organization – we've got lots going on with lots of people and lots of contractors, but [we are] firmly committed to it, and we're going to *fix it*." [Emphasis added.]

CVE DO'S AND DON'TS

Third, on October 19, 2011,[423] DHS/CRCL, in partnership with the National Counterterrorism Center (NCTC), issued a 2-page handout entitled *CVE Training Do's and Don'ts*. The introduction reads in part as follows:

> In recent years, the U.S. has seen a number of individuals in the U.S. become involved in violent extremist activities, with particular activity by American residents and citizens inspired by al Qaeda and its ideology. We know that violent extremism is not confined to any single ideology, but we also know that the threat posed by al Qaeda and its adherents is the preeminent threat we face in the homeland, targeting Muslim American communities for recruitment. Accordingly, it is urgent for law enforcement personnel to be appropriately trained in understanding and detecting *ideologically motivated criminal behavior*, and in working with communities and local law enforcement to counter domestic violent extremism.
>
> Training must be based on current intelligence and an accurate understanding of how people are radicalized to violence, and must include *cultural competency* training so that our personnel do not mistake, for example, *various types of religious observance as a sign of terrorist inclination*. Misinformation about the threat and dynamics of violent radicalization can harm our security by sending us in the wrong direction and unnecessarily creating tensions with potential community partners. [Emphasis added.]

The language in the *CVE Training Do's and Don'ts* handout is remarkably similar to the U.S. military handbook *Culture Cards: Afghanistan and Islamic Culture* we discussed in Chapter 5. The DHS document was released in September of 2011[424], i.e., just as the Great Purge was getting underway.

Importantly, tucked away in the fine print of the *CVE Training Do's and Don'ts* document is a citation for the Muslim Public Affairs Committee's publication entitled *Building Bridges to Strengthen America: Forging an Effective Counterterrorism Enterprise between Muslim Americans & Law Enforcement*.

Published on August 11, 2010,[425] *Building Bridges* discusses exotic sociopolitical topics such as "Current Theories of Radicalization and Terrorist

Recruitment and Community-Oriented Policing for Counterterrorism as a Product Extension Merger," then adds a classic bit of *taqiyya*, the *Shariah*-condoned practice of lying for the faith: "Conservative groups like the Muslim Brotherhood pose *long-term strategic threats to violent extremists* by *siphoning Muslims away from violent radicalism* into peaceful political activism." [Emphasis added.]

In Footnote 141, the bridge-builders expand on this deception:

> Hard-line Jihadist organizations like Al-Qaeda both fear and despise the Islamist political movement called the Muslim Brotherhood, in large part because the Brotherhood effectively garners support from the same constituencies that *Jihadists* are desperate to court. Because the Muslim Brotherhood and *Jihadists share a similar ideological lineage*, *Jihadists* tends to focus their criticism on the Brotherhood's willingness to participate in secular politics as a vehicle for attacking their Islamic credentials. [Emphasis added.]

As one might expect from seasoned influence operatives affiliated with an MB-linked organization like MPAC, *Building Bridges* is a masterpiece of industrial-strength propaganda and agitprop. Released right before the turmoil of the Arab Spring,[426] *Building Bridges* promoted the strategic misdirection that underpinned the U.S. government's support for the Muslim Brotherhood in Egypt: the "moderates" in the MB would form a barrier between Al-Qaeda and the greater Muslim community, and thus prevent them from joining the jihad.

UPPING THE ANTE

Finally, also on October 19, 2011,[427] a still-larger coalition of left-wing and Muslim Brotherhood-linked organizations, including CAIR, ICNA,[428] ISNA, MPAC and Islamic Relief[xlvii],[429] sent a joint letter to Homeland Security Assistant to the President John Brennan. It demanded that training materials and trainers for *not just the FBI but also the military, the Intelligence Community and the Department of Homeland Security be purged.*

In addition to statements virtually identical to those in the October 4, 2011[430] ACLU/MPAC letter, the following comments were included in this new list of threats and demands:

[xlvii] At this writing, CAIR and ISNA remain unindicted co-conspirators in the Holy Land Foundation Trial. Both groups maintain well-proven links to the Muslim Brotherhood. Also, Islamic Relief (a.k.a. IR *or* IRW), another signatory to the Red-Green axis' letter to John Brennan, has its own long history of affiliations with individuals and organizations known to have links to terrorism. On December 25, 2013, Egypt designated the MB as a terrorist organization, a move that was followed by Saudi Arabia on March 7, 2014, then quickly echoed by the UAE. In addition, on November 15, 2014, the UAE designated CAIR and IRW (and MAS) as terrorist organizations, specifically labeling IRW as a part of the global MB network.

While recent news reports have highlighted the FBI's use of biased experts and training materials, we have learned that this problem extends far beyond the FBI and has infected other government agencies, including the U.S. Attorney's Anti-Terrorism Advisory Councils,[431] the U.S. Department of Homeland Security, and the U.S. Army.

Furthermore, by the FBI's own admission, the use of bigoted and distorted materials in its trainings has not been an isolated occurrence. Since last year, reports have surfaced that the FBI, and other federal agencies, are using or supporting the use of biased trainers and materials in presentations to law enforcement officials. Disclosures of materials through a Freedom of Information Act request by civil rights organizations and in-depth reporting by *Wired* magazine show just how prevalent this issue is throughout the federal government.

The use of bigoted trainers and materials like those above is not only highly offensive, disparaging the faith of millions of Americans, but leads to biased policing that targets individuals and communities based on religion, not evidence of wrongdoing. Inaccurate and bigoted training materials also foster fear and suspicion of American Muslims amongst law enforcement and the general public, increasing discrimination, bullying, harassment and anti-Muslim violence.

Remarkably, the letter to John Brennan also included several very specific – and insolent – demands for punishment of USG law enforcement personnel (see Point 4 in Figure 2 below).

Figure 2: Excerpts of October 19, 2011 Letter to John Brennan, Assistant to the President for Counterterrorism and Homeland Security and Deputy National Security Advisor for Counterterrorism

> In response to these recent disclosures, federal officials across the country—particularly FBI field offices—have been reaching out to local Muslim communities to state that the offensive training materials do not reflect the opinion of the FBI, its field offices or the federal government. Until the following steps are taken to remedy this problem and to prevent it from recurring, we will not be confident in these assertions. We urge you to create an interagency task force, led by the White House, tasked with the following responsibilities:
>
> 1. Review *all* trainers and training materials at government agencies, including all FBI intelligence products used such as the FBI intranet, FBI library and JTTF training programs; US Attorney training programs; U.S. Department of Homeland Security, U.S. Department of Defense, and US military intranet, libraries and training materials, resources and experts;
> 2. Purge *all* federal government training materials of biased materials;
> 3. Implement a mandatory re-training program for FBI agents, U.S. Army officers, and all federal, state and local law enforcement who have been subjected to biased training;
> 4. Ensure that personnel reviews are conducted and all trainers and other government employees who promoted biased trainers and training materials are effectively disciplined;
> 5. Implement quality control processes to ensure that bigoted trainers and biased materials are not developed or utilized in the future; and
> 6. Issue guidance clearly stating that religious practice and political advocacy are protected activities under the First Amendment, not indicators of violence, and shall not be the basis for surveillance or investigation.
>
> The interagency task force should include a fair and transparent mechanism for input from the Muslim, Arab, and South Asian communities, including civil rights lawyers, religious leaders, and law enforcement experts.

IF YOU SEE SOMETHING, *DON'T* SAY ANYTHING

***

"Muslims need to become free of totalitarian Islam and the least the West can do in support is not concede an inch of its own hard-won freedom in quest of false peace with Islamists."

-Salim Mansur, How The West Was Duped, February 14, 2009

***

On October 24, 2011[432] the Red-Green axis targeted a weapon in the arsenal of the nation's first lines of defense: the Department of Homeland Security's "See Something, Say Something" campaign. According to the DHS website,[433] this is:

> ...A national campaign that raises public awareness of the indicators of terrorism and terrorism-related crime, as well as the importance of reporting suspicious activity to state and local law enforcement. Informed, alert communities play a critical role in keeping our nation safe. The U.S. Department of Homeland Security (DHS) is committed to strengthening hometown security by creating partnerships with state, local, tribal, and territorial (SLTT) governments and the private sector, as well as the communities they serve. These partners help us reach the public across the nation by *aligning their messaging* with the campaign's messages and distributing outreach materials, including Public Service Announcements (PSA's). [Emphasis added.][xlviii]

In truth, the See Something, Say Something campaign was doomed to failure from the start, because the "*something*" (i.e., the indicators of terrorism and terrorism-related crime) that Americans were exhorted to look out for was never clearly articulated. To the contrary, as this monograph makes plain, if anything, the public has been discouraged from seeing the most obvious tell-tale signs of incipient danger: adherence to *Shariah* and interest in the jihad it commands.

To make matters worse, the government's official acquiescence to *Shariah* blasphemy restrictions has made it problematic, if not actually dangerous, to "say something" about what *is* seen. Consider the neighbors of the San Bernardino jihadists who told authorities *after the attacks* that they were worried about what they

---

[xlviii] "Aligning their messaging" is a euphemism for dictating from Washington, through – among other means – control of federal funds, how state and local law enforcement officials and other, relevant non-federal agencies understand and address issues like the nature of the threat, and what can be done about it.

saw going on in the couple's garage, but they had refrained from warning anybody about it for fear of being accused of "profiling."

The attack on the See Something campaign took the form of yet another leftist-Islamist coalition letter, once again signed by prominent Muslim Brotherhood fronts like CAIR and MPAC. It was addressed to the DHS Officer for Civil Rights and Civil Liberties, Margo Schlanger. As part of their complaint about the Department's campaign, the signatories wrote:

> We are writing to follow up on a meeting request made *at the last CRCL Committee meeting* on September 26, 2011 to discuss the DHS *If You See Something, Say* Something campaign. As civil liberties, civil rights, human rights, immigrant rights, national security and privacy organizations, we are deeply concerned about how suspicious activity reporting programs, such as the DHS See Something, Say Something program, lead to racial and religious profiling and impact Arab, Middle Eastern, Muslim, Sikh, and South Asian communities. In addition, we would like to discuss what measures your office is taking to ensure accountability, transparency and oversight related to civil rights and civil liberties protections as DHS expands its work against domestic radicalization and "homegrown" terrorism. [Emphasis added.][xlix]

The clear implication of this letter is that the Red-Green axis demands that, in the interest of ensuring its members' continued cooperation (such as it is) with the Countering Violent Extremism agenda: 1) even the *reporting of* "suspicious activity" by the general public must be considered unacceptable, on the grounds that it is intolerably Islamophobic. And 2) *only* the self-appointed leftist and Islamist advocates of CRCL should be considered as legitimate intermediaries for the authorities with respect to identifying and reporting signs of possible domestic "radicalization."

PURGING THE FILES

As it happens on the same day the CAIR-MPAC letter was dispatched to Ms. Schlanger, an internal directive went out to the FBI training community. The memo was subsequently obtained by Judicial Watch[434] through a Freedom of Information Act lawsuit and provides some particularly revealing insights into the "review" – read, purging – process:

[xlix] Note that Muslim Brotherhood front groups appear to be regular attendees of Ms. Schlanger's "CRCL Committee."

On October 24, 2011 the Inspection Division (INSO), in conjunction with a team of [unidentified] Subject Matter Experts (SME's),[1] began an *impartial* review of FBI training *and reference materials* related to Islamic cultural awareness, religious interpretation, and religious history of Islam, Muslim culture, and/or Muslim, Arab, South Asian, or Middle Eastern communities. The goal of the review was to identify any material inconsistent with either constitutional or FBI core values, or otherwise inaccurate or offensive. The review was also designed to ensure all FBI training for internal and external audiences is of the highest quality.

This review was initiated following a FOIA request filed on 03/09/2010 by the American Civil Liberties Union (ACLU) in Northern California. This request, in part, asked for copies of all material used to train FBI agents on "Islam, Muslim culture, and/or Muslim, Arab, South Asian, or Middle Eastern communities in the U.S."

During this review, the SME team determined certain aspects of the identified training presentations and/or training materials are problematic and inconsistent with the criteria as set forth during the inspection. Your cooperation will ensure all CT [Counter Terrorism] training materials are accurate, *inoffensive,* consistent with FBI core values, and in strict obedience to the United States Constitution. [Emphasis added.]

The INSO directive also includes the following highly specific instructions:

1) Immediately remove the specified document(s) and report removal to INSO via EC. The EC must also be uploaded to this SharePoint site 2) by COB Tuesday, November 2, 2011, you must provide a second EC specifying the following information: a) the name of the training presenter and/or developer, b) the number of times and dates each identified presentation was given and/or the training material was used, and c) the number of recipients/attendees who were provided the presentation and their agency/community affiliation, d) the date of the last presentation.

---

[1] As noted elsewhere, the identities and affiliations of the Subject Matter Experts used in making what appear to be highly subjective (not, impartial) judgments about what should be excised from the FBI and other agencies' training curricula has been treated by the Obama administration as a closely held state secret. As Judicial Watch has reported (http://www.judicialwatch.org/press-room/press-releases/documents-obtained-by-judicial-watch-reveal-fbi-training-curricula-purged-of-material-deemed-offensive-to-muslims/), examples of such now-disclosed and controversial judgments include the following:
"Article is highly inflammatory and inaccurately argues the Muslim Brotherhood is a terrorist organization."
"The overall tenor of the presentation is too informal in the current political context."
"The Qur'an is not the teachings of the Prophet, but the revealed word of God."
"Remove references to mosques specifically as a radicalization incubator."
"Remove sweeping generality of 'Those who fit the terrorist profile best (for the present at least) are young male immigrants of Middle Eastern appearance'"
"Author seems to conflate 'Islamic militancy' with 'terrorism' and needs to define the difference and use it in their analysis."

Particularly noteworthy about this memo is the revelation that, in addition to "training" materials, the review was also supposed to examine "reference materials." Apparently, not only were potentially "offensive" CT training materials (PowerPoint presentations, etc.) subject to the purge. So were on-the-shelf reference and/or reading materials, as well. This would seem to have taken the practice of mission-disabling self-censorship a big step beyond what the Red-Green axis had demanded.

ATTORNEY GENERAL ERIC HOLDER SUPPORTS THE GREAT PURGE

As reported by the *Daily Caller*, on November 10, 2011,[435] Attorney General Eric Holder made the following statements during a Senate Judiciary Committee hearing on the FBI training materials:

> The FBI training material contained lessons that "can really undermine, really undermine, the really substantial outreach efforts that we have made and really have a negative impact on our ability to communicate effectively, as we have in the past, with this community. I almost hesitate to say 'this community,' because the reality is that we're talking about...American citizens, who have the same desires that we all have, who want their kids to be safe, who want the opportunities that this great country has to offer them."

Mr. Holder also criticized arguments that Islam's basic beliefs spur violence, or that adherence to Islamic rituals and/or style of dress are markers of "possible extremism." Those claims, he said, are "flat-out wrong."

Mr. Holder either simply changed what was once his opinion of the threat, or misremembered what he said in the run-up to the purge. On December 21, 2010,[436] the Attorney General made the following comments during an interview with *ABC News*:

> [T]he American people have to be prepared for potentially bad news. What I am trying to do in this interview is to make people aware of the fact that the threat is real, the threat is different, the threat is constant. It is one of the things that keeps me up at night. You didn't worry about this even two years ago – about individuals, about Americans, to the extent that we now do. And that is of – of great concern.
>
> The threat has changed from simply worrying about foreigners coming here, to worrying about people in the United States, American citizens – raised here, born here, and who for whatever reason, have decided that they are going to become radicalized and take up arms against the nation in which they were born.

For "whatever reason," Mr. Holder? The comment suggests that, even at that pre-Purge juncture, the Attorney General either did not understand, or at least did not care about, the source of this violent behavior. If he had not discovered its wellspring during his department's "substantial outreach efforts" and "effective communications with the Muslim American community," then just what, it must be asked, is the real purpose of these efforts?

The evident disinterest of the nation's top law enforcement officer in establishing whether authoritative Islam's basic tenets – i.e., the strategy and tactics of the global Islamic movement as found in the *Quran, Hadith* and *Shariah* – is both astonishing and symptomatic of the government's "See-No-Shariah" CVE approach. The truth is that we will never be able to address effectively the threat that Mr. Holder said kept him up at night until we all have the courage to examine honestly the true nature of the adversary we face.

THE MUSLIM-AMERICAN COMMUNITY: 'NOTHING TO SEE HERE FOLKS, MOVE ALONG'

On November 17, 2011,[437] a panel discussion featuring members of the Red-Green axis was held on Capitol Hill under the sponsorship of Congressman Bennie G. Thompson, the ranking member of the House Committee on Homeland Security. According to Rep. Thompson, the forum entitled "Islamist Radicalization: Myth or Reality?" was convened to "explore[438] the viewpoints of representatives from the Brennan Center for Justice, Center for American Progress,[439] and the American Civil Liberties Union." Faiza Patel,[440] Co-Director of the Liberty and National Security Program[441] at the Brennan Center for Justice, provided the following response to a question:

> ...I think the basic message that you know a lot of us [Muslims] have is you know you can't expect the community to behave as your partner if at the same time you're subjecting them to intense surveillance and monitoring. And that's, you know, you can't have your cake and eat it too as they say.
>
> Just coming back to New York, some of the key imams in New York City who were working with Mayor Bloomberg and with Commissioner Kelly, you would see them at every public function which involved Muslims, they would be right up there with the Mayor, they were precisely the same people who were being followed 24 hours a day over a period of years.
>
> And my point is simply that you can't do that and then turn around to those very same people and say – "Hey buddy, can you help me?" I just don't think it works. So that would be the very first thing – *get rid of these really flawed training materials, these flawed radicalization theories, and then build a*

community program where the police and the community together agree on what the problem is.

If the community doesn't believe that radicalization or extremism or extremist views or extremist Islamic ideology is a problem in their own community, then you should also understand that maybe they know what they're talking about, and not be spending police resources this way. [Emphasis added.]

Put simply, the question raised by such comments is: If the American Muslim "community" insists that "radicalization or extremism or extremist views or extremist Islamic ideology" is *not* a problem in their community is that because the community is actually free of such forces?

There are several possible alternative explanations:, 1) Such forces *are* present, but the community is willfully blind to the danger thus posed. 2) The community is so intimidated by the Islamic supremacists among them as to be unwilling to raise an alarm. And/or 3) the Muslim Brotherhood operatives being used by the authorities as interlocutors do not actually represent the community and are engaging in taqiyya towards the infidels, even as they work to suppress Muslims who do not share their views or agenda.

Whatever the answer, we must be alive to the very real possibility going forward that Islamic supremacists in our midst are unreliable arbiters of whether there is a problem, and what the rest of us can know or do about it.

PURGING THE TRAINERS

As we have seen, the Red-Green axis was insistent not only on eliminating training materials and "resources" needed to give our first lines of defense situational awareness about *Shariah* and Islamic supremacism as the wellsprings of jihad/terrorism/violent extremism. Its operatives have also sought to block those who have produced or sought to use such materials for training purposes. They have even demanded the "reeducation" of any personnel who had been exposed to them.[li]

In just the roughly year-long timeframe of the Great Purge, CAIR and/or its associates directed media attacks, smears and propaganda campaigns against such prominent counter-jihadists as, for example: Stephen Coughlin and Steven Emerson (August 10-12, 2011)[442]; Allen West (September 2, 2011)[443]; FBI Agent William Gawthrop (September 16, 2011)[444]; Robert Spencer (September 21, 2011)[445]; Pamela Geller and Robert Spencer (October 25, 2011)[446]; Adam Hasner

---

[li] See, for example, the calls for disciplining, purging and/or retraining that were included in the October 19, 2011 letter from 57 leftist and Islamist groups to then-Deputy National Security Advisor John Brennan.

and Allen West (October 28, 2011)[447]; Kamal Saleem (November 17, 2011)[448]; Nonie Darwish, Daniel Pipes and Walid Shoebat (March 23, 2012)[449]; and Zuhdi Jasser (March 27, 2012).[450]

The Hamas and Muslim Brotherhood front doing business as CAIR even sought to prevent one of their most influential opponents from addressing a *prayer breakfast* at the U.S. Military Academy. Retired Lieutenant General William G. "Jerry" Boykin is among our nation's most highly decorated military leaders. Upon learning of West Point's invitation to him, CAIR's civilization jihadists strenuously objected to it, defaming the general and demanding that he be disinvited. They were joined by the Red-Green axis in enlisting the Obama administration's help to that end.

In response to the controversy that ensued, the Military Academy issued the following statement:[451] "Lt. Gen William G. Boykin has decided to withdraw [from] speaking at West Point's National Prayer Breakfast. In fulfilling its commitment to the community, the United States Military Academy will feature another speaker for the event." A spokesperson for West Point, Theresa Brinkerhoff, told[452] Fox News via email that the U.S. Military Academy "did not decide this for him. After a conversation with our chaplain, Lt. Gen. Boykin decided to withdraw."

On January 30, 2012,[453] CAIR issued a gloating press release that read in part:

> An anti-Islam speaker, retired Lieutenant General William G. "Jerry" Boykin, has withdrawn[454] from an upcoming [February 8, 2012] prayer breakfast at the U.S. Military Academy at West Point. CAIR recently joined[455] with VoteVets.org,[456] a coalition of Iraq and Afghanistan veterans, in asking the academy to retract an invitation because of Boykin's Islamophobic views, which include a belief that "[Islam] should not be protected under the First Amendment," that there should be "no mosques in America" and that there can be no interfaith dialogue or cooperation between Muslims and Christians.
>
> "We welcome Mr. Boykin's withdrawal from this event and hope that the speaker who replaces him will offer cadets a spiritual message that promotes tolerance and mutual understanding," said CAIR National Executive Director Nihad Awad,[457] adding that CAIR has been challenging Boykin's un-American bigotry for a number of years, and that CAIR had issued an Action Alert calling on American Muslims and other people of conscience to contact the academy's superintendent to ask that he rescind Boykin's invitation.

The object of the exercise could not have been more clear, however. As the *New York Times* reported on January 30, 2012,[458] the Red-Green axis had succeeded in suppressing Gen. Boykin's freedom of speech and ability to interact with young military officers with its attacks on his character and record: "...Peter Montgomery, a senior fellow at People for the American Way,[459] a liberal advocacy group, said the West Point invitation was a mistake. West Point, Mr. Montgomery said, would have given 'a platform to someone who is publicly identified with offensive comments about Muslims and about the commander in chief.'"

FoxNews.com reported that, "[Gen.] Boykin said he doesn't believe the Obama administration has stood with the traditional values of the nation and he said the incident at West Point should serve as a wakeup call to Christians.

"The message is that people of faith and conservative Americans are losing our voice to a very well-organized and very well-funded group of very passionate people – those being the atheists and the Muslims,' Boykin said. 'They want to change the nature of our culture – and they are succeeding.'"

There has been no public condemnation of these attacks on freedom of speech by any Civil Rights and Civil Liberties official from either DHS, DOJ/FBI or the Pentagon. Where are those who profess concern about our civil rights when they have been most needed?

THE FBI AND THE PURGE

In fact, far from being stalwart defenders of our most basic constitutional rights, the CRCL advocates have done just the opposite. For example, on February 8, 2012,[460] a now-infamous meeting took place between then-FBI Director Mueller and various Islamic organizations. The purpose of the meeting was to discuss the results of a review of "inaccurate and offensive training materials" that had been conducted by [unnamed] Subject Matter Experts (SME's) chosen from the Army's Combating Terrorism Center[461] at West Point.[lii]

Among the FBI Director's invited guests[462] were members of ISNA, MPAC, the American-Arab Anti-Discrimination Committee (ADC), as well as the Arab American Institute, Interfaith Alliance, Muflehun[liii] and the ISNA-linked Shoulder To Shoulder.[liv]

[lii] A report on this meeting entitled "FBI Purges Hundreds Of Terrorism Documents In Islamophobia Probe," was posted by Spencer Ackerman at *Wired* on February 15, 2012.
[liii] The word *Muflehun* means "those who will succeed or prosper." The term comes from Quran 3.104, which says, "Let there be a people from among you that enjoins what is right, and forbids what is wrong; and they will be the successful ones (Muflehun)." The concept of "enjoining what is right, and forbidding what is wrong" is a core component of both Islamic theology and its shariah legal doctrine, which it is incumbent upon all Muslims to obey. Thus, it forms the basis of an Islamic concept known as Hisbah (Guarding Against Infringements). This all sounds fairly benign...until you understand 1) that "forbidding what is wrong" includes remaining disassociated from non-Muslim individuals and non-

On February 15, 2012,[463] the Muslim Public Affairs Council posted a press release on its homepage under the heading, "MPAC and Interfaith Leaders Meet with FBI Director Mueller to Address Concerns Regarding Training Materials." The release confirmed details, such as who attended the meeting and what prompted it:

> MPAC along with other community and interfaith organizations met with FBI Director Robert S. Mueller III and the FBI's Office of Public Affairs[464] in an effort to address concerns regarding the agency's use of inflammatory training material. The FBI provided an update on steps it has taken to rectify the matter including an extensive review and update of its material.

The press release, subtitled "Coalition Demands Continued Transparency," included these comments:

> The group also asked the FBI Director to issue a formal statement acknowledging the negative impact of these training materials on the Muslim American community. The group assembled stressed the importance of transparency by the Bureau in dealing with these matters in the future, and suggested that *a committee of community leaders and experts be assembled to review the FBI's training material.* They also requested future meetings with Mueller to continue the conversation. To date these asks have not been met or acknowledged, but MPAC and the other interfaith and community organizations are committed to working with the FBI to correct this grave mistake. [Emphasis added.]

In accordance with the victimization meme that is a hardy perennial for the U.S. Muslim Brotherhood, MPAC's president, Salam Al-Marayati,[465] criticized America's CT efforts, when he stated:

> It is a travesty that the Muslim American community has lost trust with an agency that is here to protect us. Concerned citizens will continue to report criminal activities to authorities, but now the element of mistrust has been

---

Muslin governments, including here in America, and that 2) enforcing *Hisbah* authorizes every Muslim ruler or government to intervene and, if necessary, coercively (i.e., forcibly) to "enjoin what is right, and forbid what is wrong" in order to keep everything (and everyone) in compliance with shariah law. In other words, the doctrine of *Hisbah* is much more ominous and malevolent than the Muslim Brotherhood-tied leaders of Muflehun – Imam Mohamed Magid and influence operator Suhail Khan – would have you know. In fact, under the right circumstances, it is only a small step from *Hisbah* to open jihad. What, you may ask, would be the right circumstances? The answer to that question would be *Fitna* (resistance) like "Islamophobia."

[liv] In the aftermath of the November 13, 2015 ISIS attacks in Paris, ISNA-linked "Shoulder-to-Shoulder" issued the following pro-E&D press release: We are strongest against forces that seek to divide and harm when we refuse to accept *their terms of engagement* across religious, racial, national, and ethnic lines. Together, we hope, and commit to working ever more resolutely for a peaceful, just and inclusive world. It is a second wave of tragedy when American Muslims, South Asians, Arabs, and others, so many of whom have been victims of extremist violence themselves, are the targets of violent rhetoric and backlash attacks in the aftermath of such events. [Emphasis added.]

embedded in the relationship. This undermines our pluralism, which is the best defense against any *transnational ideological threat*." [Emphasis added.]

FBI spokesman Christopher Allen confirmed[466] that the Bureau found some of the documents to be objectionable because they were inaccurate or overbroad, and others because they were in poor taste, relied on stereotypes or lacked precision. As he reported, FBI Director Robert Mueller had informed his guests that, "the FBI took the review of the training material very seriously, and he pursued the matter with urgency to ensure that this does not occur again in the future."

Apparently not satisfied with that, Imad Hamad,[467] regional director of the Michigan chapter of the Arab-American Anti-Defamation Committee, said that more needed to be done, adding, "I see it as a good step in the right direction, but it still needs some closure. We need more understanding and *more active participation in the process*." [Emphasis added.] Translation: Give the Islamic supremacists more opportunities to subvert USG policymaking from within.

On March 16, 2011,[468] then-FBI Director Mueller gave a prepared statement before the House Judiciary Committee, which included the following comments:

> The FBI understands that protecting America requires the cooperation and understanding of the public. Since the 9/11 attacks, the FBI has developed an extensive outreach program to Muslim, South Asian, and Sikh communities to develop trust, address concerns and dispel myths in those communities about the FBI and the U.S. government. As part of this effort, in 2009 the FBI established the Specialized Community Outreach Team, or SCOT,[469] composed of special agents, analysts, community outreach specialists, and personnel with language or other specialized skills.[lv] This team assists field offices with establishing new contacts in key communities.

It is important to note that, despite the assurances that the FBI "needs the cooperation and understanding of the general public," in practice, the Bureau's CVE approach focuses *almost exclusively* on outreach programs and accommodations to organizations that putatively represent the Muslim, South Asian, and Sikh communities, but that generally are dominated by Islamic supremacists. Predictably, as a result, the FBI consistently winds up ignoring, or at least misunderstanding, the true nature of the threat.[lvi]

[lv] The FBI's Specialized Community Outreach Team was established in 2009, about the same time that then-Attorney General Eric Holder established the Arab-American and Muslim Engagement Advisory Group and the DOJ's Community Relations Service (CRS) was launched.

[lvi] Consider in this regard, for example, the myriad instances in which FBI officials respond to obvious acts of jihad by insisting that they have nothing to do with "terrorism."

JUSTICE DEPARTMENT PURGE GUIDELINES

On March 20, 2012,[470] the DOJ released a memo from Deputy Attorney General James Cole,[471] entitled *Memorandum for Head of Components and United States Attorneys*. The memo included the followed revealing information:

> As the nation's principal law enforcement agency, the Department of Justice is responsible for keeping America safe and ensuring the fair and impartial administration of justice. This responsibility demands that Department representatives perform their duties consistent with the Constitution and Department values, at the highest level of professionalism, and in a manner that conveys respect for all. Training conducted or funded by the Department plays an important role in assisting the Department in fulfilling this responsibility.
>
> On September 28, 2011, I issued a memorandum to all heads of components and United States Attorneys to "carefully review all training material and presentations provided by their personnel, particularly training related to combating terrorism, countering violent extremism, and other training that may relate to ongoing outreach efforts in Arab, Muslim, Sikh, South Asian and other communities."
>
> Following my memorandum, a working group on training issues chaired by the Civil Rights Division was constituted *within the Attorney General's Arab-Muslim Engagement Advisory Group* and included representatives from each relevant component and U.S. Attorney's Office. To balance the imperatives of articulating Department-wide standards and ensuring flexibility for components in conducting their reviews of training materials, the working group drafted and unanimously submitted to my office a set of overarching principles to guide the Department's training and to ensure that all the communities we serve are respected. [Emphasis added.]

In other words, a working group penetrated by Muslim Brotherhood operatives was involved in drafting the guidelines for training that were subsequently adopted by the Justice Department. Unsurprisingly, given the Brothers' successful influence operations elsewhere within the USG, the six guidelines issued in the Cole memo were virtually identical in content and language to the CRCL-based guidelines issued by DHS, DOD, FBI, etc.

Two days after Deputy Attorney General Cole distributed his memorandum, the FBI released its own directive entitled, *The FBI's Guiding Principles Touchstone Document on Training 2012*.[472] Among the array of convoluted statements in this report, one that stood out above all to this CT specialist read as follows:

> Training must emphasize that *no investigative or intelligence collection activity* may be based *solely* on race, ethnicity, national origin, or religious affiliation.

Specifically, training must focus on behavioral indicators that have a potential nexus to terrorist or criminal activity, while making clear that *religious expression, protest activity, and the espousing of political or ideological beliefs are constitutionally protected activities* that must not be equated with terrorism or criminality absent other indicia of such offenses. [Emphasis added.]

It is impossible to expect a competent law enforcement officer to do his or her job if they follow convoluted guidelines such as these, insofar as such religious and/or ideological beliefs are often actually *the core* indicators of potential terrorist activity.

THE FBI CAPITULATES

On May 9, 2012,[473] FBI Director Mueller made plain the extent of the FBI's capitulation to the CVE approach and its abandonment of the alternative, fact-based law enforcement one in testimony before the U.S. House Committee on the Judiciary. In his prepared remarks, Mueller stated the following:

> The Bureau itself has established a CVE Office within the National Security Branch (NSB)[474] to improve our effectiveness in empowering our state, local, and community partners to assist in this effort. The duties and goals of this office include developing a better understanding of, and countering the threat of, violent extremism in the U.S., strengthening community partnerships and providing to state and local officials and to community leaders unclassified briefings regarding the threat of extremism, addressing CVE-related operational and mission-support needs, including investigations, analysis, and training, and coordinating Bureau interests with regard to CVE matters with those of other agencies to *ensure USG efforts are aligned*. [Emphasis added.]

After delivering his prepared remarks, Mueller responded to a question from now-former Representative Howard Coble about whether political correctness was a factor in how the FBI training materials were deleted. Mueller emphatically denied any political correctness was involved, even as he confirmed a few details about the amount of material that was purged.[lvii]

On July 18, 2012,[475] the February 8, 2012 FBI meeting became the subject of a FOIA request by Judicial Watch. As occurs frequently in FOIA cases, the FBI refused to respond substantively to the request, so Judicial Watch filed a lawsuit in the US District Court for the District of Columbia.[lviii] The litigation compelled the FBI to comply with the FOIA law, and produce the requested records. Many of

---

[lvii] This lively exchange can be seen on the C-SPAN website at accessed on the C-SPAN website (between 33:15-35:10).

[lviii] Judicial Watch v. FBI and U.S. Department of Justice, No. 1:12-cv-01183

these are discussed in a detailed December 5, 2013[476] Judicial Watch report entitled *U.S. Government Purges of Law Enforcement Training Material Deemed "Offensive" to Muslims.*

This Special Report concludes by stating:

> It is fair to say that not a single U.S. government employee goes to work each morning with the mission of identifying and defeating the Islamists' active measures campaigns. Large bureaucratic institutions are reluctant to "disturb" operations with examinations for deception and manipulation.
>
> Those same organizations are loath to raise those subjects in congressional appropriations requests and hearings fearing any political criticism. Until there is someone with the job of *defeating the Islamist active measures campaign targeting our nation* – and resourced to roll back the Islamists and win – the United States and her citizens are in grave peril.

CONCLUSION

It is actually incorrect that "not a single US government employee" goes to work each morning with the mission of identifying and defeating the Islamists' active measures campaigns. There are certainly many within DHS and other Federal law enforcement agencies who really do want to fulfill their oaths of office, namely to protect our country and Constitution from threats,[477] both foreign and domestic.

It *is* true, however, that people with the requisite experience and professional interest in this subject are few and far between in government today. To the extent that they are there, they are scattered through the agencies, feeling like the proverbial "voices crying in the wilderness." Fewer still have the *latitude to perform this mission effectively.*

Under these circumstances, it is hardly a surprise that, for example, personnel in the Department of Homeland Security have long suffered from "debilitating[478] morale problems." Indeed, in the wake of the Great Purge and what flowed from it, employee satisfaction at DHS plummeted to an historic low[479] in 2014, with the Department falling dead last in the annual *Best Places to Work in the Federal Government* rankings.

On February 23, 2015,[480] House Committee on Homeland Security Chairman Michael McCaul decried this historic decline in job satisfaction. He added that, "It is entirely unacceptable that DHS ranks lowest on the list of large federal agencies on the 2014 Best Places to Work survey. This once again underscores the concerning challenges the department and its components continue to face with morale."

DHS personnel have been advised by headquarters that the best way to address the problem of low morale is to *stop talking about the problem* of low morale. The verbatim quote in the internal memo issued by DHS Secretary Jeh Johnson on April 16, 2015, and which he repeated in his testimony to Congress[481] was: "My message to Congress (and the press): One of the ways we are improving morale is to stop telling workforce you suffer from low morale. We have moved on. We are no longer 'studying' the issue of morale. We are doing something about it."

What we really need to be doing, to protect our country as well as to improve the morale of those trying to serve as real first lines of defense, is to undo the damage done by the Great Purge. We must, instead, purge the U.S. government of the malign and subversive influence of the Muslim Brotherhood's operatives and get back to a fact-based and efficacious approach to countering the Global Jihad Movement.

Middlebury College Professor Jeffrey Bale[482] explored the danger of doing otherwise in his October 2013[483] study, entitled *Denying the Link between Islamist Ideology and Jihadist Terrorism: "Political Correctness" and the Undermining of Counterterrorism*, when he wrote:

> Ever since the jihadist terrorist attacks on 11 September 2001, Western policy-makers, mainstream media organizations, and even academicians have been perversely reluctant to highlight the crucial role played by Islamist ideology in motivating jihadist terrorist attacks. Indeed, the more acts of jihadist terrorism that are perpetrated, acts in which the perpetrators clearly reveal their ideological motivations, the more insistently key Western elites refuse to acknowledge those motivations.
>
> This article discusses several of the reasons for this peculiar disjuncture, and focuses in particular on the persistent efforts to whitewash certain features of Islam, demonize its critics, and even engage in apologetics for Islamism at a time when the latter, in both its violent and non-violent forms, poses a significant threat to Western democracies. One especially worrisome source and dimension of this problem is the continuing reliance of Western governments on members of Islamist advocacy organizations for advice.

This reliance was at work in – and greatly exacerbated by – the Great Purge. It continues unabated to this day, allowing hostile foreign nationals and their enablers here the chance to use our Civil Rights and Civil Liberties to try to destroy our country, rather than to ensure that we can use them to do everything possible to preserve the security and inalienable constitutional rights of American citizens.

If the power of American's civil rights and civil liberties were really being used to protect our freedoms – as our Founding Fathers meant it to be, CRCL would serve as an impenetrable shield against even the faintest hint of *Shariah* in America. As a sure proof of this commitment, we would not see our borders shattered, but rather protected, with members of the law enforcement community serving as watchmen, instead of serving as targets themselves.

Sadly, what we see today is just the opposite: CRCL is being used by the Obama administration as a sledgehammer, to pound us into submission on the anvil of Countering Violent Extremism. In the next chapter, we will see the lessons to be learned post-Purge from, among other sources, Egypt's experience with the Muslim Brotherhood before, during and after the revolution that was egged on by American policymakers.

CHAPTER 8: AFTER THE PURGE: HARD LESSONS UNLEARNED

On February 10, 2011,[484] Director of National Intelligence James Clapper appeared in open session before the House Intelligence Committee and made, as discussed in Chapter 6, his evidently scripted, and certainly malfeasant, remarks[485] about the Muslim Brotherhood's supposedly "secular" and benign nature. He was accompanied on that occasion by FBI Director Mueller, who mildly dissented from that preposterous characterization.

For example, during the hearings, Mr. Mueller confirmed that the Muslim Brotherhood was the jihadist group whose sectarian ideology inspired Osama Bin-Laden. He observed that it had affiliates in the United States and has supported terrorism, both here and overseas.

Other Obama administration intelligence officials who spoke at the hearing included: Leon Panetta, Director of the CIA; Michael Leiter, Director of the National Counterterrorism Center (NCTC); Lt. Gen. Ronald Burgess, Director of the Defense Intelligence Agency (DIA); Caryn Wagner, Under Secretary of DHS for Intelligence and Analysis (I&A);[486] Thomas Ferguson, Principal Deputy Under Secretary of Defense for Intelligence;[487] and Philip Goldberg, Assistant Secretary of State, Bureau of Intelligence and Research.[488]

EGYPT AND THE MUSLIM BROTHERHOOD

The context for this hearing with virtually the entire leadership of the Intelligence Community was the growing concern that then-Egyptian President Hosni Mubarak was preparing to resign[489] under pressure, and that a representative from the Brotherhood would become the next president of Egypt. Mubarak had repeatedly warned that his administration was the only thing keeping Brotherhood-led Islamists government from taking over that strategically located nation, which is also the Arab world's most populous one.

It turned out that Mubarak was right, but fortunately – and no thanks to President Obama and Secretary of State Hillary Clinton – only for a year. His successor, Mohamed Morsi, himself was overthrown in July of 2013 in the wake of massive popular protests largely engendered by his efforts swiftly to subject Egyptians to shariah. He was imprisoned[490] for 20 years and subsequently received a pending death sentence on May 16, 2015[491] for his role in crushing a violent prison break carried out by members of Hamas in 2011.

As these witnesses spelled out a variety of terrorist threats before the Committee, they also highlighted the Muslim Brotherhood's close connection to groups here in America. Voicing her alarm, Sue Myrick (R-NC), added: "I'm concerned that the Muslim Brotherhood is using peaceful protests in Egypt for a power grab, and our government doesn't seem to grasp their threat. *The Muslim Brotherhood isn't a danger because they are terrorists, but because they push an extremist ideology that causes others to commit acts of terrorism."*

Ms. Myrick's remarks gave the Intelligence Community that day a golden opportunity to do their duty – namely, to inform Congress and the American people about the true nature of the threat we face. But they failed to do so.

Perhaps that was because the witnesses understood all too well that the Obama administration had been actively cultivating ties to the Muslim Brotherhood, both through their front groups in this country, in Egypt and elsewhere. In fact, as we have seen, from its earliest days in office, the President and Secretary of State Hillary Clinton had been actively promoting Islamic supremacists and their agendas, including notably, the Brotherhood/Organization of Islamic Cooperation (OIC) efforts to impose shariah blasphemy laws worldwide.

For example, Mr. Obama and Mrs. Clinton had insisted that top Brothers be in the auditorium for Mr. Obama's University of Cairo speech in June 2009.[492] And they actively communicated their view that the Mubarak government should yield to popular demands that it surrender power, knowing full well the likely result would be the installation of a Muslim Brotherhood regime in its stead.

That, of course, is precisely what happened. And, as the new government was being formed in July of 2011, the Obama administration dispatched Ambassador Anne Patterson[493] to Cairo to formalize its working relationship with the Muslim Brotherhood's Morsi.

As reported by Michael Meunier, a leader of the Christian/secular[494] opposition to the Brotherhood, the Obama administration played a key role in "helping the MB ascent to power in Egypt." Meunier added that, for some time, he and many other Christian leaders had been "publically and privately warning members of Congress and the administration of the danger the Brotherhood poses, and about their desire to turn Egypt into a theocratic Islamic fascist country. Yet, we were ignored."

Mr. Meunier also observed:[495] that:

> [Amb. Patterson] seemed to favor[496] the Brotherhood and the hard line *Salafis*[497] at the expense of the secular players in Egypt. In fact, she has turned down requests for meetings from heads of political parties and other secular politicians, myself included, who oppose the Brotherhood.
>
> The MB used these high-level meetings to tell the Egyptian people that the U.S. is supporting them and does not object to their rule. Many of us reached out to U.S. officials at the State Department and complained that the U.S. policy [i.e., CVE and its associated "engagement and dialogue"]

regarding the MB was putting the secular forces in Egypt at a disadvantage because it seemed to be propping [up] the MB. But our concerns were dismissed.

'WE, THE PEOPLE'

Michael Meunier's insights into the Obama administration's attitudes were subsequently confirmed by its response to a petition posted on the White House website on July 7, 2013.[498] It called on the administration to designate the Muslim Brotherhood as a terrorist organization. The text of the petition read as follows:

> We petition the Obama administration to declare [the] Muslim Brotherhood organization as a terrorist group. [The] Muslim Brotherhood has a long history of violent killings and terrorizing opponents. Also MB has direct ties with most terrorist groups like Hamas. A book by one of their prominent figures, Sayid Qutb, called *Ma'alim Fi-Al-Tariq*[499] (a.k.a. *Milestones*, or *Signs Along the Path*) is the bible for many terrorist groups. The Muslim Brotherhood has shown in the past few days that it is willing to engage in violence and killing of innocent civilians in order to invoke fear in the hearts of its opponents. This is terrorism. We ask the U.S. government to declare [the] MB as a terrorist group for a safer future for all of us.

According to the White House's *We The People*[500] petition program launched on September 22, 2011, all requests must receive a response from the administration if 150 signatures are added within the first 30 days, and if the petition gained 100,000 signatures within the second 30 days. By July 31, 2013, the MB petition had garnered more than 136,000 signatures, with a final tally of 213,146 signatures.

To flash forward for a moment, the White House eventually rejected the "We, The People" petition. On December 1, 2014,[501] it posted a statement announcing that it would *not* designate the MB as a terrorist group. The text of this very tardy official response read as follows:

> We have not seen credible evidence[502] that the Muslim Brotherhood has renounced *its decades-long commitment to non-violence*. The United States does not condone political violence of any kind and we continue to *press actors of all viewpoints* to peacefully engage in the political process. The United States is committed to thwarting terrorist groups that pose a threat to U.S. interests and those of our partners. [Emphasis added.]

Apparently, by "press[ing] actors of all viewpoints" the Obama administration meant, among other things, cutting off[503] foreign aid and withholding military assistance from the man who had overthrown the Morsi regime and was subsequently elected Egypt's president in his own right, Abdel Fattah El-Sisi.[504] The stated U.S. goal was to "encourage the military[505] to reconcile with the Muslim Brotherhood," and to be more inclusive[506] towards them in the new Egyptian government.

CLARITY ABOUT THE BROTHERHOOD

The bizarre expectation that the U.S. government could usefully insist on the inclusion of the Muslim Brotherhood in an Egyptian government that had just removed it from power was undoubtedly promoted by the Islamic supremacists counseling the Obama administration. Recall, for example, the August 2010 MPAC publication[507] entitled *Building Bridges to Strengthen America: Forging an Effective Counterterrorism Enterprise between Muslim Americans & Law Enforcement*. It claimed counterfactually that, "Conservative groups like the Muslim Brotherhood pose long-term strategic threats to violent extremists by siphoning Muslims away from violent radicalism into peaceful political activism."

This meme is, of course, superficially reinforced by evident tactical differences between the Brotherhood and its many progeny among the violent jihadist groups like Al-Qaeda. As one of America's preeminent authorities on jihad, Raymond Ibrahim,[508] has documented, AQ leader Ayman Al-Zawahiri – a former Brotherhood member himself (as are so many other jihadist leaders today), wrote a book entitled *The Bitter Harvest*, condemning the MB for "taking advantage of the Muslim youths' fervor by...steer[ing] their onetime passionate, Islamic zeal for jihad to conferences and elections."

In another book entitled *Shariah and Democracy*, Al-Zawahiri dedicates an entire section to the premise that shariah law cannot coexist with democracy.[lix] The Muslim Brotherhood's operatives in the United States and their fellow-traveling leftist allies dispute that contention, insisting that "moderate Islamists" are committed to democratic governance. For example, as we have seen, an Islamic supremacist influence operator who deeply penetrated the Obama administration, Mohamed Elibiary, actually went so far as to declare the U.S. Constitution a shariah-compliant document.

Egypt's revolution, however, confirmed what had long been obvious. There is no disagreement between modern jihadists about their *goals* and the necessary *strategy* for achieving them – i.e., the triumph of shariah worldwide and a Caliphate (or for the Shia, an Imamate) to govern according to that Islamic code. To the extent they actually *do* differ, it is generally about the best *tactics* for achieving those goals.

[lix] See *The Al Qaeda Reader*, pp. 116-136.

This reality was captured evocatively by the Muslim Brotherhood-aligned Islamic supremacist who is now Turkey's president, Recep Tayyip Erdogan. In 1996, he candidly declared, that for him, *democracy was like a street car: "You ride it until you arrive at your destination, then you step off."*[509]

As we saw in living color in Egypt in 2011-2012, the MB's tactics initially involved "conferences (and organized protests) and elections," but then switched to a more aggressive, direct approach. After Morsi took full control, he immediately began implementing shariah law in Egypt, while he formed alliances with other *Salafi*-jihadi groups elsewhere in the Middle East.

Moreover, far from achieving the promised "moderate Islamist" alternative to jihadism of the Al-Qaeda stripe, what actually happened in Egypt was that the leaders of the new MB regime *actively colluded* with members of Al-Qaeda. In fact, after Morsi was forced out, it was discovered that he had been discussing[510] not only the implementation of shariah, but the strategy and tactics of global jihad with Muhammad Al-Zawahiri,[511] the brother of AQ leader Ayman Al-Zawahiri.[512]

One might have thought that such proof of the fraudulent nature of the assurances of moderation and loyalty to the U.S. Constitution endlessly served up by MPAC and the other Muslim Brotherhood-tied influence operations in this country would prompt the U.S. government to end – or at least reduce – their access to and sway in official policymaking circles. But, like so many other examples cited in this monograph, such evidence from Egypt did not seen make a bit of difference to their sympathizers and enablers in the Obama administration. To this day, U.S. foreign and domestic policy is shaped in important ways, if not actually dictated, by Islamic supremacists inside and outside of government.

THE JUSTICE DEPARTMENT LEAVES OPEN THE DOOR TO SHARIAH BLASPHEMY RESTRICTIONS

A case in point was on vivid display during congressional testimony on July 27, 2012[513] delivered by Thomas Perez,[514] the then-Assistant Attorney General for the DOJ's Civil Rights Division.[515] Perez, a top architect of the CVE policy in the Department of Justice, refused repeatedly to answer questions from Rep. Trent Franks, the chairman of the House Subcommittee on the Constitution and Civil Justice,[516] about whether the Justice Department would support freedom of speech with regard to religion.

Mr. Franks asked four times: "Will you tell us…that this administration's Department of Justice will never entertain or advance a proposal that criminalizes speech against any religion?"

Perez insistently equivocated with non-answers like, "It is a hard question, in the sense that when you make threats against someone," then added that he was not familiar with the context of a news report that Mr. Franks had referenced during the hearing, and that he had not seen the article. "I would have to read the article in order to understand the context of the article. What I can tell you is that the Department of Justice aggressively enforces all of the civil rights laws, including laws that protect religious authorities," Perez said.[517]

While he declined to say the Obama administration would support draft legislation from the Congress on assuring that First Amendment protections would apply to speech, the man charged with protecting civil rights at the Justice Department did say he would be willing to "look at" such an initiative.

Presumably, Mr. Franks' questions were inspired, at least in part, by Assistant AG Perez's performance at the October 19, 2011[518] summit at George Washington University. As we have seen previously, the conference was entitled,[519] *Confronting Discrimination in the Post-9/11 Era: Challenges and Opportunities Ten Years Later* and featured, along with Perez and DOJ Deputy Attorney General James Cole,[520] Islamic Society of North America President Mohamed Magid.

During the conference, Magid directly asked Perez to: 1) change the USG's rules governing terror investigations; 2) arrange more private meetings with top DOJ officials for leaders of the American Muslim community like him; 3) re-educate FBI agents who had been given "Islamophobic" training, and 4) encourage more people to oppose criticism of Islam, which he labeled "religious bigotry and hate." Magid declared that "teaching people that all Muslims are a threat to the country...is against the law and the Constitution."

As noted elsewhere, journalist Neil Munro[521] reported that, in his closing remarks, Perez did not explicitly promise whether he would comply with Mr. Magid's demands or not. But this top DOJ official did agree to call more meetings in the future. In fact, Magid has been one of the most successful Muslim Brotherhood operatives in penetrating not only the senior ranks of the Justice Department, but myriad other USG agencies at the senior-most levels and even the Oval Office.[lx]

Rep. Franks must have also been concerned that Perez did not repudiate Magid's open call for criminal punishment of people who criticize Islam and/or passages in the Quran that call for violence against non-Muslims. To the contrary,

---

[lx] See, for example, www.MuslimBrotherhoodinAmerica.com, Part 8 which describes Magid's meeting with President Obama on the eve of the latter's second "Muslim outreach" speech at the State Department in May 2011.

Perez was so conciliatory that he actually physically embraced this top Muslim Brotherhood operative on stage.

Another ominous sign at the same event was a testimonial to Perez and his colleagues by Sahar Aziz,[522] a former DHS-CRCL Senior Policy Adviser. She opined that the DOJ's "civil rights lawyers are top of the line – I say this with utter honesty – I know they can come up with a way" to redefine criticism of Islam as discrimination. In other words, to find a way to conform to UN HRC Resolution 16/18[523], notwithstanding the natty problem of the First Amendment.

Such comments by the likes of Magid and Aziz do not simply reflect troubling personal opinions. Rather, they exemplify the long-running effort by the Muslim Brotherhood, the Organization of Islamic Cooperation and other Islamic supremacists to impose shariah-based criminalization of any perceived criticism of Islam. Despite the harsh lessons of the Egyptian revolution and thanks, at least in part to the Great Purge, the U.S. government is still signaling its submission to such demands.

***

"...ISIL does not represent Islam. It is not representative in any way of the attitudes of the overwhelming majority of Muslims...And so to the degree that anyone would equate the terrible actions that took place in Paris with the views of Islam, those kinds of stereotypes are counterproductive. They're wrong. They will lead, I think, to greater recruitment into terrorist organizations over time if this becomes somehow defined as a Muslim problem as opposed to a terrorist problem. "

-President Barack Obama Press Conference
Antalya, Turkey (November 16, 2015)

***

CVE'S "BITTER HARVEST": BENGHAZI AND THE BOSTON MARATHON

Two other incidents in the post-Purge period warrant mention: the attack in Benghazi on September 11, 2012[524] and the Boston Marathon bombing on April 15, 2013.[525] Both of these jihadist incidents marked catastrophic failures in the USG's Countering Violent Extremism approach to counterterrorism.

Consider some examples of these catastrophic failures. In the Benghazi attacks, they include:

1) Using the February 17th Martyrs Brigade[526] to act as a "Quick Reaction Force"[527] to protect the Benghazi compound. Long before the attack, it was no

secret within the CT community that the Martyrs Brigade was closely affiliated with Ansar Al-Sharia[528] in Libya and with Jabhat Al-Nusrah[529] in Syria. All three of these *Salafi* jihadist groups (and many others)[530] are ideologically linked to Jamaat Al-Islamiya[531] (a.k.a. Egyptian Islamic Group),[532] which has been a Designated Foreign Terrorist Organization since October 8, 1997.[533]

Jamaat Al-Islamiya originated in Egypt in the early 1970's as the armed wing of the Muslim Brotherhood (see logo,[534] which shares the MB's crossed swords, Koran, and "Make Ready" slogan). It not only maintains an on-going alliance with Al-Qaeda, but has become a central node[535] in the worldwide network of links between Muslim Brotherhood groups and Muslim communities in the Middle East today.

The Obama administration's decision to put our personnel and resources in Benghazi under the "protection" of a known jihadist group may have reflected, at least in part, U.S. government confidence in and affinity towards the Muslim Brotherhood. But, it represents an example of deplorable, if not actually criminal, dereliction of duty[536] and contributory negligence.[537]

2) Blaming the Benghazi attacks on an obscure video about Mohammed, rather than what it really was – a coordinated jihad operation. Thanks to a cache[538] of recently released FOIA[539] documents,[540] it has now been proven that there was no basis to repeated administration claims that the attack on our facilities there amounted to a "spontaneous"[541] reaction to an anti-Muslim online video about the life of Mohammed.

In fact, the Obama administration was reportedly shipping weapons[542] from Benghazi to Syria, ostensibly in order to arm Muslim Brotherhood-backed militias[543] fighting against the regime of President Bashar Al-Assad. A now-declassified August 12, 2012[544] Defense Intelligence Agency (DIA) report served notice on the administration that the dominant forces in that insurgency were, in addition to the Brotherhood, *Salafists* and Al-Qaeda in Iraq (AQI).[545] Despite the fact that the West had essentially aligned with MB and Al Qaeda forces in order to oust Qaddafi from Libya and was now backing similar forces in Syria, Al Qaeda now saw an opportunity[546] to push the U.S. out and avenge the death of key AQ operative Abu Yahya al-Libi. So, it launched the deadly attack on the Benghazi facilities on September 11th, 2012.

3) Insisting on a fraudulent meme. As we have seen, on September 25, 2012,[547] President Obama perpetuated this false account of what happened in Benghazi during an appearance before the UN General Assembly. He once again linked the attacks to an amateur video[548] about the life of Mohammed, when he

stated: "That is what we saw play out in the last two weeks, as a crude and disgusting video sparked outrage throughout the Muslim world. Now, I have made it clear that the United States government had nothing to do with this video, and I believe its message must be rejected by all who respect our common humanity."

Worse yet, Mr. Obama went on to proclaim, "The future must not belong to those who slander the prophet of Islam." In so doing, he compounded the damage done by repeating a lie: He publicly *submitted* to the long-term MB-OIC[549] campaign[550] to confront[551] (read, criminalize) any criticism and/or defamation[552] of Islam (a.k.a. "slander").

These three examples of deplorable hubris and negligence of duty vis-à-vis the Benghazi attacks are a direct consequence of this administration's stubborn refusal to acknowledge the true nature of the threat we face today, and its deliberate collusion with the MB's seductive, but ultimately seditious, "countering violent extremism" gambit.

The CVE approach also conduced to catastrophic failures in connection with the Boston Marathon bombing:

1) Failing to "connect the dots" and respond to the "pings" in the system.[lxi] There is an old adage that applies, among other things to intelligence analysis: "Garbage in, garbage out." As long as federal law enforcement officers are officially discouraged from doing basic CT investigative work at an operational level below "probable cause," then the system will never work as it was designed to do.

In other words, we will *never* be able to connect the dots if we are prevented from putting into the system the kind of solid intelligence data that I repeatedly entered, only to be told to delete them.

2) Failing to intercept Tamerlan Tsarnaev when he returned to the United States. To this day, the facts about the elder Tsarnaev brother and his activities in Dagestan and/or Chechnya remain shrouded in mystery and confusion. We do know that while he was in Dagestan, two of his close associates, known jihadists Makhmud Nidal and William Plotnikov, were killed by Russian Special Forces.[553] Then, leaving his new Russian passport behind, Tamerlan somehow managed to avoid detention, board a flight on July 16, 2012 from the Mineralnye Vody airport to Moscow, then boarded another flight back to the United States, where he arrived on July 17, 2012.

Dots or no dots, pings or no pings, mystery and confusion aside, when Tamerlan Tsarnaev arrived at JFK airport in New York and presented his Lawful

---

[lxi] For more context on this problem, see the section in Chapter 11, "Blinding Our First Defenders to the *Pings* and *Dots*".

Permanent Resident card to a CBP Officer even the most basic line of questioning should have been enough to refer him to the Secondary inspection area for a more thorough interview. There, CT specialists may have been able to determine exactly what Tsarnaev had been doing in the volatile Caucasus Mountains, where he possibly spent time with members of the fearsome[554] jihadist group known as *Imarat Kavkaz*[555] (a.k.a. the Wolves of Jihad).

Had that happened, not only might the lives of all those who were killed and maimed nine months later in the Boston Bombing been spared, but the support system in Boston and elsewhere on which Tamerlan Tsarnaev drew might have been rolled up, as well.

The government's Countering Violent Extremism approach has created – and continues to impose – formidable disincentives for law enforcement and counter-terror specialists to 1) conduct the necessary research, and/or 2) question adequately individuals seeking entry into America (whether a U.S. citizen, legal permanent resident or foreign national).[lxii]

Far from considering a much-needed and serious course-correction in the wake of the disasters of the Great Purge and the debacles that followed – and, to varying degrees, those that flowed from it – the Obama administration has doubled down on its commitment to the disastrous CVE/CRCL approach. This attitude was particularly spectacularly evident in the February 2015 White House "Summit To Counter Violent Extremism," the subject of Chapter Nine.

[lxii] For more on the failures of the CVE policy as they relate to these two incidents, see the resources identified in Appendix VI.

CHAPTER 9: THE WHITE HOUSE SUMMIT ON COUNTERING VIOLENT EXTREMISM

It is beyond the scope of this monograph to report on the proceedings of the entire, three-day White House Countering Violent Extremism Summit in February 2015.[lxiii] We will, however, explore the extent to which this event illuminated the Muslim Brotherhood's deep penetration of the Obama administration and the impunity with which its Islamist interlocutors have responded to their perception that the U.S. government is submitting to them.

SETTING THE STAGE FOR A CVE SUMMIT

On September 10, 2014,[556] DHS Secretary Jeh Johnson spoke at the Council on Foreign Relations on the subject of homeland security and the threat of terrorism. During the course of his remarks, Mr. Johnson made the first public announcement about the proposed Countering Violent Extremism Summit. "In October, the White House will host a summit on domestic and international efforts to prevent violent extremism," he said, "and address the full life-cycle of radicalization to violence posed by the foreign fighter risk."

Five days later, then-Attorney General Eric Holder confirmed a pending October CVE Summit, while adding that:

> In order to complement the Obama administration's ongoing work to protect the American people from a range of evolving national security threats...the Department of Justice is joining with the White House, the Department of Homeland Security, and the National Counterterrorism Center [NCTC] to launch a new series of pilot programs in cities across the nation to help counter violent extremism. These programs will bring together community representatives, public safety officials, religious leaders, and United States Attorneys to improve local engagement and – ultimately – to build a broad network of community partnerships to keep our nation safe.

That October summit did not take place. But, following the jihadist attacks at the *Charlie Hebdo* office and, subsequently, at the Hypercacher kosher market in Paris on January 7 and 9, 2015, the White House announced it would host a Summit on Countering Violent Extremism on February 18, 2015, in order to: "Highlight domestic and international efforts to prevent violent extremists and their supporters from radicalizing, recruiting, or inspiring individuals or groups in the U.S. and abroad to commit acts of violence, efforts made even more imperative in light of recent, tragic attacks in Ottawa, Sydney, and Paris."

[lxiii] A comprehensive video archive of the Summit is available including Opening Day, President Barack H. Obama's speech, Secretary of State John Kerry's speech and DHS Secretary Jeh. C. Johnson's speech. Additional archived videos by Rep. Keith Ellison, Senator Al Franken and St. Paul Police Chief Tom Smith are also available.

The White House Press Secretary's official statement declared, moreover, that the CVE Summit was intended to: "Build on the strategy the White House released in August of 2011,[557] *Empowering Local Partners to Prevent Violent Extremism in the United States*, the first national strategy to prevent violent extremism domestically."

It bears restating that the August 8, 2011[558] release of the *Empowering Local Partners* document heralded the official inauguration of the CVE Policy. That white paper announced the adoption of a "Community-Based Approach, while 'enhancing federal engagement with and support to local communities that may be targeted by violent extremists.'" The evident intent of this language and the program it unveiled was to sound – and be – accommodating to American Muslim communities.

As early[559] as October 2011, however, the administration's Islamist interlocutors (notably, Brotherhood-linked groups CAIR, ISNA and MPAC) began flexing their muscles and insisting on changes in CVE initiatives that they found objectionable.[560] Having induced the Obama administration to abandon a fact-based approach to counterterrorism in favor of a civil rights-based one, the Islamic supremacists swiftly moved on to trying to sabotage the latter, dubbed Countering Violent Extremism, as well.

EARLY INDICATIONS THAT ISLAMISTS DON'T LIKE CVE

For example, on the eve of a November 14, 2014 meeting with Homeland Security Secretary Jeh Johnson, groups like CAIR Los Angeles, Asian Americans Advancing Justice Los Angeles, ACLU-Southern California, Sikh American Legal Defense & Education Fund Los Angeles, and the Islamic Shura Council of Southern California (ISCSC) issued an open letter[561] to Mr. Johnson. The opening paragraph of the letter declares:

> We the undersigned community-based and advocacy organizations that serve American Muslim and other impacted communities in Southern California urge Secretary Jeh Johnson and the Department of Homeland Security (DHS) to address our grave concerns regarding the government's proposed Countering Violent Extremism (CVE) programs. Several months ago [September 15, 2014],[562] AG Holder announced that the government would establish pilot CVE programs in three cities across the country, including Los Angeles. DHS has already spent an unknown amount of federal resources to lay the groundwork for this program in advance of today's meeting[563] with [DHS] Secretary Johnson.

Just hours before this get-together with Mr. Johnson, CAIR-LA went further, posting the following statement[564] from its Executive Director (and 2012 Democratic National Convention delegate) Hussam Ayloush[565][lxiv] on Facebook:

> We welcome Secretary Johnson initiating this meeting with Muslim religious and community leaders to discuss countering violent extremism. We do, however, have concerns about the program's adverse impact on the Muslim American community by potentially stigmatizing a religious community that has been a valuable and productive segment of the larger American society.
>
> We are also concerned about the constitutionality of such a program, under which government and law enforcement agencies may seek to determine what constitutes "acceptable" religious beliefs and practices.
>
> Constitutional rights are the cornerstone of our society and must not be suspended for any Americans. Protecting those rights requires building trust and treating the community as a partner, not as a collection of potential suspects.

What should have been a further indication of serious problems with the Obama administration's Muslim outreach efforts occurred on November 15, 2014,[566] when the United Arab Emirates designated several of the U.S. government's Islamist interlocutors – notably, CAIR, MAS and IRW – as terrorist organizations. Two days later,[567] State Department spokesman Jeff Rathke was obliged to state publicly that the U.S. government does not consider CAIR and MAS to be terrorist organizations, setting the stage for diplomatic demarches to the UAE urging that its designations of these groups be rescinded.

PLUNGING AHEAD WITH A WHITE HOUSE CVE SUMMIT

Undeterred by these warning signs of trouble with its CVE program, the White House pressed ahead with its February summit. Its January 11, 2015 statement signaled the importance the administration attached to its dealings with "the well-informed and resilient" local communities seen as models for CVE – specifically, Los Angeles, Minneapolis-St. Paul and Boston – that had taken a lead role in building "pilot frameworks."

Then, on February 4, 2015,[568] a direct reference to the pending "Summit on Countering Violent Extremism" was made in the official presidential press spokesman's readout of President Obama's White House meeting that day with so-

---

[lxiv] For more on Mr. Ayloush, who also attended the FBI Citizen's Academy, see a variety of news publications including a 2010 New York Times article, 2012 Investor Business Daily editorial and a 2012 CAIR Press Release.

called "American Muslim leaders"[569]. The hour-long event was said to have focused on "civil rights, anti-Muslim bias and extremism."

Attendees at this pre-Summit outreach meeting included Azhar Azeez[570][lxv] (the newly elected ISNA president), Mohamed Magid[571] (The outgoing ISNA President), and Hoda Hawa,[572] MPAC's Director of Policy and Advocacy.[573]

On February 6, 2015,[574] National Security Advisor Susan Rice appeared at the Brookings Institute to discuss the President's 2015 National Security Strategy.[575] During her remarks, Ms. Rice made the following comments on the administration's ongoing efforts to counter violent extremism:

> To counter today's threats, we're implementing a comprehensive counter-terrorism approach that takes account of how the enemy has evolved. As Al-Qaeda core has been decimated, we've seen the diffusion of the threat – to Al-Qaeda affiliates, ISIL, local militias, and *home-grown violent extremists*.... To meet this morphing challenge, we are combining our decisive military capabilities with local partnerships, with the financial tools to choke off funding, and the international reach of our law-enforcement and intelligence agencies. We're strengthening the capacity of weak states to govern their territory and provide for their citizens, while *countering the corrosive ideology of violent extremism.* [Emphasis added.]

Then, on February 8, 2015[576], just ten days before the White House Countering Violent Extremism Summit, a *Newsmax* report described an appearance that day on CNN by DHS Secretary Jeh Johnson:

> There are individuals living in the U.S. today who have contact with the Islamic State and other terrorist groups who have "a desire to conduct an attack." And [he said] the ability to recruit and communicate through social media has only strengthened the ability to inspire lone wolves since the days just after 9/11. "The FBI and the Department of Homeland Security do a pretty good job of tracking the travel of individuals of suspicion, of investigating potential acts of terror or material support for terrorism," adding that the government does a lot to keep track of suspected individuals, but added that the public should continue to be vigilant and report anything suspicious.

[lxv] Before becoming ISNA President, Azeez was Director of Fund Development for Islamic Relief USA (a.k.a. IRUSA, IRW or IR). IR is part of a global fundraising network that was designated as a terrorist organization by the UAE on November 15, 2014. It had previously been designated as a terrorist group by Israel on June 19, 2014. Note that these designations by friendly foreign governments predated by a number of months this White House meeting. And the U.S. government's designation of ISNA as an unindicted co-conspirator in connection with the Holy Land Foundation's material support for Hamas occurred eight years earlier. Azeez also served as founder and past president of CAIR Dallas-Fort Worth, founder and past president of the Islamic Association of Carrollton (IAC), and past president of the North Texas Islamic Council (NTIC). All three of these organizations are linked either to HLF, and/or to Mohammed Elibiary's Freedom and Justice Foundation (for details, see the Investigative Project Report on Mohammed Elibiary).

These three talking points are the ideological heart of the administration's Countering Violent Extremism doctrine: 1) individuals living in the U.S. are recruited and radicalized through social media (but with no regard to the influence of established Islamic doctrine and/or the global Muslim Brotherhood or other Islamist recruitment networks); 2) the motivation(s) behind these potential acts of terrorism or material support for terrorism remain perpetually undefined (yet, are *always* non-Islamic); and 3) the public should remain vigilant and report anything suspicious (while never providing a clear definition of what the terms "vigilant" should entail, and what "suspicious" behavior might look like).

THE ISLAMIC SUPREMACISTS PUSH BACK

Two days later,[577] the U.S. Council of Muslim Organizations (USCMO) – a newly-minted Islamist coalition with political and electoral aspirations[lxvi] – issued a challenge to Secretary Johnson, during and following a meeting with one his subordinates: Kareem Shora, the Chief of the Community Engagement Section (Civil Rights Civil Liberties, Department of Homeland Security). On February 10, 2015, the Council posted the following list of concerns on their homepage:

> In a gathering of approximately fifty U.S Muslim leaders, the U.S Council of Muslim Organizations (USCMO) hosted an all-day community forum regarding the American Muslim community's role in countering violent extremism (CVE).
>
> Session one was led by speaker Kareem Shora, Chief, Community Engagement Section, CRC-DHS. This session discussed the U.S. government's perspective on CVE since releasing their national strategy to prevent violent extremism in 2011, and Attorney General Holder's announcement in 2014 that Boston, Minneapolis, and Los Angeles are to be the pilot cities for the CVE program.
>
> The second session was held to discuss the issue of American liberty and its place in the government-led CVE initiatives. USCMO endorsed an ACLU-led [November 13, 2014][578] coalition letter that outlined concerns regarding Obama's CVE initiative.
>
> Session three was held as a collective leadership discussion. Its focus was to discuss what our appropriate role is in CVE. Efforts by extremists to recruit and spread their ideologies is a reality in some Muslim communities, *but is largely unsuccessful.*

[lxvi] For more on the USCMO, see the Center for Security Policy's Civilization Jihad Reader Series' *Star-Spangled Shariah: The Rise of America's First Muslim Brotherhood Party* (http://www.centerforsecuritypolicy.org/2015/09/15/book-release-star-spangled-shariah-the-rise-of-americas-first-muslim-brotherhood-party/).

The fourth and final session considered what actions in CVE are appropriate. As a responsible Muslim community, it is our responsibility to prevent even one successful case of extremist recruitment *even if they are few and far between*. [Emphasis added.]

The USCMO release went on to announce that:

Following the presentations, participants discussed and considered the issues at hand. In accordance with the Shura ("Consultation") process[lxvii], the USCMO embraced the following points on CVE:

- They are disappointed that the administration has not responded to our concerns that were addressed in the ACLU-led [November 13, 2014][579] letter.

- On the basis of media information and personal experience, the USCMO is very concerned that law enforcement efforts and CVE programs may be backed by intelligence-gathering activities, and other abusive law enforcement practices – particularly concerning the FBI.

- The Islamic faith and this council reject violent extremism.

- It is constitutionally questionable and morally inept that the administration for CVE seems to be singling out the Muslim community in particular.

- There are concerns over the issue that various local community leaders have had to shut down political discussions due to the fear of their words being misconstrued or misinterpreted and hasty law enforcement abuses.

- There is a noticeable lack of specification and detailed information regarding the Obama administration's current CVE initiative.

- Due to the lack of confidence in the government-led CVE, the USCMO believes it is best to support and establish community-driven practices and programs.

The following quote appeared in an apparent update to USCMO's February 10, 2015 post: "Later, on February 18, 2015, USCMO Secretary General[580] Oussama Jammal attended the White House summit on countering violent extremism, to represent and voice the concerns of the USCMO."[lxviii]

[lxvii] Shura, or Consultation, is a doctrinally prescribed element of Islamic governance, given in Sura 3:159. It is described by MB ideologue Sayyid Qutb in his "In the Shade of the Koran" where he wrote: We have here a distinctive order: "Consult with them on the conduct of public affairs." This principle, which is basic to the Islamic system of government, is established here, even when Muḥammad himself, God's Messenger, is the one who conducts public affairs. This is, then, a definitive statement which leaves the Muslim community in no doubt that consultation is central to Islamic government.

[lxviii] Based in Chicago, Oussama Jammal is closely affiliated with the Islamic supremacist Mosque Foundation and Kifah Mustafa,[lxviii] another unindicted co-conspirator in the HLF Trial. For more

WHAT 'MODEL' PROGRAMS?

In the immediate run-up to the White House CVE Summit, the Obama administration was ignominiously repudiated by three Muslim Brotherhood-tied organizations with whom it had long been partnering – and whose work it intended to showcase at the Summit.

LOS ANGELES:

First, On February 17, 2015,[581] the California-based Islamist influence operation known as Muslim Advocates[582] issued the following press release:

> Muslim Advocates is deeply troubled by the message that the administration is sending by primarily focusing on American Muslims, particularly young American Muslims, at this CVE summit. While the facts show that perpetrators who are Muslim comprise a *very tiny fraction of extremist violence* in the U.S., a summit and CVE programs that focus on Muslims send the false and dangerous message to the American people that their Muslim neighbors are a threat to their safety.
>
> By primarily focusing on Muslims, this summit and government CVE programs undermine the safety of all Americans, including American Muslims, who are living with *the very real, well-founded fear* that their neighbors may do them harm. Muslim Advocates has urged the administration to broaden the focus of the summit and is extraordinarily disappointed that it has refused to do so. [Emphasis added.]

It is worth digressing for a moment to recall that Muslim Advocates[583] is the same Islamic supremacist group that collaborated with CAIR, MPAC and the American-Arab Anti-Discrimination Committee (ADC)[584] in a May 14, 2008[585] press release entitled *Senate Homeland Security Report Lacks Substantive Analysis, Contradicts Own Recommendations*:

> Four of the country's leading Arab-American and Muslim-American advocacy organizations today issued a rare joint letter expressing strong reservations about a recently released Senate Homeland Security and Government Affairs Committee report on "homegrown terrorism." The report, issued jointly by Committee Chairman Joe Lieberman (I-CT) and ranking member Senator Susan Collins (R-ME), claims that the threat posed by violent extremists now comes "increasingly from within" the U.S. The report heavily relied upon a widely criticized and deeply flawed New York Police Department study on domestic radicalization that claimed that typical "signatures" of radicalization include wearing traditional clothing, growing a beard, or giving up cigarettes, drinking, and gambling.

---

background on Mr. Jammal, who has ties to several other pro-Hamas MB front groups in the United States, also see the Center for Security Policy web post entitled "U.S. Department of State Recruited at Muslim Brotherhood Convention" (2015) and a revealing *Chicago Tribune* article dated February 8, 2004.

The Senate Homeland Security Committee report that prompted such strong criticism from the Islamists was entitled *Violent Islamist Extremism, The Internet, and the Homegrown Terrorist Threat*. Released on May 8, 2008,[586] it was remarkably candid and informative about the nature of the threat posed by *Shariah* and its adherents. The Senate study found, among other things, that:

> Violent Islamist ideology and the terrorism it inspires pose a substantial threat to America's homeland security. The core tenets of this violent ideology are straightforward, uncompromising, and absolute. The ideology calls for the pursuit and creation of a global Islamist state – a Caliphate – that unites all Muslims – the Ummah – and is governed by Islamic law – *Shariah*. In pursuing this totalitarian goal, violent Islamists are not only encouraged to attack those who are not committed to their ideology in its purest form, including other Muslims, but are purportedly obligated to do so.

In the face of strenuous objections from the likes of Muslim Advocates and other Muslim Brotherhood-tied influence operations, such straightforward, fact-based assessments of the wellspring of Islamic supremacism and its jihad have been systematically eliminated from official discourse. But, having accomplished that feat, the practitioners of civilization jihad simply pivoted, setting their sights next on CVE – the very program that was designed to appease them by embracing a self-defeating Civil Rights and Civil Liberties-based policy approach to counter-terrorism.

MINNEAPOLIS/ST. PAUL:

At another, presumably synchronized event on February 17, 2015,[587] Somali and other Islamist leaders in Minnesota held a CAIR-sponsored press conference to raise concerns about:

> A stigmatizing and ineffective Department of Justice (DOJ) Countering Violent Extremism (CVE) pilot program, which is the subject of a White House summit on Wednesday [February 18, 2015]. Representatives from Minnesota mosques and Muslim organizations will be present, including the largest Somali mosques and organizations in St. Paul and Minneapolis.

BOSTON:

On the very day of the White House CVE Summit, Yusufi Vali,[588] executive director of the Islamic Society of Boston Cultural Center not only publicly discredited the entire premise of the event. He formally withdrew[589] the ISBCC from it.

The ISB is not only the largest mosque in the Northeast, but has numerous, longstanding and well-documented[590] ties to jihadists, as well, as discussed in Chapter 3.

In short, representatives of all three of the "well-informed and resilient local communities" that the official Countering Violent Extremism apparatus intended to play leading roles at the Summit and, far more importantly, in ferreting out and reporting on "radicalism" in their midst, openly renounced their involvement in the CVE pilot program.

THE SUMMIT GOES BUST

Matters did not improve at the CVE Summit itself.[591] Rep. Keith Ellison, the first Muslim Member of Congress – and an individual with extensive ties to Muslim Brotherhood front organizations, used his time at the event to denounce the targeting of Muslim populations. He argued that, by failing to prosecute hate crimes against Muslim communities, the U.S. government was only furthering the extremists' cause, insofar as such unchecked targeting and persecution of Muslims serves to encourage extremist behavior: "This actually helps to support the false narrative of violent extremism; [extremists] want to make the case that America hates you, is against you. Join us."

Rep. Ellison's remarks call to mind the Islamic concept of slander (*ghiba*),[592] which according to shariah[593] is considered a very serious offense, indeed possibly a capital one when the slander is perceived to be targeting Islam or its prophet. In Islam, you can slander someone even when you are telling the truth about them. Or, as is written in the *Hadith*[594] (sayings of Mohammed): "If what you say of him is true, you have slandered him, and if what you say of him is not true, you have reviled him."

In other words, from an Islamic perspective, the targeting of Muslim communities for possible violent extremists (jihadists*)* is seen as an offensive act of slander, i.e., a form of persecution, also known as *Fitnah*[595] (Opposition/Oppression).

Meanwhile, in a spectacular display of bad timing, on February 18, 2015,[596] the White House PR team released a *Fact Sheet on the White House Summit on Countering Violent Extremism*, which included the following introduction:

> This week, the White House is convening a three-day summit on Countering Violent Extremism (CVE) to bring together local, federal, and international leaders – including President Obama and foreign ministers – to discuss concrete steps the United States and its partners can take to develop community-oriented approaches to counter hateful extremist ideologies that radicalize, recruit or incite to violence. Violent extremist threats can come from a range of groups and individuals, including domestic terrorists and homegrown violent extremists in the United States, as well as terrorist groups like Al-Qaeda and ISIL.
>
> Since the release of the Strategy, local governments and communities around the United States have developed prevention frameworks that address the unique issues facing their local communities. Three cities – Greater Boston, Los Angeles, and the Twin Cities – with the leadership of representatives from the Federal Government, have created pilot programs to foster partnerships between local government, law enforcement, mayor's offices, the private sector, local service providers, academia, and many others who can help prevent violent extremism.[lxix]

This upbeat assessment of the reception CVE was getting certainly did not jive with statements from one of its putative mainstays, the ISB's Yusufi Vali, as reported in a February 18, 2015[597] *Boston Globe* article: "A top leader of Boston's Muslim community on Wednesday strenuously objected to a new Justice Department strategy to prevent disaffected youth from taking up terrorism, complaining that the effort is 'exclusively targeting the American Muslim community.'" The *Globe* report also noted:

> In a strongly worded protest to a report that U.S. Attorney Carmen M. Ortiz delivered to a White House summit on Wednesday, Yusufi Vali said he could not support the framework because the programs "are founded on the premise that your faith determines your propensity towards violence."
>
> The comments by Vali demonstrate the difficulty the Obama administration faces in taking preemptive action to prevent troubled youths from becoming

---

[lxix] If the disconnect between the Obama administration's representations about its dubious Muslim outreach partners and their hostility towards the CVE program were not alarming enough, Summit day brought yet another, jarring insight into the USG's embrace of the Muslim Brotherhood. On February 18, 2015, the Middle East Media Research Institute reported that three weeks before, several Egyptian Brotherhood members had met January 27, 2015 with White House and State Department officials. The administration also arranged for these MB operatives to meet with members of Congress and representatives of American think tanks. According to the participating Brothers' social media postings, the purpose of these meetings was to recruit U.S. support for their opposition to the Abdel Fattah El-Sisi regime in Egypt.

violent extremists, while not trampling on individual rights or singling out particular communities for scrutiny. Last fall, Boston was chosen along with Los Angeles and Minneapolis to spearhead a DOJ effort known as "Countering Violent Extremism."

Vali has been one of the local participants, and the Boston experience was the subject of a 28-page report released at the White House summit.

The referenced 28-page report, which included contributions from more than 50 people, was entitled *A Framework for Prevention and Intervention Strategies Incorporating Violent Extremism Into Violence Prevention Efforts.*[lxx] When it was released in February of 2015,[598] Massachusetts' U.S. Attorney Carmen Ortiz wrote the introduction, which included this passage:

> As U.S. Attorney, I was honored that the Greater Boston region was chosen by the White House to be one of only three pilot locations in the country to develop an approach to enhance our efforts at preventing violent extremism. Our resilience and longstanding *history of successful collaborative efforts to* [sic] *combating violence* served as the genesis for this framework and the foundation on which we will build an effective strategy to combat violent extremism locally and enable communities across the country to do the same. [Emphasis added.]

Interestingly, Vali's repudiation of the CVE program contrasts sharply with the emphasis he previously placed on the ISB's partnership with the authorities. An April 25, 2013[599] *USA Today* article, published just 10 days after the Boston Marathon bombing perpetrated by Dzhokhar and Tamerlan Tsarnaev[600] (whom he described elsewhere as "infrequent"[601] worshipers at his organization's Cambridge mosque), reported that:

> "If there were really any worry about us being extreme," he said, U.S. law enforcement agencies such as the FBI, Departments of Justice and Homeland Security would not partner with the Muslim American Society and the Boston mosque in conducting monthly meetings that have been ongoing for four years, he said, in an apparent reference to U.S. government outreach programs in the Muslim community.

How to explain the change in attitude on the part of the Boston Muslim community's putative leadership and that of its counterparts in the Twin Cities and Los Angeles – and their willingness to break publicly with the Obama administration? Could it simply reflect a perceived need to respond to criticism from within their community that, by participating in the CVE project, they are

---

[lxx] A similar report was subsequently issued by the Minneapolis-St. Paul "model community." See the April 20, 2015 study entitled *Foreign Fighters: Terrorist Recruitment and Countering Violent Extremism (CVE) Programs in Minneapolis-St. Paul.*

perhaps being disloyal to or even betraying fellow Islamists? Or could it simply be a sign of growing confidence that, after *years of highly successful infiltration and influence operations*, their hand is now sufficiently strong that they can defy the U.S. government with impunity?

TAKING BOTH PATHS – A DUAL TACTICAL APPROACH

Let us draw upon the debacle of the White House CVE Summit to drill down on these and several related questions: Why did Mr. Vali choose this precise moment, on the very eve of the CVE Summit, to publicly withdraw his support for the CVE Policy? If Muslim leaders from all three-model communities were so dissatisfied with the CVE pilot program, why did they participate in the engagement process at all?

Furthermore, why would they be so public in their protests, to renounce – indeed, sabotage – the very CRCL-based program they had repeatedly demanded and helped create? Were the Muslim leaders in these three model communities genuine friends to government officials, or subtle adversaries?

On the surface, this two-sided tactical approach (simultaneously pro/con, friend/enemy) might seem contradictory, or at the least, counter-productive. In the last few years, however, this gambit has been used very effectively by the Muslim Brotherhood's so-called "community leaders" in America, and by Brotherhood front groups in countries around the world.

To better understand this dual approach, we have to look at it from two perspectives, i.e., from 1) an Islamic doctrinal perspective, and 2) from the perspective of applied political warfare.

THE ISLAMIC DOCTRINAL IMPETUS

As discussed in Chapter 4, *Shariah* dictates that its adherents must regard an *ineffectual response* by the infidels to Muslim demands (e.g., habitual acquiescence, accommodations and submission) as a sign of weakness, not strength. Also, from an Islamic perspective, such weakness is seen as actionable divine favor, which then compels members of the Islamic community to consolidate their efforts and advance even further – to make the unbeliever "feel subdued" in the words of the Quran.

Furthermore, the concept of settling for *anything* less than total victory, and/or making what might be seen as reasonable concessions towards non-Muslims, contradict the ideology of the global Islamic movement and especially the modus operandi of the MB front groups here in America.[lxxi]

In other words, as per the Quran and the late Brotherhood ideologue, Sayyid Qutb, there is no such thing as "retreat" in Islam; the only option is to *advance*, always to advance, with every victory seen as the beginning of another step along the way, i.e., as another Milestone[602] in the path towards ultimate world-wide Islamic supremacy.

APPLIED POLITICAL WARFARE

We may derive some valuable insight from a November 11, 2015[603] editorial by MPAC Policy Analyst Saif Inam,[604] entitled *Two Sides of the Same Coin*:

> As civil rights groups mature, and as times change, whether engagement or protests takes the lead will change. However, both are needed to effectively reform policies and opinions. Instead of being diametrically opposed to each other, both should instead work in unison to achieve their similar goals.

At first glance, this statement may seem unobjectionably benign. But on a macro or global scale, this asymmetric tactical approach, is how civilization jihadist groups like the Muslim Brotherhood (which focus on "engagement") and violent jihadists like al-Qaeda (whose kinetic terrorist acts are expressed as "protests") manage to find ways to, "work in unison to achieve their similar goals."

The Islamic Movement, of which the Muslim Brotherhood is a part, understands violent jihadists like al-Qaeda and ISIS as "protest"-like expressions meant to soften non-Muslim societies to the idea of making concessions to the Brotherhood-led representatives of the Muslim community. They can be understood as the '"bad cop" in the proverbial police routine. The leadership of the Brotherhood's groups in America, on the other hand, represents the 'good cop' – who exists chiefly to receive the concessions from government, media and society at large.

The two elements waging jihadist political warfare against us at the moment are described well by David Solway in his April 12, 2010[605] article entitled, "The Return of Tariq Ramadan":

> Acts of blatant terrorism, of course, are by no means ruled out, but terrorism need no longer be exclusively violent. The jihad against the West has now adopted a double strategy. Along with its standard method of spreading fear and destruction among civilian populations at large, it *has conscripted to its cause a new breed of ostensibly peaceable ambassadors, smooth talkers, subtle academics* and *spiffy front men*.

[lxxi] This dynamic was much in evidence in the recent nuclear negotiations between Iran and the West.

But its most potent weapon in the so-called asymmetrical war that Islam is waging against the Christian and secular West is an insidious form of *persuasion*, that both clouds the mind and corrupts the will of its human targets. [Emphasis added.]

Whether it is in the context of imposing *Shariah* blasphemy codes, extorting changes in U.S. counterterrorism policy or more generally demanding submission to the Islamic supremacists' agenda, the 'good cop' Brotherhood operatives invariably exploit the threat posed by the 'bad cop' violent jihadists.

GROUPTHINK-IMPOSED WILLFUL BLINDNESS AT THE SUMMIT

Just how persuasive this Islamist version of the 'good cop-bad cop' routine can be is evident in the clueless remarks delivered at the White House CVE Summit on February 18, 2015[606] by DHS Secretary Jeh Johnson. He seemed oblivious to the fact that the administration's unctuous cultivation of the so-called "model communities" had come completely a cropper. Mr. Johnson told the invited audience:

> We in the administration and the government should give voice to the plight of Muslims living in this country and the discrimination that they face. And so I personally have committed to speak out about the situation that very often people in the Muslim community in this country face. The fact that there are 1.6 billion Muslims in the world, and *the Islamic faith is one about peace and brotherhood*. For our part, we – we ask something of you, of members of the community.
>
> First of all, I've heard over and over again, and this is where we have to depend upon people in the community, that we need to develop the counter-narrative. We've heard that over and over now. And we know that there are a number of those who have undertaken to do this. We need to take that to the next level, developing the counter-narrative. [Emphasis added.]

Mr. Johnson's comments reveal a remarkably persistent denial of the reality that the administration's Muslim interlocutors are not actually being helpful – with a "counter-narrative (counter to what, exactly?), or anything else. Examples of such abject denial bring to mind observations in a December 2014[607] Master's thesis by James E. Ricciuti, a student at the Naval Postgraduate School in Monterey, California, entitled *Groupthink: A Significant Threat to the Homeland Security of the United States*. An excerpt from the abstract of the thesis includes the following observations:

> The groupthink psychological phenomenon prevalent in the homeland security enterprise is a significant threat to the United States. Homeland

security is vulnerable to groupthink because its leaders frequently share similar backgrounds, work histories, and world-views. This similarity minimizes the chance of outside perspectives being introduced to the decision-making process, which insulates leadership from external ideas. Leaders who wish to alleviate groupthink should promote a culture in which employees are encouraged to play the role of *devil's advocate* by offering alternatives to organizational decisions and commonly held assumptions. [Emphasis added.]

In hindsight, the White House CVE Summit fiasco can be seen as a textbook case of such groupthink. First, the Obama administration was evidently completely surprised that, instead of the fanfare and acclamation it expected from Muslim community leaders, the showcased CVE pilot programs came under direct, public attack from leaders in all three of the cities the administration had chosen to work with, and had tried so hard to please.

Instead of the public endorsements that it had hoped for, the administration found itself gathering a harvest of bitter repudiation, despite years of work and more than 1,700 engagement and dialogue[608] sessions across America, the vast majority with one or more of these treacherous MB front groups. And we had confirmed by the leader of one of those groups, the Islamic Society of Boston, that its deep penetration of the U.S. government and influence operations inside the wire had been underway since at least 2009, despite the documented ties of that organization to a number[609] of prominent and dangerous jihadists.[610][lxxii]

Tragically, far from spawning a demand for "devil's advocates" and fresh thinking about the bankruptcy of the CVE strategy, the White House Summit seems to have resulted in a doubling down by the Obama administration. We see the perpetuation of its official groupthink and the continuing denial of reality about Islamic supremacism, and the threat posed by its adherents – both violent and pre-violent – that is at its core.

AFTER THE SUMMIT

This is all the more remarkable since the administration's chosen partners for their Countering Violent Extremism initiatives – which appear to be, without exception, Muslim Brotherhood fronts – have continued their intense criticism of that program. For example, on February 21, 2015,[611] the Muslim Students Association Western Region (MSA West) posted a statement entitled *Muslim*

[lxxii] See an analysis of the ISB's ties to at least 12 world-renowned jihadists at http://www.centerforsecuritypolicy.org/2015/05/13/the-dirty-dozen-president-obamas-model-mosque/

Student Associations Across CA Against Federal Government's Countering Violent Extremism Programs. The statement included the following assertions:

> We, the undersigned Muslim Student Associations (MSA's) and MSA West express grave concerns with the Countering Violent Extremism (CVE) framework. We oppose the creation of pilot programs that are planned to be launched in various cities across the nation, including Los Angeles, Boston and Minneapolis, and do not support the organizations that are aligning with CVE's programs.
>
> Furthermore, the CVE framework is rooted in the flawed "radicalization theory" which claims that there is a fixed trajectory to radicalization with indicators that, if detected early on, can be interrupted through intervention. Examples of indicators used in this theory as signs of radicalization include growing beards, increasing involvement in social activism and community issues, and "wearing traditional Islamic clothing."
>
> These so-called signs of radicalization discourage Muslims from practicing their faith, creates [sic] a sense of paranoia in the community by eroding trust amongst community members, and threatens [sic] our constitutionally protected first-amendment rights to freedom of religion, expression and assembly.

Consistent with Islamic supremacist doctrine, Muslim Brotherhood-tied influence operations are also doubling down in their determination to take down what is left of U.S. counter-terrorism policies and capabilities following their stunning humiliation of the Obama administration last February. Specifically, they are working to disassociate CVE from the Islamic community, and to deflect – and/or immunize themselves from – even minimal scrutiny from law enforcement. All the while, they are shrilly amplifying claims that they are victims of an ever-larger catalogue of putative offenses, such as harassment,[612] intimidation[613] and DHS Civil Rights and Civil Liberties violations.[614][lxxiii]

Interestingly, this tactic of deflecting criticism and blame from the Islamic community is based on the practice that the "perfect Muslim,"[615] Muhammed, charted some 1,400 years ago. It amounts to exonerating[616] the faithful from all accusations of intolerance, brutality or terrorism by deftly blaming someone else (i.e., the infernal, disbelieving "Other") for any acts of violence Muslims are doctrinally obligated to commit.[lxxiv]

[lxxiii] For much more on this subtle strategic and tactical approach, see the August 14, 2015 detailed analysis by Stephen Coughlin entitled *Exploiting Ignorance in the Post- Subversion Phase: Assessing What ISIS Wants in Light of the 'Countering Violent Extremism' Narrative.*

[lxxiv] A few examples of this Islamic doctrine being operationalized so effectively by the Muslim Brotherhood include Quranic verses: 5.51 ("Do not take the Jews and the Christians as allies"), 5.82, ("The most intense of the people in animosity toward the believers are the Jews"), 9.30-31 ("May Allah

A NEW 'MODEL COMMUNITY' FOR CVE: NEW YORK CITY?

On September 21, 2015, more than twenty civil rights, legal, and interfaith organizations sent a letter[617] New York Mayor Bill de Blasio and his top aides, urging them not to take part in the White House initiative to counter violent extremism in the United States. Among the signers were representatives from the hard Left's Brennan Center for Justice at NYU School of Law, the ACLU, and the communist front known as the National Lawyers Guild, as well as Hamas-tied groups like CAIR and MAS. Their letter claimed that the CVE program would "brand" Muslims as "inherently suspicious and somehow less American than others." It also asserted that:

> The premise of CVE programming is that the adoption or expression of extreme or "radical" ideas [places] individuals on the path toward violence, and that there are observable "indicators" to identify those "vulnerable" to radicalization, or "at risk" of being recruited by terrorist groups. *This is simply not true.* Despite years of federally funded efforts, researchers have not developed reliable criteria that can be used to predict who will commit a terrorist act. [Emphasis added.]

A follow-up article posted in *Politico* on September 24, 2015[618] reported that John Miller, NYPD's [619] Deputy Commissioner for Intelligence and Counterterrorism, said, "There has been some 'gnashing of teeth' over programs like CVE, and that even among allies in the advocacy world, there is not always consensus on the right strategy to follow."

The strategy being followed by New York City became a lot less "right" when the city in early January 2016 settled a lawsuit over NYPD surveillance of Muslims. Pursuant to that settlement reached with plaintiffs representing the Red-Green axis (including, the ACLU and several Islamic supremacist individuals and organizations and mosques tied to the 1993 WTC bombing conspiracy[lxxv]), the NYPD will be obliged to "reform" its programs for monitoring what amount to potential jihadist incubators within the Muslim community. According to the ACLU,[620] the agreed-upon reforms would entail:

- Prohibiting investigations in which race, religion, or ethnicity is a substantial or motivating factor;

---

destroy them [Jews and Christians]; how are they deluded") and 60.1 ("If you have come out for jihad in My cause and seeking means to My approval, do not take them not as friends").

[lxxv] A letter by the NYC's senior counsel responding to the Raza v. NYC case accurately describes the clear cut jihadist nature of the surveillance targets, see:
http://www.nyc.gov/html/nypd/downloads/pdf/pr/raza_et_al_letter.pdf

- Requiring articulable and factual information before the NYPD can launch a preliminary investigation into political or religious activity;

- Requiring the NYPD to account for the potential effect of investigative techniques on constitutionally protected activities such as religious worship and political meetings;

- Limiting the NYPD's use of undercovers and confidential informants to situations in which the information sought cannot reasonably be obtained in a timely and effective way by less intrusive means;

- Putting an end to open-ended investigations by imposing presumptive time limits and requiring reviews of ongoing investigations every six months;

- Installing a Civilian Representative within the NYPD, with the power and obligation to ensure all safeguards are followed and to serve as a check on investigations directed at political and religious activities; and

- Removing from the NYPD website the discredited and unscientific[621] *Radicalization in the West* report, which justified discriminatory surveillance, and affirming that the report is not and will not be relied upon to open or prolong NYPD investigations.

Tragically it is not hard to see where such accommodations to the Islamists will take the organization that has superbly performed the immensely difficult task of protecting the top jihadist target in America – New York City: The New York Police Department will have to labor under the kind of crippling constraints in terms of situational awareness and law enforcement capabilities that have rendered the nation's other front lines of defense so ill-equipped to counter the threat posed by Islamic supremacism.

As we shall see in the next chapter, Congress has done little to rectify the executive branch's extended, bipartisan indulgence in willful blindness. If it is not careful, the Republican majority on Capitol Hill will not just be guilty of passively allowing the attendant harm being done to our country. It will also be fully implicated in President Obama's disastrous Countering Violent Extremism agenda – and have to share the blame for the disaster it is inviting.

CHAPTER 10: CONGRESS AND COUNTERING VIOLENT EXTREMISM

Given all that has been written to this point about the Obama administation's abdication of its responsibility in the face of the threat of Islamic supremacism in America, one might be forgiven for assuming the United States Congress – particularly one led in both houses by the opposition party – would be holding the administration accountable for the damage it is doing to our first lines of defense. Unfortunately, you would be wrong.

Two episodes exemplify the nature and extent of the problem on Capitol Hill.

THE UNHAPPY STORY OF THE 'NATIONAL SECURITY FIVE'[lxxvi]

In June of 2012, five Members of Congress – Reps. Michele Bachmann, Louie Gohmert, Trent Franks, Lynn Westmoreland and Tom Rooney – wrote letters to the inspectors general of the Departments of State, Justice, Defense and Homeland Security and the Office of the Director of National Intelligence.[lxxvii] The correspondence respectfully requested each IG to address a pregnant question: Is there a correlation between the presence in their respective agencies, either as employees or advisors, of individuals with demonstrable ties to Muslim Brotherhood front groups, on the one hand, and the adoption by those agencies of policies favored by Islamists like the Brothers, on the other?[lxxviii]

For a month, there was essentially no response. Then, all hell broke loose. On July 12, 2012[622], Rep. Keith Ellison, himself an individual with long associations[623] with various Muslim Brotherhood fronts[624], bitterly complained about an initiative he ascribed exclusively to his colleague from Minnesota, Michele Bachmann. On July 18th, Senator John McCain took the extraordinary step of going to the Senate floor to denounce Rep. Bachmann by name[625]. He took specific umbrage at the request she and her co-signers made to the State Department's Inspector General to examine, among other things, questions about the Department's then-Deputy Chief of Staff, Huma Abedin, and her extensive family connections[626] to the Brotherhood.

In short order, other Republican legislators piled on, including: House Speaker John Boehner,[627] House Intelligence Committee Chairman Mike Rogers[628], Sen. Lindsey Graham, and Sen. Marco Rubio.[629] Ms. Bachmann's

---

[lxxvi] The phrase "National Security Five" comes from a Newt Gingrich piece available at: http://www.politico.com/story/2012/07/in-defense-of-bachmann-muslim-brotherhood-probes-079104
[lxxvii] The five letters are available at Rep. Louie Gohmert's Congressional website: http://gohmert.house.gov/news/documentsingle.aspx?DocumentID=299623
[lxxviii] The letters drew, among other things, on data developed by the Center for Security Policy and made available online at www.MuslimBrotherhoodinAmerica.com.

political career was severely damaged, and not just by the Red-Green axis,[lxxix] but at the hands of her fellow Republicans. She barely averted defeat at the polls five months later.

The message was not lost on other legislators. When combined with the harsh criticism Rep. Peter King endured when, as chairman of the House Homeland Security Committee in the Spring of 2011, he held hearings on "Islamic radicalization," every lawmaker was on notice: Taking on the Islamists could be hazardous to one's future in Congress. And, not surprisingly, scarcely any of them have exercised the sort of oversight or leadership needed to challenge, let alone *roll up*, the Muslim Brotherhood's influence operations and the Obama administration's abject submission to them.

THE 114TH CONGRESS AND CVE

Instead, Congress has all too often gone along – first, with President Bush's accommodation of the Brotherhood's operatives, starting immediately after the 9/11 attacks,[lxxx] and then during the Obama presidency. Unfortunately, at the moment, the House of Representatives is poised do something even worse: implicate itself in institutionalizing Mr. Obama's dangerous Countering Violent Extremism project.[lxxxi]

On June 25, 2015[630], Rep. Michael McCaul, the chairman of the Homeland Security Committee, introduced H.R. 2899, the "Countering Violent Extremism Act of 2015," in the House. As essayist Daniel Horowitz[631] put it: "This legislation would create a new $40 million government agency within the Department of Homeland Security – the Office for Countering Violent Extremism…tasked with working across the federal government and throughout communities to develop strategies and data concerning 'violent extremism.'"

With the initial co-sponsorship of Reps. Peter King, Buddy Carter, Daniel Donovan, John Katko, Tom Marino, Martha McSally and Bradley Walker, the bill was referred to the Congressman McCaul's committee on the same day.

[lxxix] In particular, Rep. Bachmann was savaged by leftist CNN anchor Anderson Cooper and Rep. Ellison's Islamic supremacist friends at CAIR. See: https://www.youtube.com/watch?v=X3Yhxz5f_hM
[lxxx] See *Agent of Influence: Grover Norquist and the Assault on the Right* (http://www.centerforsecuritypolicy.org/2014/03/15/agent-of-influence-grover-norquist-and-the-assault-on-the-right/).
[lxxxi] For example, on February 24, 2015, Rep. Bradley Walker introduced H. R. 1022, the "Countering Violent Extremism Grants Act," to amend the Homeland Security Act of 2002 to authorize the use of Urban Area Security Initiative (NSGP) and State Homeland Security Grant Program (HSGP) funding to "counter violent extremism."

On July 9, 2015[632], the Committee posted a press release entitled "McCaul Leads Government Efforts to Counter Violent Extremism." It announced a hearing on H.R. 2899 the following week and stated, in part:

> As violent extremist groups eagerly recruit followers inside the United States, and as recent tragic events dot the globe and also hit right here at home, House Homeland Security Committee Chairman Michael McCaul is steadfastly leading the charge to bolster U.S. efforts to counter violent extremism (CVE). Chairman McCaul announced today the House Homeland Security Committee will hold a hearing on Wednesday, July 15 [2015] to investigate whether the Government is doing enough to counter international and domestic terrorism.

The July 15, 2015[633] hearing was entitled, "The Rise of Radicalization: Is the U.S. Government Failing to Counter International and Domestic Terrorism?" In his prepared opening remarks, Mr. McCaul made the following revealing comments:

> Americans are worried about a heightened threat environment and for good reason. The number of post 9/11 homegrown terror plots in the United States has surged. In fact, there have been more U.S.-based terror plots in the first half of 2015 than any full year since 9/11. In particular, Islamist terror groups are on the march. The attack disrupted this week marks the 50th ISIS-linked terror plot against the Western world since early last year – and the 12th inside America.
>
> But while we spend billions of dollars to detect and disrupt terror attacks, we have dedicated few resources toward combating the radicalization at the root of terror. That is what countering violent extremism – or "CVE" – is all about. It is about warning communities, *helping them spot signs of radicalization, training state and local law enforcement, combating extremist propaganda*, and *developing "off-ramps" to radicalization* so we have an alternative to simply arresting young people who are preyed upon and recruited by terrorists. This is the crucial "prevention" aspect of counterterrorism. [Emphasis added.]

Incredibly, all three witnesses had been directly involved in the CVE program and/or were philosophically and professionally aligned with its leitmotif that violent extremism by right-wing constitutionalists, Tea Party activists, anti-abortion zealots and veterans constitute at least as much of a threat as does Islamic supremacism: 1) Seamus Hughes[634], Deputy Director, Program on Extremism, Center for Cyber and Homeland Security, George Washington University; 2) Farah Pandith[635], Adjunct Senior Fellow, Council on Foreign Relations and 3) Richard Cohen[636], President, Southern Poverty Law Center.

According to his GWU bio, Seamus Hughes[637] previously: "worked at the National Counterterrorism Center (NCTC), serving as a lead staffer on the U.S. government's efforts to implement the national CVE strategy; created a groundbreaking intervention program to help steer individuals away from violence through non-law enforcement means; worked closely with FBI Joint Terrorism Taskforces, Fusion Centers, and U.S. Attorney Offices; and *helped coordinate the 2015 White House Summit on CVE*. Prior to NCTC, Hughes served as the Senior Counterterrorism Advisor for the U.S. Senate Homeland Security and Government Affairs:" [Emphasis added.]

Mr. Hughes told the House committee:

> Countering Violent Extremism, commonly referred to as CVE, is an inherently amorphous term. It can be described as measures aimed at preventing individuals from radicalizing and reversing the process of those who have already radicalized. *The effort is fraught with civil rights and civil liberties concerns.* Yet CVE, if properly implemented, can help sway young people from radicalizing, thereby saving lives and enabling law enforcement to concentrate on those who have made the leap into violent militancy. On the other hand, if improperly implemented, CVE can have an adverse effect on building trust with communities.
>
> It is a delicate exercise, but one that I believe government and communities have a moral responsibility to attempt. Successful CVE efforts need support from a broad community cross-section. Some American Muslim civic groups embrace CVE efforts, while others decry it as a surveillance ruse or an effort that singles out American Muslims. In addressing these concerns, *the U.S. government would do well to listen not just to the most vocal voices, but also grassroots organizations at the local level.* [Emphasis added.]

Farah Pandith[638] held a number of positions in the Bush and Obama administration, including her appointment as the Department of State's first Special Representative[639] to Muslim Communities on June 23, 2009[640]. In addition to her current position at the Council on Foreign Relations, Ms. Pandith today is at Harvard University, home to thethe Prince Alwaleed Bin Talal Islamic Studies[641] Program, where Ms. Pandith participated in panel discussions.[642] Her testimony included the following:

> We can't create an ideological counter-movement on the backs of a few isolated government-funded programs. It requires much broader commitment and focus. Our strategy must be a cohesive, integrated and comprehensive approach to the threat we face. We must wage a battle on all fronts with money, accountability and experienced personnel. We must look at this [threat] like we would any other contagion, rooting out its hosts globally and destroying its defenses. The extremists seem all powerful, but they are not. We have yet to unleash the full power of our skills in the *soft*

power space. When we truly go "all in," we'll see how vulnerable the extremists really are. [Emphasis added.]

The final witness, Richard Cohen[643], is the president of the Southern Poverty Law Center. The SPLC today is a radical leftist organization that assiduously ignores the threat posed to U.S. constitutional freedoms by Islamic supremacists. Instead, like others in the Red side of the Red-Green axis, it assists the Islamists by promoting their memes that the real threat is from right-wing extremists afflicted with "Islamophobia" and much given to "hate-mongering."

The SPLC publishes a quarterly magazine called *Intelligence Report*,[644] which advertises itself[645] as "the nation's preeminent periodical monitoring the radical right in the U.S." A sub-section of the organization's website, *Hatewatch*[646], claims it "monitors and exposes the activities of the American radical right."

The SPLC has collaborated closely with the Islamic supremacists. On June 17, 2011[647] it published a propagandistic report entitled, *The Anti-Muslim Inner Circle*. It also supported the Muslim Brotherhood-tied Muslim Public Affairs Council in the latter's publication on December 13, 2012[648] of a report entitled *Not Qualified: Exposing the Deception Behind America's Top 25 Pseudo Experts on Islam*.

Instructively, the introduction to *Inner Circle* makes the following assertions:

> The apparent recent surge in popular anti-Muslim sentiment[649] in the United States has been driven by a surprisingly small and, for the most part, closely knit cadre of activists. Their influence extends far beyond their limited numbers, in part because of an amenable legion of right-wing media personalities – and lately, politicians like Peter King (R-NY), who held controversial hearings into the radicalization of American Muslims [in] March [2011][650] – who are eager to promote them as impartial experts or grassroots leaders. Yet, a close look at their rhetoric reveals how doggedly this group works to provoke and guide populist anger over what is seen as the threat posed by the 0.6% of Americans who are Muslim – an agenda that goes beyond reasonable concern about terrorism into *the realm of demonization*. [Emphasis added.]

Cohen's testimony amplified on these themes under the rubric of "The Rise of Radicalization: Is the U.S. Government Failing to Counter International and Domestic Terrorism?"

Not surprisingly, given the inputs of such unobjective witnesses, the Homeland Security Committee was encouraged to approve H.R. 2899 and did so by voice vote on July 15, 2012. [lxxxii]

[lxxxii] All of the procedural steps that were taken during the mark-up session can be reviewed at the Homeland Security Committee website (includes video).

The next day,[651] the Committee touted this achievement in another press release entitled "Bipartisan Support in Congress to Counter Violent Extremism," which included this statement by Chairman McCaul:

> In the face of mounting threats, our government is doing far too little to counter violent extremism here in the United States. Whether it is the long reach of international terrorists into our communities, or the homegrown hate spread by domestic extremist groups, we are ill-equipped to prevent Americans from being recruited by dangerous fanatics. Every day we wait, we cede more ground to our adversaries. I will not stand on the sidelines – asking for more reports and studies – while terrorists plot inside our communities, while people are murdered in their places of worship, and while violent extremists seek to divide our nation.

Conservatives and others concerned about the Homeland Security Committee's initiative on H. R. 2899 have warned against institutionalizing the Obama administration's CVE agenda. For instance, as soon as the Committee reported out this bill, its intent and likely consequences were sharply critiqued[652] by Daniel Horowitz in an article entitled, "Why Won't GOP Chairman Mention 'Islamic Terror' in New Bill?" This column read, in part:

> Here's the good news: Congressional Republicans finally have a bill to address the homegrown terror threat. The bad news? It has nothing to do with combating homegrown Islamic terror, and in fact, is a verbatim reflection of this administration's agenda to expunge any mention of Islam from the growing terror threat. Worse, this effort will likely enlist terrorist groups like the Muslim Brotherhood, as well as CAIR – the unindicted co-conspirator in the largest terrorism financing[653] trial in US history, the HLF Trial – in the effort to combat "extremism."
>
> Last week, the House Committee on Homeland Security, led by Rep. Michael McCaul (R-TX) passed the Countering Violent Extremism Act of 2015 out of committee by voice vote….
>
> The fact that a Republican chairman is promoting a bill that does not contain a single reference to "Islamic" terrorism should at a minimum mystify even the most moderate Republicans, and more rightfully so, anger those who realize Islamic radicals are by far the Number One domestic terrorism threat. The fact [that] *this bill creates a new agency during the Obama presidency with broad and vague powers to combat generic "extremists"* should raise goose bumps on any conservative's patriotic neck. Especially given reports as recent as February of this year that the Department of Homeland Security considers "right wing" groups to be a greater threat than Islamic terror. [Emphasis added.]

In summary, H. R. 2899 not only parrots the narratives promoted by the Obama administration and its fellow travelers about the need to embrace Civil

Rights and Civil Liberties-driven approaches to contending with a threat doctrine that must not be named and, for that among other reasons, will not be defeated.

Worse yet, if this legislation were to be approved by Congress, it would make permanent *and provide millions of dollars in funding* for the bureaucratic infrastructure that seeks to make irreversible this fatally flawed approach to countering "terrorism" – or, perhaps, even more neutered ones now being demanded by the Islamists and their allies on the Left.

In our final chapter, we will examine the impacts that such misbegotten policies and the doomed programs they dictate are having on our first lines of defense.

CHAPTER 11: CVE'S DEVASTATING IMPACT ON OUR FIRST LINES OF DEFENSE

***

"Muslim Brotherhood-affiliated organizations have succeeded in presenting themselves to U.S. federal authorities as spokesmen for Muslims and as advisors. In large part, this has been because the U.S. authorities shared the approach of their European counterparts: they dedicated themselves to combating terrorism, or violent extremism, rather than Islamist ideology per se."

> Leslie S. Lebl, "The EU, The Muslim Brotherhood and the Organization of Islamic Cooperation," Orbis, December 3, 2012

***

No study of the Obama administration's embrace of the Countering Violent Extremism approach to counter-terrorism would be complete without an assessment of its impact on the mission and morale of federal law enforcement officers and other national security professionals manning our first lines of defense.

EXTENDING THE WELCOME MAT FOR TOP JIHADISTS

A debilitating blow to the morale of those manning our first lines of defense occurred in early 2010. It took the form of a special order[654] signed personally by Secretary of State Hillary Clinton on January 20, 2010[655]. [lxxxiii]

Mrs. Clinton's order allowed Tariq Ramadan,[656] the grandson[657] of Muslim Brotherhood founder Hassan Al-Banna and a prominent Islamic supremacist in his own right, and Adam Habib,[658] another suspected supporter of Islamic terrorists, to enter the United States. In fact, after consulting with DHS Secretary Napolitano, Secretary Clinton essentially invited[659] the two jihadists to apply for visas.

While claiming publicly that she was simply exercising her exemption authority, what Mrs. Clinton really did was to engage in an act of submission to Islamic supremacism in furtherance of the pledge made by President Obama in Cairo in June of 2009 to pursue "a new relationship with Muslim communities based on mutual interest and mutual respect." This was all done in spite of major opposition from the LEO community and with a total disregard of the fact that, since 2004,[660] the State Department had repeatedly[661] denied these Islamists' previous visa requests, claiming they both presented a national security threat.

[lxxxiii] As it happens, this action occurred just a few days before the momentous January 28-29 DHS-CRCL *Inaugural Meeting* discussed in Chapter 4.

The language of the Clinton-Napolitano special order reads, in part, as follows:

> INA§212(a)(3)(B)(iv)(VI)(dd) shall not apply, for purposes of any application for non-immigrant visa or for admission as a non-immigrant, to Mr. Tariq Ramadan, relative to donations made to the *Comite de Bienfaisance et de Secours aux Palestiniens* and the *Association de Secours Palestinien* prior to 2003.

The two terrorist groups with whom Ramadan has been involved that were cited in the Special Order are noteworthy insofar as they were both[662] named as unindicted co-conspirators during the trial of the Holy Land Foundation's five Hamas fundraisers.

The Red-Green axis was gleeful over Mrs. Clinton's decision to grant visas to Mr. Ramadan and Mr. Habib. For example, a January 20, 2010[663] press release issued by the ACLU's National Security Project,[664] quoted its director, Jameel Jaffer[665], as saying: "The orders ending the exclusion of Adam Habib and Tariq Ramadan are long overdue and tremendously important. For several years, the United States government was more interested in stigmatizing and silencing its foreign critics than in engaging them."

Predictably, the Islamists' enablers at the ACLU seized upon this concession to demand more. Another of its operatives, Melissa Goodman, said:

> "The Obama administration should now conduct a broader review of visas denied under the Bush administration, reverse the exclusions of others who were barred because of their political beliefs and *retire the practice of ideological exclusion for good.*" [Emphasis added.]

MEETINGS AS SUBMISSION

Morale within the first lines of defense also suffers at the sight of spectacles discussed at length elsewhere, in which senior U.S. government officials meet – and treat – with organizations identified with our Islamic supremacist enemies.

To cite a particularly blatant example of such submission within the U.S. State Department, one such meeting involving top State Department personnel was sponsored by the Zakat Foundation and the Muslim American Society-Public Access and Civic Awareness (MAS-PACE)[666] on September 24-26, 2012,[667] just two weeks after the murderous jihadist attacks in Benghazi.

Announced speakers included representatives of American Muslims for Palestine[668] (AMP),[669] CAIR, ICNA, MAS and the Zakat Foundation of America (ZF) and U.S. officials including: Deputy Assistant Secretary of State Amb. Richard Schmierer; State Department Special Advisor Dr. Shaun Casey; Deputy

Special Coordinator in the State Department's Office of Middle East Transition Mark Ward; and Treasury Department Policy Advisor Katherine Leahy Gupta.

It is beyond comprehension why, in 2012, government officials would continue legitimating *any* of these groups by meeting with them. As we have discussed, the Justice Department has known these organizations are all known Muslim Brotherhood affiliates since at least 2004; after all, they prosecuted the Holy Land Foundation trial, and argued this very point in federal court. And since that time, several groups have been designated as terrorist organizations for these and other links to violent, subversive Islamist groups by the governments of Egypt, Israel, Saudi Arabia or the United Arab Emirates. Yet, the U.S. government continues its outreach with many of these groups to this day.

ENABLING MATERIAL SUPPORT FOR TERRORISM

Morale within the federal law enforcement community was further undermined when an important step was taken towards eliminating whatever "ideological exclusion" might still operate: On February 5, 2014,[670] a public notice was published in the Federal Register easing access to this country for those who have engaged in "limited" material support of terrorism:

> Following consultations with the Attorney General [DOJ], the Secretary of Homeland Security [DHS] and the Secretary of State [USSD] have determined that the grounds of inadmissibility at section 212(a)(3)(B) of the Immigration and Nationality Act (INA),[lxxxiv] 8 U.S.C. 1182[671](a)(3)(B), bar certain aliens who do not pose a national security or public safety risk from admission to the United States and from obtaining immigration benefits or other status.
>
> Accordingly, consistent with prior exercises of the exemption authority, the Secretary of Homeland Security and the Secretary of State, in consultation with the Attorney General, hereby conclude, as a matter of discretion in accordance with the authority granted by INA section 212(d)(3)(B)(i), 8 U.S.C. 1182[672](d)(3)(B)(i), as amended, as well as the foreign policy and national security interests deemed relevant in these consultations, that paragraphs 212(a)(3)(B)(iv)(VI)(bb) and (dd) of the INA, 8 U.S.C. 1182[673](a)(3)(B)(iv)(VI)(bb) and (dd), shall not apply with respect to an alien who provided *limited material support* to an organization described in section 212(a)(3)(B)(vi)(III) of the INA, 8 U.S.C. 1182[674](a)(3)(B)(vi)(III), or to a member of such an organization, or to an individual described in section 212(a)(3)(B)((iv)(VI)(bb) of the INA, 8 U.S.C. 1182[675](a)(3)(B)(iv)(VI)(bb),

---

[lxxxiv] 212(a)(3)(B) is the section of the Immigration and Nationality Act (INA) that authorizes Customs and Border Protection to bar entry to the United States on Terrorism-Related Inadmissibility Grounds (TRIG).

that involves (1) certain routine commercial transactions or certain routine social transactions (i.e., in the satisfaction of certain well-established or verifiable family, social, or cultural obligations), (2) certain humanitarian assistance, or (3) substantial pressure that does not rise to the level of duress, provided, however, that the alien satisfies the relevant agency authority that the alien...(~11 several exclusion clauses follow). [Emphasis added.]

In plain language, the use here of the legal term "discretion" means that the U.S. government would begin issuing entry visas and/or immigration visas (i.e., documents that would ultimately lead to citizenship) to individuals who had only provided "limited material support" to a known terrorist organization and/or to a known member of that organization, as long as such support were given as part of a "routine transaction," or in the satisfaction of certain "well-established... cultural obligations."

As a practical matter, the terms "routine transaction" and "well-established cultural obligations" offer an exception for *Zakat* from statutory restrictions on material support for terrorism. Securing such an exception became the object of an intense campaign[676] mounted by Islamic supremacists in America after the Holy Land Foundation co-conspirators were indicted on July 26, 2004[677] for providing financial support to Hamas.

The DHS-DOJ ruling also amounted to a little-noticed, but highly portentous step towards fulfilling the pledge[678] President Obama made during his so-called "New Beginning" speech in Cairo, when he declared:

> Freedom of religion is central to the ability of peoples to live together. We must always examine the ways in which we protect it. For instance, in the United States, rules on charitable giving have made it harder for Muslims to fulfill their religious obligation. That is why I am committed to working with American Muslims to *ensure that they can fulfill Zakat*.

It bears repeating in this context: shariah commands[679] that at least 1/8 of all *Zakat must* go to the support of the *mujahidin* (jihad fighters), wherever they may be in the world. By some estimates, the justification for up to half of such contributions can amount to material support for terrorism. The question occurs: Was this known to President Obama when he pledged in his speech to facilitate *Zakat*? Either way, enabling material support for terrorism – even "limited" support – only serves further to complicate the missions of our first lines of defense and undermines their ability to perform them.

ADMITTING UNVETTABLE SYRIAN REFUGEES

Law enforcement professionals are also demoralized by being told to carry out policy directions that they know endanger public safety and national security. A case in point is captured by this headline of an article published on September 11, 2015: "Homeland Security Chairman Warns U.S. Doesn't Have Proper Vetting System for 10,000 Syrian Refugees."[680]

The article describes the Obama administration's policy as follows:

> "The United States...has played a leading role in addressing the dire humanitarian crisis in the Middle East and North Africa," White House Press Secretary Josh Earnest said Thursday during the daily briefing. "One thing that [we] can do is to begin to let more Syrian refugees into the United States. This year, this fiscal year that will end this month, the U.S. is on track to take in about 1,500 Syrian refugees. The President has directed his team to scale up that number next year and he's informed his team he would like them to accept, at least make preparations, for 10,000 refugees."

The Chairman of the House Homeland Security Committee Michael McCaul warned, however, that: "The President wants to surge thousands of Syrian refugees into the United States, in spite of consistent intelligence community and federal law enforcement warnings that we do not have the intelligence needed to vet individuals from the conflict zone." He added "ISIS wants to use refugee routes as cover to sneak operatives into the West."

Three weeks later, we got a better sense of the magnitude such refugee inflows could represent. On October 1, 2015,[681] Senator Jeff Sessions insisted on specific answers about the vetting process during a two-hour hearing before the Senate Judiciary Subcommittee on Immigration and the National Interest.

The Senator cross-examined Matthew Emrich, the Acting Associate Director[682] for Fraud Detection and National Security Directorate at the U.S. Citizenship and Immigration Services (CIS),[683] after he testified[684] about refugee protection and what his written testimony described as the effort by "interagency partners to improve, refine, and enhance the security vetting regime for refugee applicants, while maintaining its integrity and rigor." The following highlights their exchange:

> Sen. Sessions: "Can you name a single computer database outside of maybe some of our own very small but valuable intelligence databases for Syria that you can check against. Does Syria have any?"
>
> Emrich: "The government does not, no sir. We check everything that we have available within U.S. holdings. As far as I'm concerned, if we haven't overturned every stone, we are in the process of overturning every stone."

Sessions: "There you go, We're turning over everything we can overturn. I don't deny that. But you don't have their criminal records, you don't have the computer database that you can check, so isn't [FBI Assistant Director for Counterterrorism Michael][685] Steinbach telling the truth?[686] That in many cases it just doesn't exist?"

Emrich: "In many countries the U.S. accepts refugees from, the country did not have extensive data holdings."

Sessions: "I'm asking you to talk to the American people. The American people are asking you a question...So aren't you left with basically looking at whatever document they produce and whatever they tell you?"

Emrich: "We have a robust screening process and these processes are continually reviewed and upgraded whenever possible, and it includes an in-depth interview with a trained U.S. government officer and is accompanied by an additional interview, an inspection rather, when the person presents him or herself at a U.S. port of entry."

Sessions: "Is there any way you can actually send someone to Iraq or Syria and see if someone actually lived on the street where they said they lived, or actually had the job he claims to have had?"

Emrich: While we do not have the ability to send an investigator to Syria, we do have resources that we can use to verify various elements of someone's testimony and story.

Sessions: "I'm sure there are things you can do, but are you saying you can independently verify with positive data on the majority of cases? Can you give me a number? Is it 50 percent, 60 percent, 80 percent?"

[Division Chief, CIS Refugee, Asylum and International Operations Directorate, Refugee Affairs Division Barbara] Strack: "I can't give you a number sir."[687]

Sessions: "And the reason is, you don't have the ability. I wish you did, but you don't."

All of these examples – the issuing of visas to known jihadists, meetings between USG officials and subversive Islamic supremacists, the enabling of material support for terrorism under the guise of *Zakat* and the admission of thousands of unvetted refugees – epitomize the Countering Violent Extremism approach in practice. They illustrate the dire operational consequences of CVE's preoccupation with what is euphemistically described as Civil Rights and Civil Liberties. They are evidence of its willful blindness toward and/or chronic disregard of the present, and prospective, threats posed to Americans by enemies committed to the destruction of our country, as well as the substitution of shariah for our constitutionally-protected civil liberties and human rights of American citizens.

THE DESTRUCTION OF OUR FIRST LINES OF DEFENSE

The continued willingness of *any* law enforcement officers and others in our first lines of defense to protect us from Islamic supremacism is all the more remarkable in light of what befell one of them: Lieutenant Colonel Matthew Dooley, U.S. Army.

In 2012, Lt. Col. Dooley was a decorated and highly regarded Army officer with a distinguished record of service and a very promising career ahead of him. At the time, he was teaching an elective course at the Joint Forces Staff College[688] of the National Defense University (NDU). It was entitled, "Perspectives on Islam and Islamic Radicalism."

Yet, at the hands of *Wired* Magazine's blogger, Spencer Ackerman – the radical leftist who is the information warfare weapon of choice for Islamists and their enablers, Lt. Col. Dooley and his course were subjected to a vicious hit piece in a May 10, 2012[689] posting entitled, "U.S. Military Taught Officers: Use 'Hiroshima' Tactics for 'Total War' on Islam." Within hours, Ackerman's broadside had made the rounds in the Defense Department.

The then-Chairman of the Joint Chiefs of Staff, Army Gen. Martin Dempsey, took the opportunity of a Pentagon press conference held that day publicly to destroy Lt. Col. Dooley's career. He said of the Joint Forces Staff College course: "It was totally objectionable, against our values and it wasn't academically sound." Gen. Dempsey added that the instructor responsible for the course was "no longer in a teaching status," even though he was still employed at the Staff College.

Ackerman posted another hatchet-job after the Dempsey press conference later on May 10th.[690] Highlights – or more accurately, *low*lights – of this screed included the following:

> For at least a year, Dooley taught an optional course at the college for lieutenant colonels, colonels, commanders and Navy captains that proposed taking a war on Islam "to the civilian population wherever necessary," which he likened to the bombardment of Dresden and nuclear destruction of Hiroshima and Nagasaki. Guest lecturers in the course encouraged those senior officers to think of themselves as a "resistance movement"[691] to Islam.
>
> Dempsey and his deputy for military education, Marine Lt. Gen. George Flynn, pulled the plug on the course last month.[692] The general said he was "quite thankful" for an unnamed military officer who brought word of the anti-Islam material to his attention. Dempsey and his staff launched an investigation into "what motivated that elective to being part of the curriculum," as he put it on Thursday, and the general also sent a letter to the heads of every military service and regional command instructing them to

jettison any similar material, as per a White House directive issued last fall...⁶⁹³

"Final judgment should await...findings [of an investigation]^lxxxv, but it's not too early to say that these excerpts are offensive (though that word may be a bit mild here)," e-mails Douglas Ollivant, a retired Army lieutenant colonel and Iraq veteran who has taught at the U.S. Military Academy at West Point. "Further, presentations like this do real harm to those trying to carefully distinguish extremism and support for it from otherwise admirable religious devotion."

The harm perpetuated [sic] on student officers "who accepted the implied authority of the instructor," Ollivant added, "is obvious."

The military is hardly alone in dealing with anti-Islam instructional material passing itself off as responsible counterterrorism. Over the years, hundreds of documents claiming "mainstream" Muslims are "violent"⁶⁹⁴ have made their way into FBI curricula, alongside internal claims that agents working on counterterrorism cases could "bend or suspend the law."⁶⁹⁵

"Plenty of U.S. military officers and troops were inspired by their service in either Iraq or Afghanistan to learn Arabic or Dari and study the peoples of the region. I left the Army in 2004, as a matter of fact, to pursue a master's degree in Middle Eastern Studies at the American University of Beirut," says Andrew Exum, a retired Army captain who now serves as a senior fellow at the Center for a New American Security. "But plenty of other officers and troops began their own amateurish studies of Islam and now, like Lt. Col. Dooley, peddle claims to know the truth about the violence and hatred at the heart of Islam. Pope's warning that a little learning can be a dangerous thing is certainly relevant here. These hucksters, like the Robert Spencers⁶⁹⁶ of the world, know just enough to make themselves sound credible to an uninformed audience and hide their prejudices under a thin layer of amateurish, ideologically motivated scholarship."

In addition to this gratuitous attack on Robert Spencer,^lxxxvi one of America's preeminent scholars about and most knowledgeable critics of authoritative Islam, Ackerman used his May 10th posts to defame several other counter-jihadist trainers who have refused to hew to the CVE/CRCL line:

For the better part of the last decade, a small cabal of self-anointed counterterrorism experts [including Shireen Burki,⁶⁹⁷ Stephen Coughlin, John Guandolo and Serge Trifkovic]⁶⁹⁸ has been working its way through the U.S. military, intelligence and law enforcement communities, trying to convince whoever [sic] it could that America's real terrorist enemy wasn't Al-

---

^lxxxv Of course, Gen. Dempsey did not "await the findings" of any investigations before publicly repudiating Lt. Col. Dooley.
^lxxxvi Robert Spencer has written some 14 books on related subjects, including several *New York Times* bestsellers.

Qaeda – but the Islamic faith itself. In his course, Dooley brought in these anti-Muslim demagogues as guest lecturers. And he took their argument to its final, ugly conclusion.

Predictably, CAIR seized immediately[699] upon this latest opportunity to wage political warfare against its opponents by issuing a press release calling for the termination of Lt. Col. Dooley. It read, in part:

> A prominent national Muslim civil rights and advocacy organization today called on the Department of Defense (DOD) to dismiss the instructor who taught fellow officers that only a "total war" on Islam would protect America, that they should use "Hiroshima" tactics, target civilian populations, and abandon the Geneva Conventions. The Washington-based Council on American-Islamic Relations (CAIR) recently applauded the DOD for dropping the Islamophobic training course attended by senior officers and for instituting a complete review of training relating to Islam and Muslims. CAIR is asking that the officer who taught that course at the Defense Department's Joint Forces Staff College in Norfolk, Va., be dismissed from his position at the college.
>
> "It is imperative that those who taught our future military leaders to wage war not just on our terrorist enemy, but on the faith of Islam itself be held accountable," wrote CAIR National Executive Director Nihad Awad in a letter to Secretary of Defense Leon Panetta. "These shocking revelations are completely out of line with the longstanding values of one of our nation's most respected institutions." Awad also called for the retraining by credible scholars of all officers who took the course and offered to coordinate a meeting between Pentagon officials and national Muslim leaders. "If left uncorrected, the biased, inaccurate and un-American training previously given to these officers will harm our nation's security, image and interests for years to come."

In other words, a Muslim Brotherhood front organization, proven in federal court to have raised funds for the designated terrorist organization Hamas, demanded the removal of a patriotic military officer for teaching about Islamic supremacism, shariah and jihad in a way the Islamists found offensive. This CAIR press release echoes the Red-Green axis' earlier demands for the disciplining, purging and/or retraining of those in the first lines of defense who had benefited from exposure to this sort of pedagogy, particularly those expressed in the October 19, 2011[700] letter sent by 57 U.S. Islamists and leftists to the then-Homeland Security Advisor to the President, John Brennan.

As with the demands made of Mr. Brennan, CAIR got its way with respect to Lt. Col. Dooley. On June 20, 2012,[701] *Reuters* reported:

> [Lt. Col. Dooley has been] relieved of teaching duties, and the course ordered redesigned to reflect U.S. policy, a military spokesman said. The

elective course at the National Defense University's Joint Forces Staff College included a slide that asserted "the United States is at war with Islam and we ought to just recognize that we are war with Islam," Pentagon officials said in April as they launched a review of the course.

Colonel David Lapan, a spokesman for the Chairman of the Joint Chiefs of Staff, said on Wednesday a review of the course found that "institutional failures and in oversight and judgment" led to the course being modified over time in a way "that portrayed Islam almost entirely in a negative way. The inquiry recommends the course be redesigned to include aspects of U.S. policy and reduce its reliance on external instruction. The elective course's military instructor has been relieved of his instructor duties until his permanent change of station, which was previously planned for 2012."

Navy Captain John Kirby, a Pentagon spokesman, said in April that Defense Secretary Leon Panetta was deeply concerned about some of the materials being taught in the course, such as the slide[702] suggesting the United States was at war with Islam. "That's not at all what we believe to be the case. *We're at war against terrorism, specifically Al-Qaeda, who has a warped view of the Islamic faith*," Kirby said. [Emphasis added.]

The Pentagon's abject capitulation to the Red-Green axis in this case is all the more egregious in light of the fact that the course on "Islamic Radicalism" was first established at the Joint Forces Staff College *in 2004 well before Lt. Col. Dooley's arrival*. Moreover, all of the external guest speakers in 2009-2010 were approved by the College's then-Commandant, Air Force Brigadier General Marvin Smoot.

In fact, earlier in the Great Purge, the Staff College's parent organization, the National Defense University, formally attested to the vetting process employed with regard to courses like Prof. Dooley's. On December 2, 2011[703] NDU Deputy Vice President for Academic Affairs Dr. Brenda Roth officially confirmed in writing[704] to the Pentagon that all the course materials at the university were vetted and approved by the University and its military command, including the content and outside guest speakers used in its course entitled "Perspectives on Islam and Islamic Radicalism."

In her memo, Roth also wrote, "The College Dean of Faculty and Academic Programs reviews and vets proposed speakers for their subject matter expertise and academic and teaching credibility. The Commandants have the final review of recommended speakers and issues invitations to those he approves."

In short, Gen. Dempsey not only disregarded[705] Dr. Roth's official report, but publicly criticized Lt. Col. Dooley and terminated him as an instructor on the grounds that the "Islamic Radicalism" course was -- notwithstanding the judgments of the professor's chain of command – unprofessional and offensive to Islam. That amounts to subjecting military training to shariah blasphemy restrictions and, in the process denying our servicemen and women what they have a "need to know."

This act of submission to Islamic supremacism is made all the more appalling for its being done on the say-so of an unidentified military officer who complained about the course's contents, Muslim Brotherhood operatives and one of their journalistic useful idiots. The JCS Chairman completed this travesty by personally ordering Lt. Col. Dooley's career-ending negative Officer Evaluation Report.[lxxxvii]

As with the message sent to legislators via the Red-Green-Republican attacks on Rep. Michele Bachmann discussed in Chapter 10, the Dooley Affair served notice on our men and women in uniform – and those in the other agencies that make up our Nation's first lines of defense, more broadly: You deviate from the party-line on the "see-no-shariah" CVE approach to homeland and national security at your peril.

The cumulative effect of the Countering Violent Extremism policies and programs has not only been to cripple those we rely upon to protect us. It has actually emboldened those against whom such protection is needed now more than ever. And it has left our nation and its people far more vulnerable, at home and abroad.

[lxxxvii] Lt. Col. Dooley, who is now being represented by the Thomas More Law Center, has notified Gen. Martin Dempsey that he may face a lawsuit for concealing "the truth about Islam" and compromising "the final bastion of America's defense against Islamic jihad and shariah, the Pentagon, to the enemy." Actions against the NDU have also been taken. For additional background information and current updates, see the Thomas More Law Center website.

EPILOGUE

The "fundamental transformation" of our first lines of defense pursuant to the Obama administration's Countering Violent Extremism doctrine has, if anything accelerated significantly over the weeks preceding the publication of this monograph.

MORE OF THE 'SEE-NO-SHARIA'

On December 2, 2015, two jihadists showed the vulnerability of virtually every city in America. Syed Farooq and his wife, Tashfeen Malik, murderously attacked his co-workers at a Christmas party in San Bernardino, California, killing 14 and wounding at least 21 others.[706]

Just hours after the shootings, President Obama began the kind of dissembling that has characterized his administration's "See-no-sharia" policy from its inception. In an interview with CBS News, he called for "common-sense gun safety laws," while urging lawmakers to pass a law preventing individuals on the "No Fly List" from legally purchasing firearms.[707]

> "*We don't yet know what the motives of the shooters are*, but what we do know is that there are steps we can take to make Americans safer. We should never think that this is just something that just happens in the ordinary course of events because it doesn't happen with the same frequency in other countries." [Emphasis added.]

The same day, presidential candidate Hillary Clinton stated on Twitter: "I refuse to accept this as normal. We must take action to stop gun violence now."[708]

PANDERING TO THE ISLAMIC SUPREMACISTS

The very next day,[709] Attorney General Loretta Lynch appeared at Muslim Advocate's 10th anniversary dinner, and made the following comments:[710]

> Now, obviously this is a country that is based on free speech, but when it edges towards violence, when we see the potential for someone to lift - *lifting that mantle of anti-Muslim rhetoric* or, as we saw after 9/11, violence against individuals who may not even be Muslims but may be perceived to be Muslims and they will suffer just as well, just as much. When we see that, *we will take action*....
>
> The fear that you have just mentioned is in fact my greatest fear as a prosecutor, as someone who is sworn to the protection of all of the American people, which is that the rhetoric will be accompanied by acts of violence. My message to not just the Muslim community, but to the entire American community is: we cannot give in to the fear that these backlashes are really based on.

> I think it's important that as we again talk about the importance of free speech we make it clear that actions predicated on violent talk are not America. They are not who we are, they are not what we do, *and they will be prosecuted*. [Emphasis added.]

Recall that, as has been documented in detail elsewhere in this monograph, Muslim Advocates has been closely allied with various other Muslim Brotherhood-affiliated organizations – including the ADAMS Center, CAIR, MAS and MPAC – in a protracted *campaign to undermine the government's law enforcement-based counter-terrorism efforts*.

The abiding hostility of the administration's chosen Muslim outreach "partners" was in evidence on December 4, 2015, when Hussam Ayloush, executive director of CAIR Los Angeles, spoke at an Los Angeles-area mosque and offered sympathy for the victims of the violence, but added that Muslims should not have to apologize for the shooting, and that there is a "big difference between condemning and apologizing."[711]

According to the *LA Times*, Ayloush maintained that after the attacks in Paris and San Bernardino, many Muslims said they felt pressure to publicly denounce terrorism, and that underlying that pressure is an expectation that they say, "Sorry."

Ayloush would have us believe that America bears responsibility for the jihad against her. During an appearance that same day on CNN, he declared: "Let's not forget that some of our own foreign policy, as Americans, as the West, have fueled that extremism." Ayloush said U.S. support for repressive regimes in the Middle East, including Egypt, "push people over to the edge. Then they become extremists. We are partly responsible. Terrorism is a global problem, *not a Muslim problem*. And the solution has to be global. Everyone has a role in it."[712]

Just two days after the shootings, Ayloush had not only exonerated Muslims from any sense of responsibility for the attacks. He had publicly blamed Americans and the West for what happened in places like San Bernardino.

On the third day following the attack, the President addressed the nation and insisted that the assailants' motives still remained unclear, but conceded:

> It is entirely possible that these two attackers were radicalized to commit this act of terror. And if so, it would underscore a threat we've been focused on for years – the danger of people succumbing to *violent extremist ideologies*.
>
> We know that ISIL and other terrorist groups are actively encouraging people – around the world and in our country – to commit terrible acts of violence, often times as lone wolf actors.

> And even as we work to prevent attacks, all of us – government, law enforcement, communities, faith leaders – need to work together to prevent people from *falling victim to these hateful ideologies*.[713] [Emphasis added.]

In a White House readout of the investigation into the San Bernardino shootings published later the same day, we also learned that:

> The President this morning received an update from FBI Director Comey, Attorney General Lynch, Secretary of Homeland Security Johnson, and his intelligence community leadership on the ongoing investigation into the horrific shootings in San Bernardino, California.
>
> The President's team highlighted several pieces of information that point to the perpetrators being *radicalized to violence* to commit these heinous attacks. The President's team also affirmed that they had as of yet uncovered no indication the killers were part of an organized group or formed part of a broader terrorist cell.[714] [Emphasis added.]

DISSEMBLING ABOUT INCONVENIENT FACTS

This narrative became more and more untenable, though, as details emerged about Syed Farooq and Tashfeen Malik. For example, we now know that Farooq was: affiliated with the *Sharia*-adherent Darul Uloom Deoband mosque in San Bernardino; well-known within the local Muslim community as a *hafiz* – someone who is revered for having memorized the Quran; affiliated with a dangerous Islamist missionary movement known as Tablighi Jamaat. We also know that, his fiancée, Tashfeen Malik, was not properly vetted before she received a K-1 marriage visa.

In addition, the weapons they used, along with the large number of homemade bombs that were found in their apartment, indicated a sophisticated level of training and planning, possibly provided during their time together in Saudi Arabia. These were, in short, individual jihadists, not "lone wolves" who had inexplicably become "radicalized" to embrace some unnamed "hateful ideology."

It is, to say the least, inconvenient that such details do not conform to the administration's memes: about the nature of the attack (i.e., that it has nothing to do with Islam); that Congress is unnecessarily concerned about visa fraud; and that foreign nationals from shariah-adherent lands can be properly vetted before being admitted into America.

There is, unfortunately, still no evidence that President Obama's team is rethinking the defective CVE policy approach underpinned by such fallacious propositions.

To the contrary, on December 7, 2015, DHS Secretary Jeh Johnson ramped up the perception of American Muslims as victims and the Obama administration as submitting to them by traveling to the Muslim Brotherhood-linked ADAMS Center.[715] There, he promised to redouble his efforts to engage with such interlocutors as part of the CVE outreach effort:

> This new phase requires a whole new approach to counterterrorism and homeland security. This must include outreach to Muslim communities across this country. Over the last two years I've been to Boston, New York, Brooklyn, suburban Maryland, Minneapolis, Chicago, Columbus, Houston, Los Angeles and other places for this purpose. One of the most meaningful discussions I've had on this tour was in June of this year, here at the ADAMS Center, with Imam Magid and other leaders of this community.

What Secretary Johnson did not mention was that, as we have seen, Islamic supremacists treated as "community leaders" from at least four of these cities (Boston, Los Angeles, Minneapolis and New York) had publicly denounced the very CVE program he was promoting at the ADAMS Center.

Mr. Johnson also neglected to note – or, apparently, take into account – that, as has been extensively documented in the preceding pages, former ISNA president Magid was among the most successful of such Muslim Brotherhood operatives in sabotaging USG policy through his access to and influence with senior administration officials, including President Obama.

We've already noted a few examples of Magid's influence operations, including how as a member of the DHS Countering Violent Extremism Working Group, Magid helped to mutate beyond recognition U.S. counterterrorism policies and programs. His calls for the re-education of FBI agents – on the grounds that "teaching people that all Muslims are a threat to the country...is against the law and the Constitution" – have discouraged such law enforcement officers from studying, let alone pursuing, jihadist subversion. And he has advanced the agenda of Islamic supremacism with his denunciations of Islamophobia, which he calls "religious bigotry and hate."[716]

A WHISTLEBLOWER REVEALS THE DAMAGE BEING DONE BY CVE

On December 10, 2015, Philip Haney – a decorated and recently retired Customs and Border Protection officer who was a founding member of the Department of Homeland Security revealed on Fox News with Megyn Kelly that he had been ordered to shut down investigations of Tablighi Jamaat that, had they been allowed to continue might have prevented the San Bernardino massacre.[717]

Haney notes that:

> "After leaving my 15 year career at DHS, I can no longer be silent about the dangerous state of America's counter-terror strategy, our leaders' willingness to compromise the security of citizens for the ideological rigidity of political correctness—and, consequently, our vulnerability to devastating, mass-casualty attack."[718]

In an op.ed. article that appeared in *The Hill* newspaper[719] on December 16, 2015, Haney documented how the Civil Rights and Civil Liberties Division at DHS, together with lawyers from the State Department, halted his investigation. His first-hand account of the sorry state of America's counter-terror effort, and the disastrous CVE policy decisions that have led to its catastrophic failure, is worth quoting at length:

> I was a firsthand witness to how these policies deliberately prevented scrutiny of Islamist groups. The two San Bernardino jihadists, Syed Farook and Tashfeen Malik, may have benefited from the administration's closure of an investigation I initiated on numerous groups infiltrating radicalized individuals into this country.
>
> While working for the Department of Homeland Security for 13 years, I identified individuals affiliated with large, but less well-known groups such as Tablighi Jamaat and the larger Deobandi movement freely transiting the United States. At the National Targeting Center, one of the premier organizations formed to "connect the dots," I played a major role in an investigation into this trans-national Islamist network. We created records of individuals, mosques, Islamic centers and schools across the United States that were involved in this radicalization effort. The Dar Al Uloom Al Islamiyah Mosque in San Bernardino was affiliated with this network and we had identified a member of it in our investigation. Farook frequented that mosque and was well-known to the congregation and mosque leadership.
>
> Another focus of my investigation was the Pakistani women's Islamist group al-Huda, which counted Farook's wife, Tashfeen Malik, as a student. While the al-Huda International Welfare Foundation distanced themselves from the actions of their former pupil, Malik's classmates told the *Daily Mail* she changed significantly while studying at al-Huda, gradually becoming "more serious and strict." More ominously, the group's presence in the U.S. and

> Canada is not without its other ties to ISIS and terrorism. In 2014, three recent former students at al-Huda's affiliate school in Canada, aged 15 to 18, left their homes to join the Islamic State in Syria.
>
> We had these two groups in our sights; if the investigation had continued and additional links been identified and dots connected, we might have given advance warning of the terrorist attack in San Bernardino. The combination of Farook's involvement with the Dar Al Uloom Al Islamiyah Mosque and Malik's attendance at al-Huda would have indicated, at minimum, an urgent need for comprehensive screening. It could also have led to denial of Malik's K-1 visa or possibly gotten Farook placed on the No Fly list.
>
> But after more than six months of research and tracking; over 1,200 law enforcement actions and more than 300 terrorists identified; and a commendation for our efforts; DHS shut down the investigation at the request of the Department of State and DHS' own Civil Rights and Civil Liberties Division. They claimed that since the Islamist groups in question were not Specially Designated Terrorist Organizations (SDTOs) tracking individuals related to these groups was a violation of the travelers' civil liberties. These were almost exclusively foreign nationals: When were they granted the civil rights and liberties of American citizens?
>
> Worse still, the administration then went back and erased the dots we were diligently connecting. Even as DHS closed my investigation, I knew that data I was looking at could prove significant to future counterterror efforts and tried to prevent the information from being lost to law enforcement.
>
> My law enforcement colleagues and I must conduct our work while respecting the rights of those we monitor. But what I witnessed suggests the Obama administration is more concerned with the rights of non-citizens in known Islamist groups than with the safety and security of the American people.

Haney understood that what his superiors at DHS, under the guidance and orders of the Obama administration, were doing was endangering America's national security. He didn't remain silent. He recounted how,

> In 2013, I met with the DHS Inspector General in coordination with several members of Congress to attempt to warn the American people's elected representatives about the threat... In retaliation, DHS and the Department of Justice subjected me to a series of investigations and adverse actions, including one by that same Inspector General.

Needless to say, such retribution sends an unmistakable signal to the rest of the workforce – i.e., that doing their jobs of protecting the American people can put such jobs at risk – and seriously undermines morale among those in the first lines of defense.

DISAPPEARING THE DOTS

It turns out that the destruction of data that might have prevented the 2015 San Bernardino attack was not the first time Philip Haney's superiors had ordered him to purge from CPB's computers damning information about Islamic supremacists.

In a second article published in *The Hill* on February 5, 2016, Haney describes how in the first year of the Obama administration his superiors at DHS demanded that he scrub key records of Muslims with links to Islamist groups[720]:

> In early November, 2009, I had been ordered by my superiors at the Department of Homeland Security to delete or modify several hundred records of individuals tied to designated Islamist terror groups like Hamas from the important federal database, the Treasury Enforcement Communications System (TECS).
>
> These types of records are the basis for any ability to "connect dots." Every day, DHS-Customs and Border Protection officers watch the comings and goings of individuals associated with known bad entities, then look for patterns. Enforcing a political scrubbing of records of Muslims greatly affected our ability to do that. Even worse, going forward, my colleagues and I were prohibited from entering the pertinent information into the database.[721]

Even as, pursuant to his orders, Haney was scrubbing the TECS database of crucial intelligence about individuals tied to Islamist groups, he was watching congressional oversight hearings on the intelligence community's failure to prevent the so-called "underwear bomber," a Nigerian jihadist named Umar Farouk Abdulmutallab, from attempting to blow up his flight from Amsterdam to Detroit on Christmas Day 2009.[722] Haney writes:

> While Members of Congress grilled Obama administration officials, demanding why their subordinates were still failing to understand the intelligence they had gathered, I was being forced to delete and scrub the record. And I was well aware that, as a result, it was going to be vastly more difficult to "connect the dots" in the future – especially *before an attack occurs*.

Following the attempted attack, President Obama threw the intelligence community under the bus for its failure to "connect the dots." He said, "this was not a failure to collect intelligence, it was a failure to integrate and understand the intelligence that we already had."[723]

Mr. Haney set the record straight:

> Most Americans were unaware of the enormous damage to morale at the Department of Homeland Security, where I worked, [President Obama's] condemnation caused. His words infuriated many of us because we knew his

administration had been engaged in a bureaucratic effort to destroy the raw material – the actual intelligence we had collected for years, and erase those dots. The dots constitute the intelligence needed to keep Americans safe, and the Obama administration was ordering they be wiped away.

THE WHITE HOUSE DOUBLES DOWN ON CVE

On December 14, 2015, less than two weeks after the San Bernardino shootings, top White House officials – including Senior Adviser Valerie Jarrett, Domestic Policy Council Director Cecilia Munoz, and Deputy National Security Adviser Ben Rhodes – met with not only Mohamed Magid, but such other Islamic supremacist individuals and organizations as: Hassan Shibly, the executive director of CAIR; Muslim Advocates Farhana Khera; Maya Berry, executive director of the Arab-American Institute (AAI); and Hoda Hawa, director of policy and advocacy with the Muslim Public Affairs Council (MPAC).[724]

The ostensible purpose of the meeting was to discuss religious discrimination, and presumably to follow-up on President Obama's remarks to the nation on December 6, 2015, when he declared: "Moreover, *the vast majority of terrorist victims around the world are Muslim*. If we're to succeed in defeating terrorism we must enlist Muslim communities as some of our strongest allies, rather than push them away through suspicion and hate."[725]

The question is not whether anyone should be "push[ed] away through suspicion and hate." There are, however, ample, fact-based grounds for distancing U.S. policymakers from, rather than embracing, Muslim Brotherhood-affiliated operatives and their groups. Let us recall that, to this day, CAIR and Magid's organization, ISNA, remain unindicted co-conspirators in the 2008 Holy Land Foundation trial, while MPAC, also a close ally of CAIR, was founded by self-proclaimed members of the Muslim Brotherhood.

In other words, these are not benign, "moderate" Muslim groups, and the administration should not be maintaining outreach and/or engagement and dialogue programs with them.[726]

This is a point courageously made by one Muslim American who is genuinely committed to moderation and reform in Islam, Dr. Zuhdi Jasser. He serves as president of the American Islamic Forum for Democracy (AIFD) and helped organize a Muslim Reform Movement[lxxxviii] that, on December 6, 2015 issued a declaration that says, in part: "We oppose institutionalized sharia. sharia is

---

[lxxxviii] http://muslimreformmovement.org/

man-made." Of the White House meeting with Muslim Brotherhood-tied individuals and groups, Jasser said:

> Partnering with such organizations sends the wrong message to the American people. I think it says a lot when the president uses those organizations that have an ACLU-type mentality. They should have a seat at the table. That's fine. [727]
>
> But not to include groups, which have completely different focuses about counter-radicalization, counter-Islamism, creates this monolithic megaphone for demonization of our government and demonization of America that ends up radicalizing our community.

THE ISLAMISTS NEXT GAMBIT ON CAPITOL HILL

On December 17, 2015, some 85 members of the House of Representatives put forward House Resolution 569, which condemns "violence, bigotry, and hateful rhetoric towards Muslims in the United States."

Here are three examples of the Resolution's numerous problematic passages:

> Whereas the victims of *anti-Muslim hate crimes and rhetoric* have faced physical, verbal and emotional abuse because they were Muslim or believed to be Muslim....
>
> Whereas the rise of hateful and anti-Muslim speech, violence, and cultural ignorance plays into the *false narrative* spread by terrorist groups of Western hatred of Islam, and can encourage certain individuals to react in extreme and violent ways....
>
> Resolved that the House of Representatives...declares that the *civil rights and civil liberties* of all United States citizens, including Muslims in the United States, should be protected and preserved.[728] [Emphasis added.]

There is an eerie similarity in style and substance between the language of H.R. 569 and that of UN Resolution 16/18. After all, they are born of the same Islamist agenda: suppressing freedom of speech that "offends" Muslims:

> Reaffirming...the obligation of States to *prohibit discrimination* on the basis of religion or belief and to implement measures to guarantee the equal and effective protection of the law.
>
> 1. Expresses deep concern at the continued serious instances of derogatory stereotyping, negative profiling and stigmatization of persons based on their religion or beliefs, as well as programs and agendas pursued by extremist organizations and groups aimed at creating and perpetuating *negative stereotypes* about religious groups, in particular when condoned by Governments.

...

3. Condemns any advocacy of religious hatred that constitutes *incitement to discrimination, hostility* or violence, whether it involves the use of print, audio-visual or electronic media or any other means.[729] [Emphasis added.]

At this writing, it remains to be seen whether the Republican-controlled Congress will act at all, let alone favorably, on this endorsement of the Organization of Islamic Cooperation-Muslim Brotherhood agenda for our submission.

'GLOBAL ENGAGEMENT' OR UNILATERAL DISARMAMENT IN THE WAR OF IDEAS

On January 7, 2016, President Obama's national security team – including Attorney General Loretta Lynch, FBI Director James Comey, Homeland Security Adviser Lisa Monaco, National Intelligence Director James Clapper, National Security Agency Director Michael Rogers and Deputy Secretary of State Anthony Blinken, traveled to Silicon Valley, to meet with senior executives from Apple, Facebook, LinkedIn, Microsoft, Twitter and YouTube.[730]

According to the agenda, the purpose of the meeting was to find innovative ways to use technology to "disrupt paths to radicalization to violence and identify recruitment patterns."[731]

The next day, press accounts revealed that the revamped counter-messaging operation is to be run out of a proposed new "Global Engagement Center." It turns out that this idea was actually put in train at the February 2015 White House Summit on Countering Violent Extremism (see Chapter 9) and a subsequent international CVE meeting at the UN General Assembly in September 2015.

According to a State Department press release, Michael D. Lumpkin, Assistant Secretary of Defense for Special Operations/Low-Intensity Conflict, was appointed to direct the Global Engagement Center, which will employ a strategy defined by:

1. Drawing upon data and metrics to develop, test and evaluate themes, messages and messengers.

2. Building narratives around thematic campaigns on the misdeeds of our enemy (e.g., poor governance, abuse of women, narratives of defectors), not the daily news cycle.

3. Focusing on driving third-party content, in addition to our own.

4. Nurturing and empowering a global network of positive messengers.[732]

Note that there is not a word anywhere about Islamism or the Quran, let alone the more complex topics of jihad or sharia. The closest the Global Engagement Center's strategy comes is to cite certain attributes of Islamic supremacism under the rubric "misdeeds of our enemy."

But there is not the slightest hint of acknowledgment of the ideology that drives not only ISIS, but every other Islamic *Salafi* group operating in the world today – including the Muslim Brotherhood.

As with the administration's earlier efforts that tried to engage with ISIS terrorists and *Jihadist* sympathizers, but ignored basic Islamic doctrines, it is highly likely that this new CVE effort at the proposed Global Engagement Center will also come to be characterized as "embarrassing, ineffective and distressing" and perhaps even "providing jihadists with a stage to voice their arguments."[733]

Even if such outcomes do not eventuate, it is already clear that Silicon Valley has stepped onto the slippery slope of conforming to shariah blasphemy restrictions in its treatment of social media posts that might prove offensive to Muslims. For example, on January 4, 2016, Andrew C. McCarthy described new rules adopted by Twitter at the start of the New Year as follows:

Twitter has announced new regulations on content communicated via its social-networking service. They are prohibitions on speech similar in effect to Resolution 16/18. As usual, this is shrewdly done under the guise of suppressing "hate" speech. In fact, the regulations cast a much wider net that potentially calls for the suppression of political and educational speech. Twitter's policy, called "Hate content, sensitive topics, and violence," is here.

The policy states that it applies to "Twitter Ads," but goes on to explain that these "paid advertising products" include all "Tweets," as well as "trends and accounts."

The policy is then spelled out in question-and-answer form. Here is the relevant part (the italics are mine):

> What's the policy? Twitter prohibits the promotion of hate content, sensitive topics, and violence globally.
>
> ACM: Note from the get-go: We are not just talking about the incitement of violence here. Twitter is laying the groundwork to regulate discussions of any topics it deems "sensitive."
>
> What products or services are subject to this policy? This policy applies, but is not limited, to: Hate speech or advocacy against an individual, organization or protected group based on race, ethnicity, national origin, color, religion, disability, age, sex, sexual orientation, gender identity, veteran status or other protected status.

ACM: Note that this prohibition expressly goes beyond "hate speech" (which itself is an absurdly subjective term), additionally banning "advocacy against" people or groups based on, among other things, "religion" (as well as "other protected status" — who knows what that means?)[734]

On February 9, 2016, Twitter announced the establishment of a "Trust and Safety Council" that would draw upon, among others "community groups with an acute need to prevent abuse, harassment, and bullying" to help the company "strike the right balance between fighting abuse and speaking truth to power."[735]

THERE GOES NEW YORK

Finally, on the very same day that the administration announced that it would partner with Silicon Valley technology companies to revamp its counter-messaging operation, and establish a new Global Engagement Center, the American Civil Liberties Union declared victory in its long-running assault on what had been the gold-standard of American counter-terrorism law enforcement: the New York Police Department. The ACLU posted the following announcement on its website:

> The ACLU, the NYCLU, and the CLEAR project at CUNY Law School filed a lawsuit in June 2013 challenging the New York City Police Department's discriminatory and unjustified surveillance of New York Muslims. We were later joined by the law firm of Morrison & Foerster LLP.

The plaintiffs included three religious and community leaders, two mosques, and one charitable organization, all of whom were subject to the NYPD's unconstitutional religious profiling program. In January 2016, a settlement to the lawsuit was announced after the NYPD agreed to reforms barring investigations on the basis of race, religion, or ethnicity.[736]

The terms of the settlement included the following, portentous provisions:

1. Prohibiting investigations in which race, religion, or ethnicity is a substantial or motivating factor

2. Requiring articulable and factual information before the NYPD can launch a preliminary investigation into political or religious activity

3. Requiring the NYPD to account for the potential effect of investigative techniques on constitutionally protected activities such as religious worship and political meetings

4. Limiting the NYPD's use of undercovers and confidential informants to situations in which the information sought cannot reasonably be obtained in a timely and effective way by less intrusive means

5. Putting an end to open-ended investigations by imposing presumptive time limits and requiring reviews of ongoing investigations every six months

6. Installing a Civilian Representative within the NYPD, with the power and obligation to ensure all safeguards are followed and to serve as a check on investigations directed at political and religious activities

7. Removing from the NYPD website the discredited and unscientific *Radicalization in the West* report, which justified discriminatory surveillance, and *affirming that the report is not and will not be relied upon to open or prolong NYPD investigations* [Emphasis added.]

Especially troubling is the purging of the report mentioned in Point 7. It was issued on August 13, 2007 and entitled *Radicalization in the West: The Homegrown Threat*.[737] This study, which carefully examined a dozen terrorist-related cases, was prepared by two top NYPD Intelligence Division officials, Senior Intelligence Analysts Mitchell D. Silber and Arvin Bhatt.

A section of the report entitled *Radicalization* provides the following summary: "An assessment of the various reported models of radicalization leads to the conclusion that the radicalization process is composed of four distinct phases: Stage 1 (Pre-Radicalization), Stage 2 (Self-Identification), Stage 3 (Indoctrination) and Stage 4 (Jihadization)."

The *Radicalization* summary also lists these five observations:

1. Each of these phases is unique and has specific signatures;

2. All individuals who begin this process do not necessarily pass through all the stages;

3. Many stop or abandon this process at different points;

4. Although this model is sequential, individuals do not always follow a perfectly linear progression;

5. Individuals who do pass through this entire process are quite likely to be involved in   the planning or implementation of a terrorist act.

Another section of the report entitled *Findings* includes the following critical observations:

1. Al-Qaeda has provided the inspiration for homegrown radicalization and terrorism; direct command and control by al-Qaeda has been the exception, rather than the rule among the case studies reviewed in this study.

2. The four stages of the radicalization process, each with its distinct set of indicators and signatures, are clearly evident in each of the nearly one dozen terrorist-related case studies reviewed in this report.

3. In spite of the differences in both circumstances and environment in each of the cases, *there is a remarkable consistency in the behaviors and trajectory of each of the plots across all the stages.*

4. This consistency provides *a tool for predictability.* [Emphasis added.]

Despite the claims of the ACLU, this is not "discredited and unscientific information." In fact, it is just the opposite. For example, the two highlighted phrases above – noting the "remarkable consistency" that "provides a tool for predictability" – are ignored at our peril. They are, after all, basic, essential components in any successful law enforcement effort to protect our country from the threat of terrorism. Another name for this process of fact-based identification of relevant trends and adapting appropriate responses is "connecting the dots."

Removal of *Radicalization in the West: The Homegrown Threat* from the New York Police Department website, and the explicit banning of its use in any future law enforcement actions, is the result of the inevitable application of the Great Purge at the federal level to one of America's most important local, albeit strategic, first lines of defense. Excising from the NYPD's situational awareness information said to be "offensive and discriminatory" to Muslims – but that, actually is simply an impediment to the efforts of Islamic supremacists bent on compelling our submission – simply ensures that New York City will be exposed to greater danger than ever.

CONCLUSION - WHERE DO WE GO FROM HERE?

At this point in time, it is both astonishing, and ominous, that we continue disarming ourselves at the behest of Muslim Brotherhood front groups, in collusion with the Red part of the Red-Green axis (in particular, leftist "civil rights organizations," such as the ACLU), and with the open endorsement and cooperation of the Obama administration.

Today, U.S.-based Muslim Brotherhood front groups are allowed to use the civil rights and civil liberties-based CVE policy as a protective shield. Despite all the evidence to the contrary, these front groups and their influence operators have largely succeeded in obscuring any connection between our accession to the Islamic supremacy they promote and the steady rise in *Jihad* attacks in the U.S. and around the world. Worse yet, the Obama administration continues making overtures and concessions to them in both domestic and foreign policy.

Until the U.S. government acknowledges the fact that the Global Islamic Movement is based on the tenets of shariah, and allows its first lines of defense to operate on the basis of that immutable reality by adjusting our counter-terrorism policies and programs accordingly, CVE efforts like a revamping of our counter-messaging operations in a new "Global Engagement Center" will not only be unavailing.

We will find ourselves increasingly vulnerable to vastly more – and ever-more toxic – civilization jihad. And, in due course, we will be subjected to more and more lethal acts of violent jihad, some of which will likely make those of Ft. Hood, San Bernardino and even 9/11 pale by comparison.

ACTION RECOMMENDATIONS

USG: EXECUTIVE BRANCH

- The White House must adopt a new National Security Strategy that reflects the realities of the threat from the Global Jihad Movement and effective approaches to defeating it, starting with the abandonment of the policy known as "Countering Violent Extremism."

- As with Egypt, Saudi Arabia and the United Arab Emirates, the U.S. government must designate the Muslim Brotherhood as a Foreign Terrorist Organization (FTO) for its role in indoctrinating, recruiting, training, and facilitating global terrorism. If necessary the FTO statute should be improved to more appropriately address and sanction the Muslim Brotherhood and other Terrorist Support Entities (TSEs) for their role in materially supporting existing foreign terrorist organizations around the globe.

- The U.S. Government must take steps to identify the Muslim Brotherhood and its various front organizations as a hostile foreign power, and direct U.S. counterintelligence assets to treat known or suspected Muslim Brotherhood members in the same manner as any other foreign intelligence threats.

- All Muslim Brotherhood-tied organizations must be barred from positions of influence in or with the U.S. government.

- All Muslim Brotherhood-tied advisors/appointees must be removed from positions of influence in or with the U.S. government.

- The USG must issue policy guidance barring anyone with Muslim Brotherhood ties from instructing, teaching or training in federally funded or sponsored courses.

- Federal agencies must proactively seek out and utilize for government training experts and instructional materials that "connect the dots" – showing the essential links between Islamic supremacism, the jihad it pursues (both violently and stealthily), and authoritative Islamic doctrines, laws, scriptures and practices.

- The State Department must overhaul its immigration and refugee resettlement criteria, procedures and programs. The goal would be to establish a vetting process that will deny entry into the United States to those coming from nations in which Islamic supremacism is the norm and who there is reason to believe do – or will – seek to engage in jihad or otherwise impose shariah in this country. Such ideological affinities must, henceforth, be considered a bar to admission to the United States.

- The next administration must reverse the joint DHS and State Department finding of February 5, 2014, which eased entry into the United States for aliens who are known to have provided "limited" material support to an organization described under the Terrorism-Related Inadmissibility Grounds of the Immigration and Naturalization Act (section 212(a)(3)(B)(vi)(III)).

- The Department of Justice must release to the Congress the documents made available to the defense in the 2007-2008 Holy Land Foundation trial and prosecute the unindicted co-conspirators in that case.

- The Department of Defense must revise and adopt rules of engagement for conflicts in Muslim countries, as elsewhere, to maximize the prospects for military success and force protection, not winning hearts and minds.

- The Department of Homeland Security must formally review investigations terminated in the name of conforming to Civil Rights/Civil Liberties dictates, pursuant to the CVE approach, and assess the damage done by the associated destruction of relevant data bases with a view to reconstituting them and reopening the inquiries they supported.

USG: LEGISLATIVE BRANCH

- Congress must abandon efforts to establish a Countering Violent Extremism Office within the Department of Homeland Security. Instead, it should work with DHS to enforce the Immigration and Naturalization Act, and re-establish a fact and enforcement based immigration and counter-terrorism policy

- As suggested by members of Congress as early as 2012, comprehensive oversight hearings must be conducted to assess the extent of Muslim Brotherhood penetration of and influence within U.S. domestic and foreign policy-making agencies including: the White House, the Departments of Defense, Homeland Security, Justice, and State and the Intelligence Community.

- Congress must legislatively establish standards for excluding would-be immigrants, asylum-seekers and refugees who there is reason to believe do – or will – seek to engage in jihad or otherwise impose shariah in this country.

- Statutes governing refugee resettlement programs must be updated to ensure that local jurisdictions – i.e., states, counties and municipalities – are included in the entire decision-making process.

USG: JUDICIAL BRANCH

- The judiciary must try the unindicted co-conspirators in the 2008 Holy Land Foundation Hamas terror-funding case.

- The FBI, in cooperation with other Federal and local law enforcement agencies, must be afforded the latitude to pursue evidence-based investigations into Islamic terrorism and especially the indoctrination process at U.S. mosques, madrassas, Islamic societies and centers and Muslim Brotherhood front groups.

U.S. SOCIETY: ACADEMIA

- School districts across the country must restore courses in civics, American history and the U.S. Constitution to K-12 curricula.

- School administrators, school boards, teachers and parents must ensure that K-12 textbooks celebrate American heroes, history, traditions and values and not give preferential treatment to the study of Islam.

- Propagandizing and proselytizing course curricula and materials must not be used if they are the products of Muslim Brotherhood associates or apologists for Islamic supremacism, jihad and shariah.

- Academic institutions must be discouraged from accepting endowments and other donations that would allow influences from foreign countries, individuals or groups whose agenda favors Islamic supremacism. All such donations must be publicly disclosed.

- Academic institutions must not make special accommodations on campus for Muslims that are not offered equally to others.

- Academic institutions must not allow what amount to shariah blasphemy restrictions to prevent professors, guest speakers and students from expressing opposition to Islamic supremacism on campus.

U.S. SOCIETY: LAW ENFORCEMENT

- Federal, state, county and local law enforcement must cut ties to all Muslim Brotherhood-affiliated individuals and groups.

- Muslim Brotherhood-affiliated individuals or groups who are currently serving as advisors or instructors for local law enforcement should be terminated and replaced with subject matter experts able and willing to address the roots of Islamic terrorism in shariah and the jihad it commands.

- State and local officers must enforce U.S. and state laws already on the books regarding incitement to violence and sedition.

- Local law enforcement officers must be equipped to understand – and authorized to work against – jihad, individual jihad and other criminal offenses associated with shariah-adherent Muslim communities (including but not limited to multiple and/or underage and forced marriages, Islamic divorce laws, domestic abuse, female genital mutilation, honor killing and religiously motivated hate crimes).

U.S. SOCIETY: MEDIA

- News organizations must afford editors, hosts, reporters and guests the latitude to understand and address forthrightly national security and other threats arising from shariah and jihad (both the violent and civilization kind).

U.S. SOCIETY: WORKPLACE

- Workplace rules must be defined and applied *equally*. There must be no acquiescence to demands from Muslim Brotherhood-affiliated groups and individuals for exemptions and/or special treatment in facility usage, clothing/uniforms, breaks/time-off or other accommodations not offered to others.

APPENDIX I: HIGHLIGHTS OF THE HOLY LAND FOUNDATION CHRONOLOGY

January 24, 1995	First designation of Hamas as a terrorist organization, by Executive Order 12947, which also designates Islamic Gamaat (aka Al-Gamaat Al-Islamiyya or Jamaa Islamia), founded in 1964 as an armed branch of the Muslim Brotherhood in Lebanon, but with origins in Egypt
October 8, 1997	The Secretary of State designates Hamas as a Foreign Terrorist Organization (FTO), making it illegal for anyone in the US to provide material support or resources to Hamas
December 4, 2001	HLF designated as terrorist organization, all financial assets frozen
July 26, 2004	Federal Grand Jury in Dallas, TX returns 42-count indictment against HLF
September 24, 2004	USG files *Restraining Order* to preserve HLF assets for forfeiture
September 2004	Ungar family files *Motion for Summary Disposition* to vacate USG restraining order
December 8, 2004	HLF liable for $156M damages for aiding/abetting Hamas in death of American citizen David Boim
November 30, 2005	*Second Superseding Indictment* filed after original October 04, 2004 date was postponed
April 4, 2006	*Motion for Summary Disposition* to vacate USG restraining order denied

February 1, 2007	Judge Joe Fish denies CAIR, ISNA and NAIT *Joint Motion and Memorandum for a Bill of Particulars* (a.k.a. *Defendants' Motion*) for evidence (proof) that HLF singled out families for aid because they were related to members of Hamas.
May 29, 2007	Government's *Trial Brief* filed (providing background facts and details of MB groups in America)
May 29, 2007	CAIR, ISNA, NAIT and CAIR leader Omar Ahmad publicly identified as Unindicted Co-Conspirators
July 16, 2007	HLF criminal trial begins in the Northern District of Texas, Dallas
July 20, 2007	Khalil Meek complains U.S. Islamic charities unfairly scrutinized and persecuted
August 14, 2007	CAIR files Motion For Leave To File A Brief Amicus Curiae Instanter (a.k.a. Amicus Brief)
August 28, 2007	Letter to AG Alberto Gonzales from Peter Hoekstra and Sue Myrick re ISNA Convention
October 22, 2007	Judge Joe Fish declares mistrial because of deadlocked jurors (aka Hung Jury)
December 28, 2007	U.S. Court of Appeals 7th Circuit, Chicago reverses $156M decision (not for HLF-affiliated American Muslim Society and Quranic Literacy Society)

February 13, 2008	HLF case scheduled for second jury trial
June 18, 2008	CAIR, ISNA and NAIT *Motion for Equitable Relief* from being named as Unindicted Co-Conspirators (i.e., they request their names be removed)
July 10, 2008	ISNA press release on mistrial; includes reasons for filing *Motion for Equitable Relief*
July 21, 2008	CAIR, ISNA and NAIT response to USG defense against *Motion for Equitable Relief*
September 22, 2008	Second HLF criminal trial begins
November 03, 2008	Appeal of $156 million in damages in Boim Case upheld by US Court of Appeals 7th Circuit, Chicago
November 24, 2008	**Guilty verdicts returned on all 108 counts against 5 HLF defendants**
December 04, 2008	Court upholds $156 million in damages against both HLF-affiliated organizations in Boim case.
July 01, 2009	USG files *Memorandum Opinion Order* to counter CAIR, ISNA and NAIT *Motion for Equitable Relief*; District Clerk for Northern District of Texas files *Amicus Curaie Brief* in support of Unindicted Co-Conspirators' First and Fifth Amendment Rights (includes Order to seal the list of Unindicted Co-Conspirators, i.e., *Appendix A*)

February 12, 2010	DOJ Letter to Sue Myrick (R-NC) re the Unindicted Co-Conspirator status of CAIR
March 31, 2010	Declination of Prosecution of Omar Ahmad CAIR
June 13, 2010	Judge faults HLF lawyer Nancy Hollander for not disclosing she dropped HLF as a client
October 19, 2010	Appeal for reversal of HLF convictions filed, US Court of Appeals 5th Circuit, New Orleans
April 14, 2011	"Did Obama and Holder Scuttle Terror Finance Prosecutions?" article by Patrick Poole, PJ Media
April 15, 2011	Rep. Peter King letter to AG Eric Holder re: failure to prosecute CAIR, ISNA and NAIT
April 26, 2011	Eric Holder: Bush Administration Declined to Prosecute CAIR [no mention of ISNA/NAIT]
April 29, 2011	US Attorney James T. Jacks in Dallas says the Obama White House did not meddle in case
June 28, 2011	Judicial Watch sues DOJ for documents re *Declination of Prosecution* of Omar Ahmad
July 14, 2011	*Appeal for Dismissal* filed in US Court of Appeals 5th Circuit, New Orleans

September 01, 2011	Opening arguments in *Appeal Hearing* scheduled
December 07, 2011	U.S. Court of Appeals 5th Circuit, New Orleans affirms all HLF convictions and sentences
February 17, 2012	U.S. Court of Appeals 5th Circuit, New Orleans issues *Order Denying Petition for Rehearing*
May 17, 2012	Four HLF defendants file petition for *Writ of Certiorari* with US Supreme Court
June 07, 2012	Eric Holder Ducks Congress's Questions About HLF Trial
October 29, 2012	U.S. Supreme Court petition for Writ of Certiorari is rejected
February 02, 2014	USG submits argument against *Petition For Relief* filed by Mohammad El-Mezain

APPENDIX II: OTHER SPECIALLY DESIGNATED GLOBAL TERRORIST ORGANIZATIONS LINKED TO HAMAS

These organizations are highlighted here to show that the Holy Land Foundation was just one part of a much larger network of international MB front groups involved in the support of Hamas. That remains the case to this day.

- Al Aqsa Foundation; Designated May 29, 2003

- Association de Secours Palestinien; Designated August 21, 2003

- Commité de Bienfaisance et de Secours aux Palestiniens (*aka* Association for Palestinian Aid, Palestine Relief Committee, Palestinian Aid Council, Palestinian Aid Organization, Palestinian Relief Society *or* Relief Association for Palestine); Designated August 22, 2003

- Global Relief Foundation (*aka* GIF Foundation, Secours Mondial or FSM); Designated October 18, 2002

- Interpal (*aka* Palestinian Relief and Development Fund); Designated August 21, 2003

- Palestinian Association in Austria (PVO); Designated August 21, 2003

- Sanabil Association for Relief and Development; Designated August 21, 2003

APPENDIX III: DEPARTMENT OF JUSTICE LETTER TO REP. SUE MYRICK REGARDING CAIR'S TIES TO HAMAS

U.S. Department of Justice

Office of Legislative Affairs

Office of the Assistant Attorney General Washington, D.C. 20530

FEB 1 2 2010

The Honorable Sue Myrick
U.S. House of Representatives
Washington, DC 20515

Dear Congresswoman Myrick:

This responds to your letter, dated October 21, 2009, to the Attorney General requesting information regarding the evidence and findings by the Department of Justice and the FBI which resulted in the Council on American Islamic Relations (CAIR) being named as an unindicted co-conspirator of the Holy Land Foundation for Relief and Development in *United States v. Holy Land Foundation et al.* (Cr. No. 3:04-240-P N.D.TX.). An identical letter has been sent to the other Members who joined in your letter. We apologize for the delay in responding.

Enclosed are four copies of the trial transcripts on CD-ROM that contain testimony and other evidence that was introduced in that trial which demonstrated a relationship among CAIR, individual CAIR founders, and the Palestine Committee. Evidence was also introduced that demonstrated a relationship between the Palestine Committee and HAMAS, which was designated as a terrorist organization in 1995. Specifically, the enclosed CD-ROM's contain:

1. A Palestine Committee document recovered in the search of Ismail Elbarasse's Virginia residence that Special Agent (SA) Lara Burns refers to in her testimony (File titled "Elbarasse Search 19." This is the original Arabic version and starting on page six is the English translation of the document);

2. Testimony of SA Lara Burns (file titled "HLF Transcripts Burns 9-29-08." The relevant portion begins on page 186, line 6 and continues);

3. Testimony of SA Lara Burns (File titled "HLF Transcripts Burns 10-07-08." The relevant portions begin on page 99, line 12 and continues to page 101, line 10; and page 148 lines 5-25. This transcript also contains a discussion between defense counsel Dratel and Judge Solis on page 149, line 5 through page 151, line 7).

APPENDIX IV: TIMELINE OF MUSLIM BROTHERHOOD FRONTS' INVOLVEMENT IN CVE POLICYMAKING[lxxxix]

[lxxxix] Either **MPAC, ISNA** and/or **CAIR** participated in each of these key 'turning-point' events. Most of these events occurred *after* the Holy Land Foundation (HLF) verdicts in 2008. **Note: ISNA** and **CAIR** remain *Unindicted Co-Conspirators* in the HLF Trial, along with the International Institute of Islamic Thought (**IIIT**) and Association of Muslim Social Scientists (**AMSS**). The Muslim American Society (**MAS**) and American Muslim Council (**AMC**), once led by Abdulrahman Alamoudi, are also represented below.

March 1998	Seven Muslim Organizations Establish National Coordination Council [AMC, CAIR, ISNA & MPAC]
April 1, 1999	A Position Paper On US Counterterrorism Policy – Total Anti-U.S. Attacks, 1998 [MPAC]
November 24, 1999	**Salam Al-Marayati [MPAC]**, "Muslims in America," News Hour with Jim Lehrer, PBS [Pro-Hezbollah]; Al-Marayati has visited the WH *at least* 6 times with Paul Monteiro, Associate Director of the WH Office of Public Engagement, on September, 17, 2009; June 8, 2010; July 14, 2010; July 16, 2010; June 29, 2011 and July 28, 2011
October 16, 2001	AG Ashcroft Meets With Muslim, Arab Leaders [MPAC, represented by Wright Mahdi Bray]
December 4, 2001	**Holy Land Foundation for Relief and Development (HLF)** designated under EO 13224 and 12947 of providing millions of dollars of material and logistical support to HAMAS
February 13, 2002	FBI Director Meets With Key US Leaders of National Arab, Muslim and Sikh Organizations [MPAC, CAIR and AMC]
May 31, 2002	HLF re-designated under EO 13224 and 12947
November 13, 2002	Joint Arab-American, Muslim-American Statement [AMC and CAIR]
February 28, 2003	FBI Director Meets with Muslim, Sikh, and Arab-American Leaders [AMC and MPAC]
April 1, 2003	MPAC Joins Advisory Committee to FBI's DC Field Office
April 2, 2003	MPAC Attends FBI Advisory Committee Meeting in DC Field Office
September 1, 2003	A Position Paper On US Counterterrorism Policy – American Muslim Critique & Recommendations [MPAC]

May 20, 2004	Arab and Muslim-American Organizations Condemn Israeli Killings [**MPAC** and **CAIR**]
July 9, 2004	DOJ, FBI Reinforce Commitment to Working with Leaders of Muslim, Sikh and Arab-American Communities
July 26, 2004	Federal Grand Jury in Dallas, TX returns 42-count indictment against **HLF**
October 27, 2005	**MPAC** Attends Five Government Hosted *Iftars* During Ramadan
November 19, 2005	Muslim American Identity: Present and Future [**MPAC, CAIR** and **ISPI** in Chicago, IL]
November 20, 2005	**MPAC** (Muslim Public Affairs Council) Aligns With **CAIR**
December 16, 2005	State, Justice Will Appear At **MPAC**, Causing Concern
January 08, 2006	Attorney General Alberto Gonzalez Meets With Prominent Muslim American Groups
January 11, 2006	Muslim and Arab Leaders Meet With FBI On Domestic Surveillance Reports [**CAIR** and **MAS**]
December 04, 2006	U.S. Government Officials Meet With Prominent American Muslim Leaders To Discuss Islamophobia [**ISNA** and **MPAC**]
January 23, 2007	**Muslim Public Affairs Council** Honored by FBI
February 22, 2007	**MPAC** Meets with DHS Secretary Chertoff and FBI Director Robert S. Mueller III
February 26, 2007	FBI Director Robert S. Mueller III meets with leaders from **MPAC**, the Arab American Institute (AAI), the American Arab Anti-Discrimination Committee (ADC) and Muslim Advocates at FBI headquarters in Washington, D.C.
May 08, 2007	Security Agency Enlisting Muslims To Rebut Radicals (DHS Secretary Chertoff)
January 2008	*Words Matter Memo* released
February 13, 2008	**HLF case scheduled for second jury trial**

May 14, 2008	Senate Homeland Security Report Lacks Substantive Analysis, Contradicts Own Recommendations [**MPAC** and **CAIR**]
October 14, 2008	U.S.-Muslim Engagement Project: Changing Course, A New Direction For US Relations with the Muslim World
November 24, 2008	108 Guilty Verdicts In HLF Trial Announced
June 4, 2009	President Obama *A New Beginning* speech at Al-Azhar, Cairo with MB leaders
August 12, 2009	**MPAC** Participates in Government Interagency Meeting
October 23, 2009	**DOJ** Should Show Congress Damning Evidence on **CAIR**, Reps Say
December 5, 2009	Remarks of Tom Perez At **MPAC** 2009 National Conference
January 12, 2010	As **DOJ** Seeks Liaison Partners, A Muslim Group's Prominence Grows [Thomas Perez and **MPAC**]
January 28, 2010	Inaugural Meeting DHS Secretary Napolitano and Muslim Community (**MPAC**, **ISNA** and **MAS**)
February 12, 2010	**DOJ** Response Letter To Representative Sue Myrick on **CAIR** Evidence
February 17, 2010	Napolitano Meets with Muslim Brotherhood Leaders [**MPAC** and **ISNA**]
Spring 2010	CVE Working Group – Homeland Security Advisory Council
March 4, 2010	Urge President Obama and Congress to Make Appointments to Privacy and Civil Liberties Board [**MPAC**]
March 12, 2010	**DOJ**: **CAIR**'s Unindicted Co-Conspirator Status Upheld
June 16, 2010	Letter to Senator Joseph Lieberman **Also see:** http://www.mpac.org/issues/national-security/mpac-sends-letter-to-sen.-lieberman-challenging-use-of-religious-terminology-in-national-security.php

June 17, 2010	MPAC and ISPU Will Hold A Briefing On CVE ('Perspectives on Countering Violent Extremism and Radicalization')
August 3, 2010	Coalition Letter to FBI Director Robert S. Mueller III [MPAC, ISNA and CAIR]
August 13, 2010	[MPAC, ISNA and CAIR] Building Bridges to Strengthen America – Forging An Effective Counterterrorism Enterprise Between Muslim Americans and Law Enforcement [MPAC]
August 31, 2010	Direct Access' Stimulus Grants for the Muslim Brotherhood [MPAC, CAIR, ISNA and IIIT]
Unknown 2011	Helping Our Officers Work With Muslims Communities – Increasing Cultural Competency [Memo, Copy on file with Author]
February 25, 2011	MPAC and King Hearings Talking Points
March 6, 2011	National Security Adviser Stresses Muslims Part of 'American Family' During Speech at ADAMS Center
April 14, 2011	Top DOJ Officials Abandon CAIR Terror Finance Prosecutions
2011-2012	The *Year of the Great Purge* begins
September 15, 2011	MPAC Letter to FBI Dir. Robert S. Mueller III Asking for Explanation on Islamophobic Trainings
September 16, 2011	Muslim Groups Press FBI, DOJ On Anti-Islamic Training [MPAC and Muslim Advocates]
October 4, 2011	Letter To FBI Dir. Robert S. Mueller III [MPAC, ISNA, CAIR, MSA and ACLU;]
October 5, 2011	MPAC Co-Signs Letter to FBI Demanding Reformation in Flawed, Anti-Muslim Training
October 19, 2011	Salam Al-Marayati, "*The Wrong Way To Fight Terrorism,*" Los Angeles Times
October 19, 2011	Letter To John Brennan from 57 Muslim Groups Regarding Purge of Islamophobic Training Material

October 24, 2011	Letter to Margo Schlanger To Discuss "*If You See Something, Say Something*" [**MPAC** and **CAIR**]
October 24, 2011	CAIR-Chicago Reps To Speak At CIOGC-MPAC Conference [**MPAC** and **CAIR**]
February 8, 2012	FBI Dir. Robert S. Mueller III Meets With American Muslim Community
February 15, 2012	MPAC and Interfaith Leaders Meet with FBI Dir. Robert S. Mueller III to Address Concerns Regarding Training Materials
March 27, 2012	Senator Richard J. Durban Letter To **FBI** Director Robert S. Mueller III
May 17, 2012	**MPAC** One Of The Key Players In The Counter-Radicalization Debate
August 6, 2012	**MPAC** Press Conference to Call on Romney to Denounce Bachmann's Witch Hunt
August 20, 2012	CVE/Community Engagement National Conference [*Muflehu* is led by M. Magid, now former president of **ISNA**
September 24-26, 2012	MAS-PACE holds first American Muslim Leadership Conference [**CAIR, ICNA, MAS**]
March 11, 2013	**MPAC** DC Director Meets With President In Preparation For Trip To Middle East
March 14, 2013	President Obama Meets With **MPAC** Prior To Middle East Trip
May 28, 2013	**MPAC** Tackles Violent Extremism And Online Radicalization At Two DC Events
April 24, 2014	Letter: Muslim Groups Call on 9-11 Museum to Edit Insufficiently Vetted Film [**MPAC** and **CAIR**]
August 5, 2014	Meeting between US Council of Muslim Organizations and DHS officials [**MPAC**]
August 14, 2014	Letter to Lisa O. Monaco and DHS Against Law Enforcement Bias
November 13, 2014	Asian Americans Advancing Justice Letter to DHS Secretary Johnson [**CAIR** and **ISCSC**]

December 18, 2014	Letter to Lisa O. Monaco, Assist. to President for HS, Deputy National Security Adviser, Office of the HS Advisor
February 4, 2015	Obama Meets With American Muslims Leaders In White House [**MPAC** and **ISNA**]
February 13, 2015	The Los Angeles Framework For Countering Violent Extremism [**MPAC**]
February 17, 2015	White House Summit On Countering Violent Extremism [**MPAC**] and Salam Al-Marayati]
February 18, 2015	White House Summit On Countering Violent Extremism [**MPAC** and Salam Al-Marayati]
March 23, 2015	DHS Secretary: Reading Quran Reminds Me of Quintessential American Values [**MPAC Award Banquet**]
June 15, 2015	Muslim Public Affairs Council Has White House Meetings [**MPAC**]
July 20, 2015	Why Won't GOP Chairman Mention 'Islamic Terror' In New Bill? [**MPAC**]
September 2, 2015	No, ISIS Doesn't Represent Islam [Editorial by MPAC's Salam Al-Marayati]
September 21, 2015	Letter to NY Mayor Bill de Blasio Protesting CVE Program [**CAIR, MAS** and **ACLU**]

[1] Quoted in Scaparrotti, C. (November 27, 2012). "Joint Publication 3-13: Information Operations" *Defense Technical Information Center.* Retrieved February 9, 2016 from http://dtic.mil/doctrine/new_pubs/jp3_13.pdf.

[2] Paul, R. (January 13, 1944). "Report to the Secretary on the Acquiescence of this Government in the Murder of the Jews". *U.S. Department of the Treasury.* Retrieved February 9, 2016 from http://www.jewishvirtuallibrary.org/jsource/Holocaust/treasrep.html.

[3] "Morgenthau Biography "(n.d.). "Henry Morgenthau, Jr. Biography." *Jewish Virtual Library.* Retrieved February 9, 2016 from http://www.jewishvirtuallibrary.org/jsource/biography/Morgenthau.html.

[4] McCarthy, A. (2008). *Willful Blindness: A Memoir of the Jihad.* United States: Encounter Books.

[5] "Bylaws". (n.d.). "An introduction to the by laws of Palestine Committee in North America And Canada". *The Investigative Project on Terrorism.* Retrieved February 9, 2016 from http://www.investigativeproject.org/documents/24-bylaws-of-the-palestine-committee-of-the-muslim.pdf.

[6] IPT News. (November 12, 2008). "HLF Redux: The Philadelphia Meeting," *The Investigative Project on Terrorism.* Retrieved February 9, 2016 from http://www.investigativeproject.org/859/hlf-redux-the-philadelphia-meeting. Transcripts of FBI surveillance tapes of the meeting are available at the Northern District of Texas federal court website. Retrived February 9, 2016 from http://coop.txnd.uscourts.gov/judges/hlf2.html

[7] "Bylaws". (n.d.). " An introduction to the by laws of Palestine Committee in North America And Canada" *The Investigative Project on Terrorism.* Retrieved February 9, 2016 from http://www.investigativeproject.org/documents/24-bylaws-of-the-palestine-committee-of-the-muslim.pdf.

[8] King, P. (April 15, 2011). "King Letter to AG Holder on Holy Land Foundation Decision." *House Committee on Homeland Security.* Retrieved February 9, 2016 from https://homeland.house.gov/document/king-letter-attorney-general-holder/.

[9] "Commission" (n.d.) "Commission on British Muslims." *Runnymede.* Retrieved February 9, 2016 from http://www.runnymedetrust.org/projects/commissionOnBritishMuslims.

[10] "OIC". (n.d.) "Homepage of the Organization of Islamic Cooperation." *Organization of Islamic Cooperation.*
Retrieved February 9, 2016 from http://www.oic-oci.org/oicv2/home/?lan=en.

[11] Goodenough, P. (2010, December 22). "U.N. Passes Religious 'Defamation' Resolution Sponsored by Islamic Nations, But Support Dwindles." *CNS News.*
Retrieved February 9, 2016 from http://www.cnsnews.com/news/article/un-passes-religious-defamation-resolution-sponsored-islamic-nations-support-dwindles.

[12] Charbonneau, L. (2011, December 19). "UN Condemns Religious Intolerance, Drops "Defamation" Line For First Time in Years." *Reuters.*
Retrieved February 9, 2016 from http://blogs.reuters.com/faithworld/2011/12/19/un-condemns-religious-intolerance-drops-defamation-line-for-first-time-in-years/.

[13] "DHS Homepage". (n.d.) "Homepage." *Department of Homeland Security Office of Civil Rights and Civil Liberties*. Retrieved February 9, 2016 from http://www.dhs.gov/office-civil-rights-and-civil-liberties.

[14] Lormel, D. (n.d.). "Holy Land Foundation... The Retrial." *Counterterrorism Blog*. Retrieved February 9, 2016 from http://counterterrorismblog.org/2008/11/holy_land_foundationthe_retria.php.

[15] "Executive Order" (September 24, 2001). "Executive Order Blocking Property and Prohibiting Transactions With Persons Who Commit, Threaten to Commit, or Support Terrorism." *Yale Law School Library*. Retrieved February 9, 2016 from http://avalon.law.yale.edu/sept11/execord_924.asp.

[16] "Operation Greenquest"(October 25, 2001). "Feds Launch 'Operation Green Quest.'" *CBS News*. Retrieved February 9, 2016 from http://www.cbsnews.com/news/feds-launch-operation-green-quest/.

[17] "Affidavit" (October, 2003). "Affidavit in support of the application for search warrant." *The Investigative Project on Terrorism*. Retrieved February 9, 2016 from https://www.investigativeproject.org/documents/case_docs/891.pdf.

[18] "Terrorism Financing". (February 20, 2004). "Investigations of Terrorist Financing, Money Laundering, and Other Financial Crimes." *United States General Accounting Office*. Retrieved February 9, 2016 from http://www.gao.gov/new.items/d04464r.pdf.

[19] "FBI OIG Report" (July, 2007) "Coordination Between FBI and ICE on Investigations of Terrorist Financing." *Department of Homeland Security Office of the Inspector General*. Retrieved February 9, 2016 from https://www.oig.dhs.gov/assets/Mgmt/OIG_07-55_Jul07.pdf.

[21] El-Naggar, M. (March 21, 2002). "'Operation Green Quest' Singles Out Muslims." *IslamOnline.net*. Retrieved February 9, 2016 from https://web.archive.org/web/20020619210251/http://www.islamonline.net/english/News/2002-03/22/article10.shtml.

[22] Mauro, R. (April 2, 2003). "International Institute of Islamic Thought." *The Clarion Project*. Retrieved February 9, 2016 from http://www.clarionproject.org/analysis/international-institute-islamic-thought.

[23] Sharp, J. (February 8, 2005). "The Middle East Partnership Initiative: An Overview." *CRS Report to Congress*. Retrieved February 9, 2016 from http://www.dtic.mil/get-tr-doc/pdf?AD=ADA459129.

[24] "MEPI Homepage." (n.d.). "Middle Eastern Partnership Initiative Homepage" *U.S. Department of State*. Retrieved February 9, 2016 from http://mepi.state.gov/.

[25] Pandith, F. (July 15, 2015). "The Rise of Radicalization: Is the U.S. Government Failing to Counter International and Domestic Terrorism." *Council on Foreign Relations*. Retrieved February 9, 2016 from http://docs.house.gov/meetings/HM/HM00/20150715/103739/HHRG-114-HM00-Wstate-PandithF-20150715.pdf.

[26] "Words Matter Memo". (January, 2008). "Terminology to Define the Terrorists: Recommendations From American Muslims." *Department of Homeland Security Office of Civil rights and Civil Liberties*. Retrieved February 9, 2016 from http://www.dhs.gov/xlibrary/assets/crcl_terminology_paper_final_3_10_08.pdf.

[27] "DOJ HLF Convictions Press Release". (November 24, 2008). "Federal Jury in Dallas Convicts Holy Land Foundation and Its Leaders for Providing Material Support to Hamas Terrorist Organization."

U.S. Department of Justice. Retrieved February 9, 2016 from http://www.justice.gov/archive/opa/pr/2008/November/08-nsd-1046.html.

[28] "DOJ HLF Sentencing Press Release". (May 27, 2009). " Federal Judge Hands Downs Sentences in Holy Land Foundation Case: Holy Land Foundation and Leaders Convicted on Providing Material Support to Hamas Terrorist Organization." U.S. *Department of Justice.* Retrieved February 9, 2016 from http://www.justice.gov/opa/pr/federal-judge-hands-downs-sentences-holy-land-foundation-case

[29] "CVE Homepage." (n.d.). "Countering Violent Extremism Homepage". *Department of Homeland Security.* Retrieved February 9, 2016 from http://www.dhs.gov/topic/countering-violent-extremism.

[30] Kerry, J. (August 7, 2013). "Remarks at the launch of the Office of Faith-Based Community Initiatives." *United States Department of State.* Retrieved February 9, 2016 from http://www.state.gov/secretary/remarks/2013/08/212781.htm.

[31] Baran, Z. (2008, February 27). "The Muslim Brotherhood's U.S. Network." *The Counterjihad Report.* Retrieved February 9, 2016 from http://counterjihadreport.com/2012/07/29/the-muslim-brotherhoods-us-network/.

[32] Obama, B. (2009, June 4). "Remarks by the President at Cairo University 06-04-2009." *The White House Office of the Press Secretary.* Retrieved February 9, 2016 from https://www.whitehouse.gov/the-press-office/remarks-president-cairo-university-6-04-09.

[33] "Executive Order 12947" (January 25, 1995). "Executive Order 12947 Prohibiting Transactions With Terrorists Who Threaten To Disrupt the Peace in the Middle East Discussions." *Government Printing Office.* Retrieved February 9, 2016, from https://www.gpo.gov/fdsys/pkg/FR-1995-01-25/pdf/X95-110125.pdf

[34] "Treasury Press Release" (December 4, 2001) "Treasury Department Press Release: Shutting Down the Terrorist Financial Network" U.S. Treasury Department Retrieved February 9, 2016 from http://avalon.law.yale.edu/sept11/treas_027.asp

[35] Ibid.

[36] "Trial Brief". (May 29, 2007) "Government Trial Briefing: United States of America Vs. The Holy Land Foundation et al.". *The Investigative Project on Terrorism.* Retrieved February 9, 2016 from http://www.investigativeproject.org/documents/case_docs/422.pdf

[37] Lefkowitz, J. (November 15, 2007). "The 1993 Philadelphia Meeting: A Road Map for Future Muslim Brotherhood Actions in the U.S." *NEFA Foundation.* Retrieved February 9, 2016 from http://www.anti-cair-net.org/93Phillyfinal.pdf

[38] "Bylaws" (n.d.). "The Bylaws of the Palestine Committee." *The Investigative Project.* Retrieved February 9, 2016 from http://www.investigativeproject.org/documents/24-bylaws-of-the-palestine-committee-of-the-muslim.pdf

[39] "Oslo Accord". (n.d.). "Details of the Oslo Accords." *Palestine Facts.* Retrieved February 9, 2016from http://www.palestinefacts.org/pf_1991to_now_oslo_accords.php

[40] "FTO List". (October 8, 1997) "Foreign Terrorist Organizations". *U.S. Department of State.* Retrieved February 9, 2016, from http://www.state.gov/j/ct/rls/other/des/123085.htm

[41] "U.S. Government Trial Brief." (N.D.) *U.S. vs. Holy Land Foundation et al. U.S. Northern District Court.* Retrieved February 9, 2016 from http://www.investigativeproject.org/documents/case_docs/422.pdf

[42] Beam, C. (2009, June 9). "Why is the color green so important in the Muslim world?" *Slate Magazine*. Retrieved February 9, 2016 from http://www.slate.com/articles/news_and_politics/explainer/2009/06/islamic_greenwashing.html

[43] "DOJ HLF Convictions Press Release". (November 24, 2008). "Federal Jury in Dallas Convicts Holy Land Foundation and Its Leaders for Providing Material Support to Hamas Terrorist Organization." *The United States Department of Justice*. Retrieved February 9, 2016 from http://www.justice.gov/archive/opa/pr/2008/November/08-nsd-1046.html

[44] Lormel, D. (November 17, 2008). "Holy Land Foundation: The Retrial." *Counterterrorism Blog*. Retrieved February 9, 2016 from http://counterterrorismblog.org/2008/11/holy_land_foundationthe_retria.php

[46] "TSEC MB report" (May 27, 2014) "The Muslim Brotherhood Report Sabotaging the Miserable House through the Process of Settlement and Civilization Jihad". (2014, May 27) *Terrorism and Security Experts of Canada*. Retrieved February 9, 2016 from https://docs.google.com/file/d/0B6tM70447biiTmotZUF0MWV0Nnc/edit?pli=1

[47] "ISNA". (n.d.). "ISNA Homepage". *The Islamic Society of North America*. Retrieved February 9, 2016 from http://www.isna.net/

[48] IPT News. (n.d.) "Islamic Society of North America: An IPT Investigative Report." *The Investigative Project on Terrorism*. Retrieved February 9, 2016 from https://www.investigativeproject.org/documents/misc/275.pdf

[49] "CAIR." (n.d.). "CAIR Homepage". *The Council on American Islamic Relations*. Retrieved on January 12, 2016 from http://www.cair.com/

[50] CAIR. (June 13, 2010). "Articles of Incorporation and Certification of Incorporation Document. *Cairunmasked Project*. Retrieved February 9, 2016 from http://cairunmasked.org/wp-content/uploads/2010/06/DC52-1887951_Incorporation_Bylaws.pdf

[51] Mauro, R. (February 10, 2013). "Declassified FBI Memos Reveal the ISNA was Identified as Brotherhood Front as Early as 1987". *Clarion Project*. Retrieved February 9, 2016 from http://www.clarionproject.org/analysis/islamic-society-north-america-isna#

[52] Mauro, R. (February 11, 2013). "North American Islamic Trust (NAIT) holds the titles of over 325 properties in 42 states." *The Clarion Project*. Retrieved February 9, 2016, from http://www.clarionproject.org/analysis/north-american-islamic-trust-nait#_ftn2

[53] IPT News. (n.d.) "The Muslim Students Association". *The Investigative Project on Terrorism*. Retrieved February 9, 2016, from https://www.investigativeproject.org/documents/misc/31.pdf

[54] IPT News. (n.d.) "The North American Islamic Trust". *The Investigative Project on Terrorism*. Retrieved February 9, 2016 from http://www.investigativeproject.org/documents/misc/708.pdf

[55] "IIIT" (n.d.). "Homepage of the International Institute of Islamic Thought". *International Institute of Islamic Thought*. Retrieved February 9, 2016, from http://iiit.org/

[56] King, P. (April 15, 2011). "King Demands Answers from Holder on Decision Not to Prosecute CAIR, its Co-Founder, and other Unindicted Co-Conspirators in Holy Land Foundation Case" *House Committee on Homeland Security*. Retrieved February 9, 2016 from https://homeland.house.gov/press/king-demands-answers-holder-decision-not-prosecute-cair-its-co-founder-and-other/

[57] King, P. (April 15, 2011). King Letter to AG Holder on Holy Land Foundation Decision". *Homeland Security Committee*. Retrieved February 9, 2016 from https://homeland.house.gov/document/king-letter-attorney-general-holder/

[58] Kirby, S. (2015, November 12). Why Americanized Muslim Reformers Are Failing. *Front Page Magazine*. Retrieved February 9, 2016 from http://www.frontpagemag.com/fpm/260743/why-americanized-muslim-reformers-are-failing-dr-stephen-m-kirby

[59] Remarks at the Launch of the Office of Faith-Based Community Initiatives. *United States Office of Secretary of State*. (2013, August 7). Retrieved February 9, 2016 from http://www.state.gov/secretary/remarks/2013/08/212781.htm

[60] "Counterterrorism Fact sheet" (n.d.). "Fact Sheet: National Strategy for Counterterrorism." *The White House*. Retrieved February 9, 2016 from https://www.whitehouse.gov/the-press-office/2011/06/29/fact-sheet-national-strategy-counterterrorism

[61] Obama, B. (September 24, 2014). "Excerpt from Remarks As Prepared for Delivery by President Barack Obama to the United Nations General Assembly." *Fox News Network*. Retrieved February 9, 2016 from http://nation.foxnews.com/2014/09/24/isis-watches-obama-tells-un-america-will-never-be-war-islam-wont-base-entire-foreign

[62] King, P. (April 15, 2011). King Letter to AG Holder on Holy Land Foundation". *House Committee on Homeland Security*. Retrieved February 9, 2016 from https://homeland.house.gov/document/king-letter-attorney-general-holder/

[63] Pipes, D. (June 18, 2002). "[The American Muslim Council:] 'Mainstream' Muslims?" *Middle East Forum*. Retrieved February 9, 2016 from http://www.meforum.org/4093/the-american-muslim-council-mainstream-muslims

[64] Markon, J. (October 16, 2004). "Muslim Activist Sentenced to 23 years for Libya Contacts." Retrieved February 9, 2016 from http://www.washingtonpost.com/wp-dyn/articles/A36718-2004Oct15.html

[65] Jacobsen, M. (October 16, 2003). "Memorandum for the Record: Interview for FBI Special Agent Wade Ammerman." *New York Times*. Retrieved February 9, 2016 from http://www.nytimes.com/interactive/2015/08/26/magazine/30mag-awlaki-document-2.html?_r=0

[66] Killough, A. (September 11, 2014). "Strong reaction to Obama statement: 'ISIL is not Islamic'" *CNN News Network*. Retrieved February 9, 2016 from http://www.cnn.com/2014/09/10/politics/obama-isil-not-islamic/index.html

[67] Laub, Z. (2014, January 15). "Egypt's Muslim Brotherhood." *Council on Foreign Relations*. Retrieved February 9, 2016 from http://www.cfr.org/egypt/egypts-muslim-brotherhood/p23991

[68] King, P. (April 15, 2011). "King Letter to AG Holder on Holy Land Foundation Decision". *House Homeland Security Committee*. Retrieved February 9, 2016 from https://homeland.house.gov/document/king-letter-attorney-general-holder/

[69] Howerton, J. (June 7, 2012). "Eric Holder Ducks Congress's Questions About Massive Terrorism Financing Trial". *The Blaze*. Retrieved February 9, 2016 from http://www.theblaze.com/stories/2012/06/07/eric-holder-ducks-congresss-questions-about-massive-terrorism-financing-trial/

[70] Poole, P. (April 14, 2011). "Did Obama and Holder Scuttle Terror Finance Prosecutions?" *PJ Media*. Retrieved February 9, 2016 from https://pjmedia.com/blog/did-obama-and-holder-scuttle-terror-finance-prosecutions/

[72] Waterman, S. (October 6, 2011). "Islam content spurs FBI review of anti-terror training." *Washington Times*. Retrieved February 9, 2016 from http://www.washingtontimes.com/news/2011/oct/6/islam-content-spurs-fbi-review-of-anti-terror-trai/

[73] CAIR-TX (n.d.) "Who We Are." *CAIRTexas.com*. Retrieved February 9, 2016from http://cairtexas.com/about-us/who-we-are/

[74] Al-Arian, L. (November 26, 2008). "Verdict Against Holy Land Charity Could Have a Chilling Effect on the Muslim Community". *Alternet*. Retrieved February 9, 2016 from http://www.alternet.org/story/108740/verdict_against_holy_land_charity_could_have_a_chilling_effect_on_the_muslim_community

[75] Shariah Finance Watch. (August 28, 2012). "How Zakat Funds Jihad." *Center for Security Policy*. Retrieved February 9, 2016from http://www.shariahfinancewatch.org/blog/2012/08/28/how-zakat-funds-jihad/

[76] Ahmad Ibn Naqib al-Misri. (July 1, 1997). "Book H- Zakat" from *Reliance of the Traveler: The Classic Manual of Islamic Law*. Trans. Nu Ha Mim Keller. *Amana Publications*. Retrieved February 9, 2016 from http://shariahthethreat.org/wp-content/uploads/2011/04/reliance_of_the_traveller.pdf

[77] Schilling, C. (June 25, 2010). "White House welcomes Shariah finance specialist." *WND News*. Retrieved February 9, 2016from http://www.wnd.com/2010/06/170617/

[78] "Runnymede" (n.d.). "Publications & Resources." *Runnymede Trust*. Retrieved February 9, 2016 from http://www.runnymedetrust.org/publications/currentPublications.html

[79] "The Commission" (n.d.). "The Commission on British Muslims," *Runnymede Trust*. Retrieved February 9, 2016, from

http://www.runnymedetrust.org/projects/commissionOnBritishMuslims

[80] Runnymede Trust *(1994). A Very Light Sleeper: The Persistence and Dangers of Anti-Semitism*. The Runnymede Trust. London.

[81] Muslim Museum UK. (January 17, 2014). "Runnymede Trust Researches Islamophobia". *Runnymede Trust*. Retrieved February 9, 2016, from http://muslimmuseum.org.uk/runnymede-trust-researches-islamophobia/

[82] ibid.

[83] Conway, G. (February, 1997). *Islamophobia: A Challenge for Us All. The Runnymede Trust*. Retrieved February 9, 2016, from http://www.runnymedetrust.org/uploads/publications/pdfs/islamophobia.pdf

[84] Muslim Museum UK. (January 17, 2014). "Runnymede Trust Researches Islamophobia". *Runnymede Trust*. Retrieved February 9, 2016, from http://muslimmuseum.org.uk/runnymede-trust-researches-islamophobia/

[85] "The Commission" (n.d.). "The Commission on British Muslims," *Runnymede Trust*. Retrieved February 9, 2016, from

http://www.runnymedetrust.org/projects/commissionOnBritishMuslims

[86] Stone, R. (June 2, 2004). Islamophobia: Issues, Challenges, and Action. *Trentham Books* (London).Retrieved February 9, 2016, from http://www.insted.co.uk/islambook.pdf

[87] "Letter to the Editor". (June 21, 2013) "Letter to the Editor of the Times Newspaper". *Runnymede Trust*. Retrieved February 9, 2016, from http://www.runnymedetrust.org/uploads/Full Text of Letter to the Editor 21 June 2013.pdf

[88] Stone, R. (2004, June 2). *Islamophobia: Issues, Challenges, and Action. Trentham Books* (London).Retrieved February 9, 2016, from http://www.insted.co.uk/islambook.pdf

[90] Mauro, R. (2013, February 4). "Association of Muslim Social Scientists of North America". *The Clarion Project.* Retrieved February 9, 2016, from http://www.clarionproject.org/analysis/association-muslim-social-scientists-north-america

[91] "IIIE" (n.d.) "Homepage of the Institute of Islamic Information and Education". IIIE.net. Retrieved February 9, 2016 from http://www.iiie.net/

[92] Ali, M. (November 1, 1997). *Islamophobia in America. State University of New York (SUNY) – Brockport Publications.* Retrieved February 9, 2016, from http://www.ilaam.net/PDF/Islamophobia.pdf

[93] "The Sunnah" (n.d.). "Sunnah: Sayings and Teachings of Prophet Muhammad" *Sunnah.com.* Retrieved February 9, 2016, from http://sunnah.com/

[94] "Al Sirat." (n.d.). "The Al-Sirat: *Dictionary Online.* Retrieved February 9, 2016, from http://dictionary.reference.com/browse/al-sirat

[95] "Hudood." (1973). "The Hudood Laws " *The Islamic Constitution of Pakistan.* Retrieved February 9, 2016, from http://www.pakistani.org/pakistan/legislation/hudood.html

[96] Baiannoie, M. (December 27, 1996). "Definition of the Word Deen and the Word Islam." *Islamic Center of North Carolina.* Retrieved February 9, 2016, from http://www.islam1.org/khutub/Defn__of_Deen_&_Islam.htm

[97] "The Charter" (n.d.). "The Charter of the Organisation of the Islamic Conference." *Organization of the Islamic Cooperation.* Retrieved February 9, 2016, from http://www.comcec.org/TR_YE/Yeni_Site_Dokumanlar/Basic_Documents/OIC_Charter.pdf

[98] "Al Quds" (n.d.) "Al-Qud Al-Shariff and Palestine." *The Islamic Educational Scientific and Cultural Organization.* Retrieved February 9, 2016, from http://www.isesco.org.ma/al-quds-al-sharif-palestine/

[99] "UN Res.181" (November, 29, 2002), "United Nations, 1947, Resolution 181 approves the creation of Israel, the Jewish State". Facts of Israel.com Retrieved February 9, 2016, from http://www.factsofisrael.com/blog/archives/000520.html

[100] "Ten-Year Program". (December 1, 2005). "Ten-Year Program of Action to Meet the Challenges Facing the Muslim Ummah in the 21st Century." *The Organisation for Islamic Cooperation.* Retrieved February 9, 2016, from http://www.oic-oci.org/ex-summit/english/10-years-plan.htm

[101] Kendal, E. (2008, March 26). "OIC: Eliminating 'defamation' of Islam". *Islamic Research Foundation International.* Retrieved February 9, 2016, from http://www.irfi.org/articles/articles_2051_2100/oic - eliminating 'defamation' of islamhtml.htm

[102] "Islamophobia Observatory" (n.d.) "The Islamophobia Observatory of the Organisation for Islamic Cooperation," (n.d.). *Organisation for Islamic Cooperation.* Retrieved February 9, 2016, from http://www.oic-oci.org/oicv2/page/?p_id=182&p_ref=61&lan=en

[103] "Thirty-fourth Session" (May, 1, 2007). "The Thirty-Fourth session of the Islamic Cabinet of Foreign Ministries." *The Organisation for Islamic Cooperation.* Retrieved February 9, 2016, from http://www.oic-oci.org/34icfm/english/main.htm

[104] "Islamophobia Worst Form of Terrorism" (May 17, 2007). "Islamophobia Worst Form of Terrorism". *Arab News Network.* Retrieved February 9, 2016 from http://www.arabnews.com/node/298472

[105] Islamophobia. (n.d.). *The Organisation for Islamic Cooperation*. Retrieved February 9, 2016, from http://www.oic-oci.org/oicv2/page/?p_id=182&p_ref=61&lan=en

[106] KUNA (March 13, 2008). "OIC Islamophobia Observatory Presents First Report to Islamic Summit." *Kuwait News Agency*. Retrieved February 9, 2016, from http://twocircles.net/2008mar13/oic_islamophobia_observatory_presents_first_report_islamic_summit.html#.VpZ6xHlRHct

[107] Peter, H. (2012). *Current Themes in Imer Research: Number 13*. Malmo University Publishing (Malmo). Retrieved February 9, 2016, from http://www.mah.se/upload/Forskningscentrum/MIM/CT/CT 13.pdf

[108] Charbonneau, L. (December 19, 2011). "UN condemns religious intolerance, drops 'defamation' line for first time in years." *Reuters News*. Retrieved February 9, 2016 from http://blogs.reuters.com/faithworld/2011/12/19/un-condemns-religious-intolerance-drops-defamation-line-for-first-time-in-years/

[109] Wasala, R. (December 7, 2014). "UN resolutions for combating defamation of religions". *Lankaweb News-Sri Lanka*. Retrieved February 9, 2016, from http://www.lankaweb.com/news/items/2014/12/07/un-resolutions-for-combating-defamation-of-religions/

[110] "Act XLV of 1860". (October 6, 1860). "Pakistani Penal Code Act XLV of 1860". *Financial Monitoring Unity, Pakistan Government*. Retrieved February 9, 2016, from http://www.fmu.gov.pk/docs/laws/Pakistan Penal Code.pdf

[111] BBC News. (2014, November 6) "What are Pakistan's Blasphemy Laws?" *British Broadcasting Corporation*. Retrieved February 9, 2016, from http://www.bbc.com/news/world-south-asia-12621225

[112] Wikipedia. (n.d.) "Blasphemy Laws." *Wikipedia Foundation*. Retrieved February 9, 2016, from https://en.wikipedia.org/wiki/Blasphemy_law

[113] BBC News. (March 17, 2011). "Malaysian Christian lawyer barred from Shariah courts". *British Broadcasting Corporation*. Retrieved February 9, 2016, from http://www.bbc.com/news/world-asia-pacific-12768939

[114] "UN RES. 6/164". (February 21, 2007). "United Nations General Assembly Resolution 6/164: Combating Defamation of Religions". *United Nations General Assembly*. Retrieved February 9, 2016, from http://www.refworld.org/cgi-bin/texis/vtx/rwmain?page=search&docid=45fe69342

[115] Khan, A. (January 1, 2007), Combating Defamation of Religions. *The American Muslim*. Retrieved February 1, 2016, From http://works.bepress.com/abu_kashif/35/

[116] "Combating Defamation of Religions". (August 29, 2007.) "Combating defamation of religions: Report of the Secretary-General A/62/288". *United Nations General Assembly*. Retrieved February 9, 2016, from http://www.refworld.org/docid/473313242.html

[117] "UN Press Release." (April 13, 2004). "Commission Adopts Resolutions on Combating Defamation of Religions; Right to Development." *United Nations General Assembly*. Retrieved February 9, 2016, from http://www.un.org/press/en/2004/hrcn1082.doc.htm

[118] "HRC Res. 7/19". (March 27, 2008). "Human Rights Council Resolution 7/19: Combating defamation of religions." *United Nations Human Rights Council*. Retrieved February 9, 2016, from http://ap.ohchr.org/documents/E/HRC/resolutions/A_HRC_RES_7_19.pdf

[119] "IFEX Press Release". (March 31, 2000). "UN resolution on defamation of religions goes against free speech, say IFEX members". *International Freedom of Expression Exchange.* (2010, March 31). Retrieved February 9, 2016, from http://www.ifex.org/international/2010/03/31/defamation_religions/

[120] Pakistan and the Combating Defamation of Religions UN Resolution. (2010, April 19). *Grand Trunk Road Web Page.* Retrieved February 9, 2016, from https://grandtrunkroad.wordpress.com/2010/04/19/pakistan-and-the-combating-defamation-of-religions-un-resolution/

[121] Chamberlain-Donahoe, E. (March 25, 2010). "Combatting Defamation of Religions: U.S. Explanation of Vote." *U.S. Mission to Geneva.* Retrieved February 9, 2016, from https://geneva.usmission.gov/2010/03/25/combatting-defamation-of-religions-u-s-explanation-of-vote/

[122] Human Rights Watch. (January 11, 2016). "King Salman's First Year of Rule Marked by Sustained Assault on Free Expression". *International Freedom of Expression Exchange.* Retrieved February 9, 2016, from https://www.ifex.org/saudi_arabia/2016/01/11/sustained_assault_on_free_expression/

[123] Committee on the Elimination of All Forms of Racial Discrimination (January 4, 1969). "International Convention on the Elimination of All Forms of Racial Discrimination". *United Nations Office of the High Commissioner on Human Rights.* Retrieved February 9, 2016, from http://www.ohchr.org/EN/ProfessionalInterest/Pages/CERD.aspx

[124] "Combating Intolerance". (March 22, 2012). "Combating Intolerance, Incitement to Violence and Violence Against Persons, Based on Religion/Belief" *OIC Human Rights: Human Rights in Islamic Countries.* Retrieved February 9, 2016, from https://oichumanrights.wordpress.com/2012/03/22/hrc-resolution-combating-intolerance-negative-stereotyping-and-stigmatization-of-and-discrimination-incitement-to-violence-and-violence-against-persons-based-on-religion-or-belief/

[125] Limon, M., Ghanea, N., & Por, H. (n.d.). "URG Policy Report: Combatting global religious intolerance." *Universal Rights Group.* Retrieved February 9, 2016, from http://www.universal-rights.org/urg-policy-reports/combatting-global-religious-intolerance-the-implementation-of-human-rights-council-resolution-1618/

[126] Esman, A. (2011, December 30). "Could You Be A Criminal? US Supports UN Anti-Free Speech Measure". *Forbes Online.* Retrieved February 9, 2016, from https://web.archive.org/web/20120108094147/http://www.forbes.com/sites/abigailesman/2011/12/30/could-you-be-a-criminal-us-supports-un-anti-free-speech-measure

[127] "Section 295C" (October 12, 1986). *Pakistan Criminal Code: Section 295C.* Retrieved February 9, 2016, from http://www.thepersecution.org/archive/10_c.html

[128] Clinton, H. (July 15, 2011)."Remarks at the Organization of the Islamic Conference (OIC) High-Level Meeting on Combating Religious Intolerance". *U.S. Department of State.* Retrieved February 9, 2016, from http://www.state.gov/secretary/20092013clinton/rm/2011/07/168636.htm

[129] Ibid.

[130] Johnson-Cook, S. (December 12, 2011). Remarks for Istanbul Process Conference. *U.S. State Department.* Retrieved February 9, 2016, from http://www.state.gov/j/drl/rls/rm/2011/178640.htm

[131] Cheruppa, H. (February 18, 2013). "OIC gears up to get denigration of religions criminalized." Saudi Gazette, retrieved January 14, 2016, from https://web.archive.org/web/20130220112839/http://www.saudigazette.com.sa/index.cfm?method=home.regcon&contentid=20130218153611

[132] Solaker, G. (2014, June 27). "Ekmeleddin Ihsanoglu, Turkish Opposition Candidate, Says 'Religion And Politics Should Be Kept Separate." *The Huffington Post.* Retrieved February 9, 2016, from http://www.huffingtonpost.com/2014/06/27/ekmeleddin-ihsanoglu-religion-politics_n_5536908.html

[133] United Nations High Commissioner on Human Rights. (March 23, 1976). *The International Covenant on Civil and Political Rights* Retrieved January 14, 2016, from http://www.ohchr.org/en/professionalinterest/pages/ccpr.aspx

[134] "Rabat Plan" (October 5, 2012). "Rabat Plan of Action on the prohibition of advocacy of national, racial or religious hatred that constitutes incitement to discrimination, hostility or violence". *Office of the High Commissioner for Human Rights.* Retrieved February 9, 2016 from http://www.ohchr.org/Documents/Issues/Opinion/SeminarRabat/Rabat_draft_outcome.pdf

[135] United Nations Human Rights Office of the High Commissioner. *United Nations Human Rights Homepage.* Retrieved February 9, 2016 from http://www.ohchr.org/EN/pages/home.aspx

[136] Shea, N. (2012, December 3). "American Again Submits to the Istanbul Process." *National Review Online* Retrieved February 9, 2016 at https://nationalreview.com/corner/334647/america-againsubmits-istanbul-process-shea

[138] Kozak, M. (June 2, 2013). "Statement By U.S. on the Way Forward with Istanbul Process". *U.S. Mission Geneva* Retrieved on January 13, 2006 at https://geneva.usmission.gov/

[139] Khan, A. (2014). *Doha Meeting Report for Advancing Religious Freedom.* Doha International Center for Interfaith Dialogue (Doha). Retrieved on February 9, 2016 from https://www.academia.edu/10450135/Doha_Meeting_Report_for_Advancing_Religious_Freedom_2014

[140] "Fifth Session" (June 3, 2015) "Fifth Session of the Istanbul Process". *International Federation of Human Rights.* Retrieved February 9, 2016 from http://IMG/PDF/fidh_written_submission_5thsession_of_the_istanbul_process-2.pdf

[141] Cheruppa, H. (February 18, 2013). "OIC gears up to get denigration of religions criminalized". *Saudi Gazette* Retrieved February 1, 2016, from https://web.archive.org/web/20130220112839/http://www.saudigazette.com.sa/index.cfm?method=home.regcon&contentid=20130218153611

[142] ABC News. (January 19, 2015) "10 killed in anti-Charlie Hebdo riots in Niger." *Australian Broadcasting Corporation.* Retrieved February 9, 2016 from http://www.abc.net.au/news/2015-01-20/charlie-hebdo-protesters-torch-45-churches-in-niger/6026534

[143] BrandeisNOW. (2009, April 21). "Professor Jytte Klausen talks about cartoon cataclysm in NOW interview". *Brandeis NOW.* Retrieved February 9, 2016, from http://www.brandeis.edu/now/2009/august/klausenbook.html

[144] 10 killed in anti-Charlie Hebdo riots in Niger. (2015 January, 19). ABC News. Retrieved on February 9, 2016 from http://www.abc.net.au/news/2015-01-20/charlie-hebdo-protesters-torch-45-churches-in-niger/6026534

[145] Report on Islamophobia. October 2013-April 2014: Presented to the 41st Council on Foreign Ministers (2014, June 8-9). Retrieved on February 9, 2016 http://www.oic-oci.org/oicv2/upload/islamophobia/2014/en/reports/islamphoba_7th_report_2014.pdf

[146] Limon, M., Ghanea, N., & Por, H. (n.d.). "URG Policy Report: Combatting global religious intolerance." *Universal Rights Group.* Retrieved February 9, 2016, from http://www.universal-

rights.org/urg-policy-reports/combatting-global-religious-intolerance-the-implementation-of-human-rights-council-resolution-1618/

[147] Watson, D. (February 6, 2002). "Testimony of AD Dale Watson in front of the Senate Select Committee on Intelligence." (February 6, 2002). *The Federal Bureau of Investigation*. Retrieved February 9, 2016 from https://www.fbi.gov/news/testimony/the-terrorist-threat-confronting-the-united-states.

[148] "About Us". (n.d.). "FBI Counterintelligence: About Us". *The Federal Bureau of Investigation Counterintelligence Division*. Retrieved February 9, 2016 from https://www.fbi.gov/about-us/investigate/counterintelligence/counterintelligence.

[149] "Richard Colvin Reed." (n.d.) "FBI History: Richard Colvin Reed". *The Federal Bureau of Investigation*. Retrieved February 9, 2016 from https://www.fbi.gov/about-us/history/imagesimages/timeline/january_2002.png/view.

[150] FBI Press Release. (February 13, 2002). "Director Meets with Key U.S. Leaders of National Arab, Muslim, and Sikh Organizations." (2002, February 13). *FBI National Press Office*. Retrieved February 9, 2016 from https://www.fbi.gov/news/pressrel/press-releases/value-of-the-continuing-assistance-from-the-arab-muslim-and-sikh-communities-in-the-overall-effort-to-provide-greater-security-for-all-americans.

[151] MPAC Press Release (April 1, 2003). "MPAC joins advisory committee to FBI's DC field office." (2003, April 1). *Muslim Public Affairs Council*. Retrieved February 9, 2016 from http://www.mpac.org/programs/government-relations/mpac-joins-advisory-committee-to-fbis-dc-field-office.php.

[152] IPT News. (n.d.) "Nihad Awad." *The Investigative Project on Terrorism*. Retrieved February 9, 2016 from http://www.investigativeproject.org/profile/113/nihad-awad.

[153] Traditional Values Coalition Press Release. (July 1, 2008) "TVC Tells Connolly: Return Contributions From Radical Islamic Lobby." *Saudi Watch*. Retrieved February 9, 2016 from https://saudiwatch.wordpress.com/2008/07/01/tvc-tells-connolly-return-contribution-from-radical-islamic-lobby/#more-54.

[154] "Who are We." (n.d.). "Council on American Islamic Relations: Who We Are". *Council on American-Islamic Relations*. Retrieved February 9, 2016 from http://www.cair.com/about-us/cair-who-we-are.html.

[155] "FBI Press Release." (2002, February 13). *FBI National Press Office*. Retrieved February 9, 2016 from https://www2.fbi.gov/pressrel/pressrel02/director021302.htm.

[156] Gaffney, F. (2002, June 28). "The truth about the AMC." *Fox News*. Retrieved February 9, 2016 from http://www.foxnews.com/story/2002/06/28/truth-about-amc.html.

[157] "MPAC joins advisory committee to FBI's DC field office." (2003, April 1). *Muslim Public Affairs Council*. Retrieved February 9, 2016 from http://www.mpac.org/programs/government-relations/mpac-joins-advisory-committee-to-fbis-dc-field-office.php.

[158] IPT News. (n.d.). "Nihad Awad." *The Investigative Project on Terrorism*. Retrieved February 9, 2016 from http://www.investigativeproject.org/profile/113/nihad-awad.

[159] IPT News. (n.d.). "Profile: Hamas." *The Investigative Project on Terrorism*. Retrieved February 9, 2016 from http://www.investigativeproject.org/profile/129/hamas.

[160] "Executive Order 12947". (January 23, 1995). "Executive Order 12947: Prohibiting Transactions With Terrorists Who Threaten To Disrupt the Middle East Peace Process." *The U.S. Federal Register*. Retrieved February 9, 2016 from https://www.gpo.gov/fdsys/pkg/FR-1995-01-25/pdf/X95-110125.pdf

[161] "FTO List" (n.d.). "Foreign Terrorist Organizations." *Bureau of Counterterrorism, U.S. Department of State.* Retrieved February 9, 2016 from http://www.state.gov/j/ct/rls/other/des/123085.htm.

[162] The Scrapbook. (June 17, 2002). "Guess Whose Coming To Lunch", *The Weekly Standard.* Volume 007, Issue 39. Retrieved February 9, 2016 from http://www.usasurvival.org/home/ck62102.shtml.

[163] "DOJ Press Release". (October 15, 2004). "Abdurahaman Alamoudi Sentenced to Jail in Terrorism Financing Case." *U.S. Department of Justice.* Retrieved February 9, 2016 from http://www.justice.gov/archive/opa/pr/2004/October/04_crm_698.htm

[164] "Attachment A" (n.d.) "Attachment A: List of Unindicted Co-Conspirators and/or Joint Venturers." *United States vs. Holy Land Foundation et al.* Retrieved February 9, 2016 from https://www.investigativeproject.org/documents/case_docs/423.pdf

[165] IPT News. (n.d) "Behind the Façade: The Muslim Public Affairs Council." *The Investigative Project on Terrorism.* Retrieved February 9, 2016 from http://www.investigativeproject.org/documents/misc/358.pdf.

[166] ICSC. (n.d.). "Homepage: Islamic Center of Southern California". *The Islamic Center of Southern California.* Retrieved February 9, 2016 from http://icsconline.org/.

[167] "Hassan al-Banna." (n.d.). *Encyclopedia of the Middle East.* Retrieved February 9, 2016 from http://www.mideastweb.org/Middle-East-Encyclopedia/hassan_al_banna.htm.

[168] "FBI Director Meets with Muslim, Sikh, and Arab-American Leaders." (2003, February 28). *FBI National Press Office.* Retrieved February 9, 2016 from http://iipdigital.usembassy.gov/st/english/texttrans/2003/03/20030304113646sdomowit@pd.state.gov0.0325281.html#axzz3mYzcgvGJ.

[169] MPAC Press Release. (March 1, 2003). "MPAC Meets with FBI Director Mueller." (2003, March 1). *Muslim Public Affairs Council.* Retrieved February 9, 2016 from http://www.mpac.org/programs/anti-terrorism-campaign/mpac-meets-with-fbi-director-mueller.php.

[170] "Homepage: ADC." (n.d.). *Arab-American Anti-Discrimination Committee.* Retrieved February 9, 2016 from http://www.adc.org/.

[171] AAI. (n.d.). "Homepage: Arab American Institute." *Arab American Institute.* Retrieved February 9, 2016 from http://www.aaiusa.org/.

[172] The Islamic Institute. (n.d). "Homepage: The Islamic Institute." *The Islamic Institute.* Retrieved February 9, 2016 from http://www.theislamicinstitute.org/.

[173] MPAC Press Release. (April 2, 2003). "MPAC Attends FBI Advisory Committee Meeting in DC Field Office." *Muslim Public Affairs Committee.* Retrieved February 9, 2016 from http://www.mpac.org/programs/government-relations/mpac-attends-fbi-advisory-committee-meeting-in-dc-field-office.php.

[174] FBI Press Release (July 9, 2004). "Department of Justice, FBI Reinforces Commitment to Working with Leaders of Muslim, Sikh, and Arab-American Communities.". *FBI National Press Office.* Retrieved February 9, 2016 from https://www.fbi.gov/news/pressrel/press-releases/department-of-justice-federal-bureau-of-investigation-reinforce-commitment-to-working-with-leaders-of-muslim-sikh-and-arab-american-communities.

[175] MPAC Press Release (January 11, 2006). "Muslim & Arab Leaders Meet with FBI on Domestic Surveillance Reports." *Muslim Public Affairs Council.* Retrieved February 9, 2016 from http://www.mpac.org/programs/anti-terrorism-campaign/muslim-arab-leaders-meet-with-fbi-on-domestic-surveillance-reports.php.

[176] Muslim Advocates (n.d.). "Homepage: Muslim Advocates." *Muslim Advocates*. Retrieved February 9, 2016 from https://www.muslimadvocates.org/.

[177] ADAMS Center. (n.d.). "Homepage: All-Dulles Area Muslim Society Center." (n.d.). *ADAMS Center*. Retrieved February 9, 2016 from http://www.adamscenter.org/.

[178] Guandolo, J. (March 9, 2015). "ADAMS Center in Sterling, VA: Jihad Central." *The Counter Jihad Report*. Retrieved February 9, 2016 from http://counterjihadreport.com/tag/imam-mohamed-magid/.

[179] MPAC Press Release. (January 11, 2006). "Muslim & Arab Leaders Meet with FBI on Domestic Surveillance Reports." *Muslim Public Affairs Council*. Retrieved February 9, 2016 from http://www.mpac.org/programs/anti-terrorism-campaign/muslim-arab-leaders-meet-with-fbi-on-domestic-surveillance-reports.php.

[180] FBI Counterterrorism Division (May 10, 2006.) "The Radicalization Process: From Conversion to Jihad." *FBI*. Retrieved February 9, 2016 from http://media.cygnus.com/files/cygnus/document/OFCR/2012/JAN/theradicalizationprocessfromco_10619306.pdf.

[181] The Religion of Peace (n.d.) "List of Islamic Terror Attacks from 2011." *The Religion of Peace.com* Retrieved February 9, 2016 from http://www.thereligionofpeace.com/attacks-2011.htm.

[182] MPAC Press Release. (October 5, 2011). "MPAC Co-Signs Letter to FBI Demanding Reformation in Flawed Anti-Muslim Training.". *Muslim Public Affairs Council*. Retrieved February 9, 2016 from http://www.mpac.org/programs/government-relations/mpac-co-signs-letter-to-fbi-demanding-reformation-in-flawed-anti-muslim-training.php.

[183] ACLU. (n.d.). "Homepage: American Civil Liberties Union." (n.d.). *American Civil Liberties Union*. Retrieved February 9, 2016 from https://www.aclu.org/.

[184] "DeBlasio Letter". (September 21, 2015). "Letter from CAIR and ACLU Et Al. to New York City Mayor Bill DeBlasio." *Politico New York*. Retrieved February 9, 2016 from http://www.capitalnewyork.com/sites/default/files/092115%20Coalition%20Letter%20to%20Mayor%20Re%20CVE.pdf.

[185] MPAC Press Release. (February 28, 2007). "MPAC Meets with DHS Secretary Chertoff & FBI Director Mueller." *Muslim Public Affairs Council*. Retrieved February 9, 2016 from http://www.mpac.org/programs/government-relations/mpac-meets-with-dhs-secretary-chertoff-fbi-director-mueller.php.

[186] IPT News. "Profile: Salam al-Marayati." (n.d.). *The Investigative Project on Terrorism*. Retrieved February 9, 2016 from http://www.investigativeproject.org/profile/114/salam-al-marayati.

[187] "Ali-Salaam Award". (December 6, 2007). "Muhammad Ali-Salaam Given Award by FBI !?!?" *The Miss Kelly Weblog*. Retrieved February 9, 2016 from http://misskelly.typepad.com/miss_kelly_/2007/12/muhammad-ali-sa.html.

[188] Rosso, P. (August 9, 2014). "Community Advocate Muhammad Ali-Salaam honored in Roxbury." *Boston.com*. Retrieved February 9, 2016 from http://www.boston.com/yourtown/news/roxbury/2013/08/hold_muhammad_ali-salaam_honored_in_roxbury.html.

[189] FBI Podcast (April 4, 2014)."FBI Director's Community Leadership Awards Podcast." (2014, April 4). *FBI Podcasts and Radio*. Retrieved February 9, 2016 from https://www.fbi.gov/news/podcasts/thisweek/the-directors-community-leadership-awards.mp3/view.

[190] Schilling, A. (December 4, 2007). "Boston Muslim Community Leader Receives Law Enforcement Award." *Muslim American Society: Boston Chapter*. Retrieved February 9, 2016 from https://web.archive.org/web/20080108050107/http:/www.masboston.org/index.php?action=view&id=65&module=newsmodule&src=@random41940a897e943.

[191] ICNE (n.d.) "Homepage: Islamic Council of New England." *The Islamic Council of New England*. Retrieved February 9, 2016 from http://islamiccouncilne.org/.

[192] ADC-Michigan (September 8, 2011). "BRIDGES 10th Anniversary Reception, September 9, 2011." *Arab America*. Retrieved February 9, 2016 from http://www.arabamerica.com/bridges-10th-anniversary-reception-september-9-2011/.

[193] "MAS Boston." (n.d.). "Muslim American Society-Boston." *Islamic Society of Boston Cultural Center*. Retrieved February 9, 2016 from http://isbcc.org/mas-boston/.

[194] Rosso, P. (2013, August 9). "Community Advocate Muhammad Ali-Salaam honored in Roxbury." *Boston.com*. Retrieved February 9, 2016 from http://www.boston.com/yourtown/news/roxbury/2013/08/hold_muhammad_ali-salaam_honored_in_roxbury.html.

[195] Serjeant, J. (November 15, 2007). "L.A. Police Drop Controversial Muslim Mapping Plan." *Reuters News*. Retrieved February 9, 2016 from http://www.reuters.com/article/us-usa-security-muslims-idUSN1560353720071115.

[196] IPT News (n.d.) "Dossier: Muslim American Society" *The Investigative Project on Terrorism*. Retrieved February 9, 2016 fromhttp://www.investigativeproject.org/documents/misc/85.pdf.

[197] Jones, B. and Cullinane, S. (July 3, 2013). *Cable News Network*. Retrieved February 9, 2016 from http://www.cnn.com/2013/07/03/world/africa/egypt-muslim-brotherhood-explainer/index.html.

[198] El-Hudaibi, M. (February 1, 2010). "The Principles of the Muslim Brotherhood." *Ikhwan Web*. Retrieved February 9, 2016 from http://www.ikhwanweb.com/article.php?id=813&ref=search.php.

[199] Rosso, P. (2013, August 9). "Community Advocate Muhammad Ali-Salaam honored in Roxbury." *Boston.com*. Retrieved February 9, 2016 from http://www.boston.com/yourtown/news/roxbury/2013/08/hold_muhammad_ali-salaam_honored_in_roxbury.html.

[200] "Ali-Salaam Award". (December 6, 2007). "Muhammad Ali-Salaam Given Award by FBI !?!?" *The Miss Kelly Weblog*. Retrieved February 9, 2016 from http://misskelly.typepad.com/miss_kelly_/2007/12/muhammad-ali-sa.html

[201] Hanson, J. (May 13, 2015). "The Dirty Dozen- President Obama's Model Mosque." *Center for Security Policy*. Retrieved February 9, 2016 from http://www.centerforsecuritypolicy.org/2015/05/13/the-dirty-dozen-president-obamas-model-mosque/.

[202] Pipes, D. (October 29, 2003). "The Islamic Society of Boston & the Politicians' Red Faces." *Daniel Pipes: Middle East Forum*. Retrieved February 9, 2016 from http://www.danielpipes.org/blog/2003/10/the-islamic-society-of-boston-the.

[203] APT (n.d.). "Homepage: Americans for Peace & Tolerance."*Americans for Peace & Tolerance*. Retrieved February 9, 2016 from http://www.peaceandtolerance.org/.

[204] ISBCC. (October 23, 2013). "Hossam Al-Jabri: Lessons from the Quran (video)." *Islamic Society of Boston Cultural Center*. Retrieved February 9, 2016 from http://isbcc.org/hossam-al-jabri-the-quran/.

[205] IPT News. "Jamal Badawi: Enduring Link to ISNA's Radical Past." (2012, May 8). *Investigative Project on Terrorism.* Retrieved February 9, 2016 from http://www.investigativeproject.org/3569/jamal-badawi-enduring-link-to-isna-radical-past.

[206] "ISB Complaint" (2015). "Complaint and Jury Trial Demand". *Islamic Society of Boston et al. vs. Boston Herald et al.* Retrieved February 9, 2016 from http://www.jewssupportthemosque.org/files/ISB_Complaint.pdf.

[207] Mauro, R. (December 10, 2013). "Profile: The Islamic Society of Boston." *The Clarion Project.* Retrieved February 9, 2016 from http://www.clarionproject.org/analysis/islamic-society-boston.

[208] Sperry, P. (September 7, 2014). "Boston bombers; mosque tied to ISIS." *The New York Post.* Retrieved February 9, 2016 from http://nypost.com/2014/09/07/jihadi-behind-beheading-videos-linked-to-notorious-us-mosque/?utm_campaign=SocialFlow&utm_source=NYPTwitter&utm_medium=SocialFlow.

[209] APT (September 3, 2015). "Boston Globe in Cover-up of Islamist Network in New England." *Americans for Peace & Tolerance,* Retrieved February 9, 2016 from https://creepingsharia.wordpress.com/2015/09/03/boston-globe-in-cover-up-of-islamist-network-in-new-england/.

[210] Center for Security Policy. (August 11, 2015). "The Islamic Society of Boston's Building Controversy." *Center for Security Policy.* Retrieved at http://www.centerforsecuritypolicy.org/2015/08/11/the-islamic-society-of-bostons-building-controversy/.

[211] "MAS Boston." (n.d.). "Muslim American Society-Boston." *Islamic Society of Boston Cultural Center.* Retrieved February 9, 2016 from http://isbcc.org/mas-boston/.

[212] "Margo Schlanger Brief Bio." (n.d.). "University of Michigan Law School Faculty: Margo Schlanger". *University of Michigan Law.* Retrieved February 9, 2016 from http://www.law.umich.edu/FacultyBio/Pages/FacultyBio.aspx?FacID=mschlan.

[213] Al-Hajal, K. (December 20 2008). "ADC fights to keep doors open amid economic downturn." *The Arab American News.* Retrieved February 9, 2016 from http://www.arabamericannews.com/news/news/id_1798/ADC-fights-to-keep-doors-open-amid-economic-downturn.html.

[214] FBI Directorate of Intelligence. (January 28, 2008.) "Counterterrorism Analytical Lexicon. *FBI Directorate of Intelligence: Counterterrorism Division.* Retrieved February 9, 2016 from http://www.cryptocomb.org/FBI-Counter-Terrorism-Analytical-Lexicon.pdf

[215] DHS Office of Intelligence and Analysis (November 10, 2011). "Domestic Terrorism and Homegrown Violent Extremism Lexicon." *DHS Office of Intelligence and Analysis.* Retrieved February 9, 2016 from https://info.publicintelligence.net/DHS-ExtremismLexicon.pdf.

[216] Halper, D. (July 13, 2014). "Holder: "Homegrown Violent Extremists… Keep Me Up at Night." *The Weekly Standard.* Retrieved February 9, 2016 from http://www.weeklystandard.com/article/holder-homegrown-violent-extremists-keep-me-night/796475.

[217] FBI Podcast (February 15, 2013). "Homegrown Violent Extremism." *FBI Podcasts and Radio.* Retrieved February 9, 2016 from https://www.fbi.gov/news/podcasts/thisweek/homegrown-violent-extremism.mp3/view.

[218] Gill, K. (n.d.). "Oaths of Office For Federal Officials." *About.com.* Retrieved February 9, 2016 from http://uspolitics.about.com/od/usgovernment/a/oaths_of_office_4.htm.

[219] Argiriou, S. (n.d). "Terry Stop Update: The Law, Field Examples and Analysis," FLETC.GOV Retrieved February 9, 2016 from https://www.fletc.gov/sites/default/files/imported_files/training/programs/legal-division/downloads-articles-and-faqs/research-by-subject/4th-amendment/terrystopupdate.pdf

[220] DHS CRCL (January, 2008). "Terminology to Define the Terrorists: Recommendations from American Muslims." *DHS Office of Civil Rights and Civil Liberties.* Retrieved February 9, 2016 from http://www.dhs.gov/xlibrary/assets/dhs_crcl_terminology_08-1-08_accessible.pdf.

[221] UPI. (March 18, 2010). "FBI Urges Outreach to Halt Radicalization." *Allied Media Corp.* Retrieved February 9, 2016 from http://www.allied-media.com/law_enforcement/FBI_urges_outreach_to_halt_radicalization.html.

[222] "About" (n.d.) "Homepage: Allied Media Corp." *Allied Media Corp.* Retrieved February 9, 2016 from http://www.allied-media.com/index.html.

[223] CAIR Press Release. (August 3, 2010). "Coalition Concerned that Anti-Islam Leader Trained FBI." *Common Dreams.* Retrieved February 9, 2016 from http://www.commondreams.org/newswire/2010/08/03/coalition-concerned-anti-islam-leader-trained-fbi.

[224] Ibid.

[225] American Freedom Defense Initiative. (April 29, 2013). "AFDI/SIOA Calls for Closure of Mosques That Breed Jihad Terror." *Stop Islamization of America.* Retrieved February 9, 2016 from http://freedomdefense.typepad.com/sioa/.

[226] "DOJ Guidance" (December 8, 2014.) "Guidance or Federal Law Enforcement Agencies Regarding the Use of Race, Ethnicity, Gender, National Origin, Religion, Sexual Orientation, or Gender Identity." *U.S. Department of Justice.* Retrieved February 9, 2016 from http://www.justice.gov/sites/default/files/ag/pages/attachments/2014/12/08/use-of-race-policy.pdf.

[227] Durbin, R. (March 27, 2012). "Sen. Durbin Letter to FBI Director Mueller III." *National Public Radio.* Retrieved February 9, 2016 from http://www.npr.org/blogs/thetwo-way/2012/fbi-training-letter.pdf.

[228] Peralta, E. (March 28, 2012). "FBI Pulls Offensive Counterterrorism Training Materials. *National Public Radio.* Retrieved February 9, 2016 from http://www.npr.org/sections/thetwo-way/2012/03/28/149564721/fbi-pulls-offensive-counterterrorism-training-materials.

[229] Durbin, R. (March 27, 2012). "Sen. Durbin Letter to FBI Director Mueller III." *National Public Radio.* Retrieved February 9, 2016 from http://www.npr.org/blogs/thetwo-way/2012/fbi-training-letter.pdf.

[230] FBI Bulletin (May 28, 2015). "Militia Extremists Expand target Sets to Include Muslims." *FBI Intelligence Bulletin Counterterrorism Division.* Retrieved February 9, 2016 from https://info.publicintelligence.net/FBI-MilitiaTargetingMuslims.pdf.

[231] Inskeep, S. (July 27, 2005). "Shifting Language: Trading Terrorism for Extremism." *NPR* Retrieved February 9, 2016 from http://www.npr.org/templates/story/story.php?storyId=4772826.

[232] Stevenson, R. (August 4, 2005). "President Makes It Clear: Phrase Is 'War on Terror.'" *The New York Times.* Retrieved February 9, 2016 from http://www.nytimes.com/2005/08/04/politics/president-makes-it-clear-phrase-is-war-on-terror.html?_r=1.

[233] Associated Press (April 7, 2007). "Hoyer Meets Official from Egypt's Banned Muslim Brotherhood." *Fox News*. Retrieved February 9, 2016 from http://www.foxnews.com/story/2007/04/07/hoyer-meets-official-from-egypt-banned-muslim-brotherhood.html.

[234] BBC News. (December 25, 2013). "Profile: Egypt's Muslim Brotherhood." *BBC News*. Retrieved February 9, 2016 fromhttp://www.bbc.com/news/world-middle-east-12313405.

[235] IkhwanWeb. (January 16, 2012). "Profile of Dr. Mohamed Katatni, FJP's Nominee for Parliament Chairman." *IkhwanWeb*. Retrieved February 9, 2016 from http://www.ikhwanweb.com/article.php?id=29561.

[236] Londono, E. (February 8, 2011.) "Muslim Brotherhood Eyes Comeback in Egypt. *The Washington Post*, 1-2. Retrieved February 9, 2016 from http://www.washingtonpost.com/wp-dyn/content/article/2011/02/07/AR2011020706037.html.

[237] Bureau of International Information Programs (September 24, 2013). "Introducing John Berry, U.S. Ambassador to Australia." (2013, September 24). Retrieved February 9, 2016 from http://iipdigital.usembassy.gov/st/english/video/2013/09/20130923283364.html#axzz3mx4y2wrd.

[238] "Francis Ricciardone, Jr." (n.d.). "Biography of U.S. Ambassador to Turkey Francis J. Ricciardone, Jr." *U.S. Embassy Turkey* Retrieved February 9, 2016 from http://turkey.usembassy.gov/ambassador_francis_j_ricciardone.html.

[239] "Jon B. Alterman" (n.d.). "Biography of Jon B. Alterman." *Center for Strategic International Studies*. Retrieved February 9, 2016 from http://csis.org/expert/jon-b-alterman.

[240] DHS CRCL (January, 2008). "Terminology to Define the Terrorists: Recommendations from American Muslims." *DHS Office of Civil Rights and Civil Liberties*. Retrieved February 9, 2016 from http://www.dhs.gov/xlibrary/assets/dhs_crcl_terminology_08-1-08_accessible.pdf.

[241] "Michael Chertoff" (n.d.). "Biography of Michael Chertoff, Homeland Security Secretary 2005 - 2009." *Department of Homeland Security*. Retrieved February 9, 2016 fromhttp://www.dhs.gov/michael-chertoff-homeland-security-secretary-2005-2009.

[242] Sutherland, D. (August 10, 2010). "Homeland Security Office for Civil Rights and Civil Liberties: A One-Year Review." *The Heritage Foundation*. Washington, D.C. Retrieved February 9, 2016 from http://www.heritage.org/research/lecture/homeland-security-office-for-civil-rights-and-civil-liberties-a-one-year-review.

[243] DHS CRCL (January, 2008). "Terminology to Define the Terrorists: Recommendations from American Muslims." *DHS Office of Civil Rights and Civil Liberties*. Retrieved February 9, 2016 from http://www.dhs.gov/xlibrary/assets/dhs_crcl_terminology_08-1-08_accessible.pdf.

[244] Zambelis, C. (July 11, 2006). "Florida African-American Group Inspired by al-Qaeda Ideology." *The Jamestown Foundation Terrorism Focus, Vol.3 Issue. 27*. Retrieved February 9, 2016 from http://www.jamestown.org/single/?tx_ttnews%5Btt_news%5D=834#.VpUtAcArLPB

[245] Joesclyn, T. (December 5, 2011). "DC court: Iran showed al Qaeda how to bomb embassies." *The Long War Journal*. Retrieved February 2, 2016 from http://www.longwarjournal.org/archives/2011/12/dc_court_iran_showed.php

[246] Phillips, J. (August 14, 2012). "Muslim Brotherhood Consolidates Control over Egypt." *Daily Signal*. Retrieved February 9, 2016 from http://dailysignal.com/2012/08/14/muslim-brotherhood-consolidates-control-over-egypt/.

[247] Wheat, T. (April 8, 2012). "Obama Administration Courts the Muslim Brotherhood." *Daily Signal.* Retrieved February 9, 2016 fromhttp://dailysignal.com/2012/04/18/obama-administration-courts-the-muslim-brotherhood/.

[248] Real Clear Politics (January 20, 2015). "Earnest: "The World is not at war with Islam;" We're at war with those who carry out attacks in the name of Islam." *Real Clear Politics.* Retrieved February 9, 2016 from http://www.realclearpolitics.com/video/2015/01/20/josh_earnest_world_not_at_war_with_islam_war_with_those_who_carry_out_attacks_in_name_islam.html.

[249] Kuruvila, M. (June 5, 2007). "Security agency enlisting Muslims to rebut radicals: Idea is to engage young minds in ideological battle." *SFGate.* Retrieved February 9, 2016 fromhttp://www.sfgate.com/news/article/Security-agency-enlisting-Muslims-to-rebut-2557543.php

[250] Frieden, T. (October 16, 2001). "Ashcroft meets with Muslim, Arab leaders." *Cable News Network.* Retrieved February 9, 2016 fromhttp://www.cnn.com/2001/US/10/16/ashcroft.arab.meet/index.html

[251] FBI Press Release. (July 9, 2004). "Department Of Justice, FBI Reinforce Commitment to Working with Leaders of Muslim, Sikh and Arab-American Communities." Federal Bureau of Investigation. Retrieved February 9, 2016 from https://www.fbi.gov/news/pressrel/press-releases/department-of-justice-federal-bureau-of-investigation-reinforce-commitment-to-working-with-leaders-of-muslim-sikh-and-arab-american-communities.

[252] IPT News (n.d.). "Who is Kifah Mustapha: An IPT Investigative Report:," *Investigative Project on Terrorism.* Retrieved February 9, 2016 fromhttp://www.investigativeproject.org/documents/misc/440.pdf.

[253] Lee, M. (April 24, 2008). "'Jihadist' Booted from Government Lexicon." *Associated Press.* Retrieved February 9, 2016 from http://web.archive.org/web/20080505185757/http:/ap.google.com/article/ALeqM5i3X6Gha4z-MCq9pU0vC4FWqDCXrwD908CUGO0.

[254] CNN (May 8, 2008). "Agency Urges Caution with Terrorist Language." *Cable News Network.* Retrieved February 9, 2016 from http://www.cnn.com/2008/US/05/30/terrorist.terms/index.html?section=cnn_latest.

[255] Emerson, S. (April 25, 2008). "Dangerous World Games." *The Investigative Project on Terrorism.* Retrieved February 9, 2016 from http://www.investigativeproject.org/653/dangerous-word-games#.

[256] Emerson, S. (May 2, 2008). "Investigative Project Releases Gov't Memos Curtailing Speech in War on Terror." Investigative Project on Terrorism. Retrieved February 9, 2016 from http://www.investigativeproject.org/659/investigative-project-releases-govt-memos-curtailing-speech.

[257] Global Muslim Brotherhood Daily Watch. (May 4, 2008). "Analysis: DHS Memo Supports Muslim Brotherhood Influence Over U.S. Counter-Terrorism Language." The Global Muslim Brotherhood Daily Watch. Retrieved February 9, 2016 from http://www.globalmbwatch.com/2008/05/04/analysis-dhs-memo-supports-muslim-brotherhood-influence-counter-terrorism-language/.

[258] Spencer, R. (May 29, 20089). "The great war against nothing in particular." *Jihad Watch.* Retrieved February 9, 2016 fromhttp://www.jihadwatch.org/2008/05/the-great-war-against-nothing-in-particular.

[259] Seibold, M. (May 21, 2008). "'Words matter': Homeland Security rolls out newspeak campaign, cautions against use of terms like 'jihadists,' 'Islamic terrorists,' 'Islamists' and 'holy warriors'." Jihad Watch. Retrieved February 9, 2016 fromhttp://www.jihadwatch.org/2008/05/words-matter-homeland-security-rolls-out-newspeak-campaign-cautions-against-use-of-terms-like-jihadi.

[260] Napolitano, J. (February 9, 2011). "Testimony of Secretary Janet Napolitano Before the United states House of Representatives Committee on Homeland Security, "Understanding the Homeland Threat Landscape- Considerations for the 112th Congress." House Committee on Homeland Security. Retrieved February 9, 2016 from http://www.dhs.gov/news/2011/02/09/secretary-napolitanos-testimony-understanding-homeland-threat-landscape.

[261] Der Spiegel. (March 16, 2009). "Interview with Homeland Security Secretary Janet Napolitano: 'Away From the Politics of Fear'." *Spiegel Online.* Retrieved February 9, 2016 from http://www.spiegel.de/international/world/interview-with-homeland-security-secretary-janet-napolitano-away-from-the-politics-of-fear-a-613330.html.

[262] Napolitano, J. (February 9, 2011). "Testimony of Secretary Janet Napolitano Before the United states House of Representatives Committee on Homeland Security, "Understanding the Homeland Threat Landscape- Considerations for the 112th Congress." *House Committee on Homeland Security.* Retrieved February 9, 2016 from http://www.dhs.gov/news/2011/02/09/secretary-napolitanos-testimony-understanding-homeland-threat-landscape.

[263] Malik, S.K. (1992) *The Quranic Concept of War.* Adam Publishers & Distributors.(Delhi) Retrieved February 9, 2016 from https://azelin.files.wordpress.com/2010/08/general-s-k-malik-the-quranic-concept-of-war.pdf.

[264] "Quran 3:110". (n.d.) "The Quran: English Meanings Sura 3: Verse 110". *Sahih International.* Retrieved February 9, 2016 from http://corpus.quran.com/translation.jsp?chapter=3&verse=110

[265] "CVE" (n.d.) "Countering Violent Extremism: DHS Priorities for Understanding and Countering Violent Extremism." *Department of Homeland Security.* Retrieved February 9, 2016 from http://www.dhs.gov/topic/countering-violent-extremism.

[266] "DHS's Approach" (n.d.) "DHS's Approach to Countering Violent Extremism." *Department of Homeland Security.* Retrieved February 9, 2016 from http://www.dhs.gov/dhss-approach-countering-violent-extremism.

[267] "CVE". (n.d.) "Countering Violent Extremism: DHS Priorities for Understanding and Countering Violent Extremism." *Department of Homeland Security.* Retrieved February 9, 2016 from http://www.dhs.gov/topic/countering-violent-extremism.

[268] Judicial Watch. (July 29, 2010). "Documents Uncovered by JW Detail Meeting between DHS Secretary Napolitano and Controversial Islamic 'Community Leaders'." Judicial Watch Retrieved February 9, 2016 from http://www.judicialwatch.org/press-room/press-releases/documents-uncovered-jw-detail-meeting-between-dhs-secretary-napolitano-and-controversi/.

[269] Pollock, R. (February 17, 2010). "Napolitano meets with Muslim Brotherhood Leaders." *PJ Media.* Retrieved February 9, 2016 from https://pjmedia.com/blog/napolitano-meets-with-muslim-brotherhood-leaders-pjm-exclusive/.

[270] Sweir, R. (March 18, 2014). "An Analysis of President Obama's Terrorism Doctrine." *The Counter Jihad Report.* Retrieved February 9, 2016 from http://counterjihadreport.com/2014/03/18/an-analysis-of-president-obamas-terrorism-doctrine/.

[271] HSAC (n.d.) "The Homeland Security Advisory Council." *Department of Homeland Security.* Retrieved February 9, 2016 from http://www.dhs.gov/homeland-security-advisory-council.

272 Judicial Watch. (July 29, 2010). "Documents Uncovered by JW Detail Meeting between DHS Secretary Napolitano and Controversial Islamic 'Community Leaders'." *Judicial Watch* Retrieved

February 9, 2016 from http://www.judicialwatch.org/press-room/press-releases/documents-uncovered-jw-detail-meeting-between-dhs-secretary-napolitano-and-controversi/.

[273] IPT News (n.d.) "Dossier: Muslim American Society" *The Investigative Project on Terrorism*. Retrieved February 9, 2016 from http://www.investigativeproject.org/documents/misc/85.pdf.

[274] "Islamic Society of North America: An IPT Investigative Report." (n.d.) *Investigative Project on Terrorism*. Retrieved February 9, 2016 from https://www.investigativeproject.org/documents/misc/275.pdf.

[275] "Muslim Student Association: The Investigative Project on Terrorism Dossier." (n.d.) *Investigative Project on Terrorism*. Retrieved February 9, 2016 fromhttp://www.investigativeproject.org/documents/misc/84.pdf.

[276] McCarthy, A. (August 7, 2012). "The History of MPAC". *National Review Online*. Retrieved February 9, 2016 fromhttp://www.nationalreview.com/article/313257/history-mpac-andrew-c-mccarthy

[277] "Hossam Al-Jabri: Lessons from the Quran." (2013, October 22). *Islamic Society of Boston Cultural Center*. Retrieved February 9, 2016 fromhttp://isbcc.org/hossam-al-jabri-the-quran/.

[278] Spencer, R. (2008, December 9). Controversial Boston mosque tied to Muslim Brotherhood's "grand jihad in eliminating and destroying Western civilization from within." *Jihad Watch*. Retrieved February 9, 2016 from http://www.jihadwatch.org/2008/12/controversial-boston-mosque-tied-to-muslim-brotherhoods-grand-jihad-in-eliminating-and-destroying-we.

[279] Kofol, A. (2001, October 4). "Expert Panelists Discuss Islam." *The Harvard Crimson*. Retrieved February 9, 2016 from http://www.thecrimson.com/article/2001/10/4/expert-panelists-discuss-islam-last-night/?page=single.

[280] Elibiary, M (March 15, 2010) "Muslim Radicalization at Roxbury Mosque." *Vimeo*. Retrieved February 9, 2016 from https://vimeo.com/12048080.

[281] Clarke, R. (October 22, 2003). "Statement of Richard A. Clarke Before the United states Banking Committee." *Investigative Project on Terrorism*. Retrieved February 9, 2016 fromhttp://www.investigativeproject.org/documents/testimony/54.pdf.

[282] Judicial Watch. (February 4, 2010). "Judicial Watch FOIA: David O'Leary emails." *Judicial Watch*. Retrieved February 9, 2016 from http://www.judicialwatch.org/files/documents/2010/dhs-napolitano-jan-meeting-docs-excerpt-1.pdf.

[283] "Office of Legislative Affairs". (n.d.) "Office of Legislative Affairs: Mission, Leadership and Organization" *Department of Homeland Security*. Retrieved February 9, 2016 from http://www.dhs.gov/about-office-legislative-affairs.

[284] CRCL. (n.d.) "Civil Rights and Civil Liberties: Compliance Branch." *Department of Homeland Security*. Retrieved February 9, 2016 from http://www.dhs.gov/complaints.

[285] HSAC. (n.d.) "Homeland Security Advisory Council." (n.d.) *Department of Homeland Security*. Retrieved February 9, 2016 from http://www.dhs.gov/homeland-security-advisory-council.

[286] Pollock, R. (February 17, 2010). "Napolitano meets with Muslim Brotherhood Leaders." *PJ Media*. Retrieved February 9, 2016 fromhttps://pjmedia.com/blog/napolitano-meets-with-muslim-brotherhood-leaders-pjm-exclusive/.

[287] "DHS Read Out." (January 28, 2010). "Readout of Secretary Napolitano's Meeting with Faith-Based Community Leaders."*Department of Homeland Security*. Retrieved February 9, 2016

fromhttp://www.dhs.gov/news/2010/01/28/readout-secretary-napolitanos-meeting-faith-based-and-community-leaders.

[288] "Walid Phares." (n.d.) "Author Biography: Walid Phares". *Simon & Schuster*. Retrieved February 9, 2016 from http://authors.simonandschuster.com/Walid-Phares/68356551.

[289] "About FDD." (n.d.) "About the Foundation for Defense of Democracies". *Foundation for Defense of Democracies*. Retrieved February 9, 2016 from http://www.defenddemocracy.org/about-fdd.

[290] Kouri, J. (February 2, 2011). "Napolitano, Muslim Brotherhood affiliates met secretly". *Examiner.com*. Retrieved February 9, 2016 from: https://web.archive.org/web/20121015103704/http://www.examiner.com/article/napolitano-muslim-brotherhood-affiliates-met-secretly

[291] "CVE Working Group" (2010) "Recommendations of the DHS Countering Violent Extremism Working Group." *Homeland Security Advisory Council*. Retrieved February 9, 2016 from http://www.dhs.gov/xlibrary/assets/hsac_cve_working_group_recommendations.pdf.

[292] Temple-Raston, D. (July 18, 2011). "Terrorist Training Casts Pall Over Muslim Employee." *NPR*. Retrieved February 9, 2016 from http://www.npr.org/2011/07/18/137712352/terrorism-training-casts-pall-over-muslim-employee.

[293] "Mohammed Magid" (n.d.) "ISNA President: Imam Mohammed Magid." *Islamic Society of North America*. Retrieved February 9, 2016 from http://www.isna.net/mohamed-magid.html.

[294] Mauro, R. (June 25, 2014). "Homeland Security's Mohammed Elibiary: Caliphate Inevitable." The Clarion Project. Retrieved February 9, 2016 from http://www.clarionproject.org/analysis/homeland-securitys-mohammed-elibiary-caliphate-inevitable.

[295] Mauro, R. (n.d.). "A Window on the Muslim Brotherhood in America: An Annotated Interview with DHS Advisor Mohammed Elibiary," *Center for Security Policy*. Retrieved February 9, 2016 fromhttp://www.centerforsecuritypolicy.org/wp-content/uploads/2013/09/Elibiary-Occasional-Paper-1001.pdf.

[296] Clarion Project. (n.d.) "Shukri Abu Baker." *The Clarion Project*. Retrieved February 9, 2016 from http://www.clarionproject.org/category/tags/shukri-abu-baker.

[297] DHS Press Release (October 18, 2010). "Secretary Napolitano Swears in Homeland Security Advisory Council Members." *Department of Homeland Security Office of the Press Secretary*. Retrieved February 9, 2016 fromhttp://www.dhs.gov/news/2010/10/18/secretary-napolitano-swears-homeland-security-advisory-council-members.

[298] "Dalia Mogahed." (n.d.) "Author Profile: Dalia Mogahed". *The Huffington Post*. Retrieved February 9, 2016 from http://www.huffingtonpost.com/dalia-mogahed/.

[299] IPT News (April 15, 2010). "Dalia Mogahed: A Muslim George Gallup or Islamist Ideologue?" The Investigative Project on Terrorism. Retrieved February 9, 2016 fromhttp://www.investigativeproject.org/1904/dalia-mogahed-a-muslim-george-gallup-or-islamist.

[300] White House Press Release (April 6, 2009). "President Obama Announces Additional Members of Advisory Council on Faith-Based and Neighborhood Partnerships." The White House Office of the Press Secretary. Retrieved February 9, 2016 from https://www.whitehouse.gov/the-press-office/president-obama-announces-additional-members-advisory-council-faith-based-and-neigh

[301] "OFNP" (n.d.) "About The Office of Faith-based and Neighborhood Partnerships." *The White House*. Retrieved February 9, 2016 from https://www.whitehouse.gov/administration/eop/ofbnp.

[302] "Nadia Roumani." (n.d.). "American Muslim Civic Leadership Institute Staff". *Center for Religion and Civic Culture University of Southern California*. Retrieved February 9, 2016 from http://crcc.usc.edu/events-and-training/amcli/staff/.

[303] "AMCLI Alumni." (n.d.). "AMCLI National Program Alumni (2008-2013)." *Center for Religion and Civic Culture University of Southern California* Retrieved February 9, 2016 from http://crcc.usc.edu/events-and-training/amcli/alumni/.

[304] ACLU (August 15, 2013) "Muneer Awad v. Paul Zirax, Oklahoma State Board of Elections, Et Al." American Civil Liberties Union. Retrieved February 9, 2016 from https://www.aclu.org/cases/muneer-awad-v-paul-ziriax-oklahoma-state-board-elections-et-al.

[305] IPT News (April 29, 2010). "CAIR's Next Generation Radical." *The Investigative Project on Terrorism*. Retrieved February 9, 2016 from http://www.investigativeproject.org/3730/cair-next-generation-radical.

[306] IPT News. (December 23, 2010). "Dawud Walid Unhinged." *The Investigative Project on Terrorism*. Retrieved February 9, 2016 from http://www.investigativeproject.org/2438/dawud-walid-unhinged

[307] "Zahir Latheef." (n.d.) "Islamic Scholarship Fund Recipient Zahir Latheef". *Islamic Scholarship Fund*. Retrieved February 9, 2016 from http://islamicscholarshipfund.org/recipients/zahir-latheef/.

[308] "Zahir Latheef." (n.d.) "Profile: Zahir Latheef." *zoominfo*. Retrieved February 9, 2016 from http://www.zoominfo.com/p/Zahir-Latheef/449473479.

[309] Pipes, D. (June 1, 2007). "MPAC, CAIR, and Praising Osama Bin Laden." *The Investigative Project on Terrorism*. Retrieved February 9, 2016 from http://www.investigativeproject.org/271/mpac-cair-and-praising-osama-bin-laden.

[310] Ibid

[311] LAPD News Release (February 14, 2007). "Islamic Symposium." *Los Angeles Police Department*. Retrieved February 9, 2016 from http://www.lapdonline.org/rampart_news/news_view/34680.

[312] "Affiliates." (n.d.). "Islamic Relief: Affiliates and Alliances." *Islamic Relief USA*. Retrieved February 9, 2016 from http://irusa.org/affiliates-and-alliances/.

[313] Al Arabiya News. (November 15, 2014). "UAE Blacklists 82 groups as 'terrorist'." *Al Arabiya News*. Retrieved February 9, 2016 from http://english.alarabiya.net/en/News/middle-east/2014/11/15/UAE-formally-blacklists-82-groups-as-terrorist-.html.

[314] "MPAC-NY" (n.d.). "MPAC New York Board." *Muslim Public Affairs Council*. Retrieved February 9, 2016 from http://www.mpac.org/chapters/new-york-city-ny.php.

[315] IPT News. (n.d.) "Haris Tarin." *The Investigative Project on Terrorism*. Retrieved February 9, 2016 from http://www.investigativeproject.org/documents/misc/717.pdf.

[316] MPAC Press Release (February 23, 2012). "MPAC Meets with Defense Dept. Officials about Quran Burning in Afghanistan." Muslim Public affairs Council. Retrieved February 9, 2016 from http://www.mpac.org/issues/national-security/mpac-meets-with-defense-dept.-officials-about-quran-burning-in-afghanistan.php.

[317] Feoktistov, I. and Jacobs, C. (April 7, 2015). "As Boston Bombing Trial Continues, Boston Muslim Leaders Upend Obama's Plan to Counter Violent Extremism." *The Counter Jihad Report*. Retrieved February 9, 2016 from http://counterjihadreport.com/tag/yusufi-vali/.

[318] IPT News (n.d.) "Islamic Society of Boston." *The Investigative Project on Terrorism*. Retrieved February 9, 2016 from http://www.investigativeproject.org/mosques/531/islamic-society-of-boston.

[319] IPT News. (n.d.) "Muslim American Society: The Investigative Project on Terrorism Dossier." *The Investigative Project on Terrorism*. Retrieved February 9, 2016 from http://www.investigativeproject.org/documents/misc/85.pdf.

[320] Pipes, D. (June 1, 2007). "MPAC, CAIR, and Praising Osama Bin Laden." *The Investigative Project on Terrorism*. Retrieved February 9, 2016 fromhttp://www.investigativeproject.org/271/mpac-cair-and-praising-osama-bin-laden.

[321] "About us" (n.d.) "About Us: The Arab American Association of New York." *Arab American Association of New York*. Retrieved February 9, 2016 from http://www.arabamericanny.org/about-us/.

[322] "Linda Sarsour." (n.d.) "Champions Giving Back to the Community: Linda Sarsour." *The White House* Retrieved February 9, 2016 from https://www.whitehouse.gov/champions/giving-back-to-community/linda-sarsour.

[323] "DeBlasio Letter". (September 21, 2015). "Letter from CAIR and ACLU Et Al. to New York City Mayor Bill DeBlasio." *Politico New York*. Retrieved February 9, 2016 from http://www.capitalnewyork.com/sites/default/files/092115%20Coalition%20Letter%20to%20Mayor%20Re%20CVE.pdf.

[324] "Millions for Justice March." (October 10, 2015). *C-Span*. Retrieved February 9, 2016 from http://www.c-span.org/video/?328654-1/millions-justice-march&start=6097.

[325] Kraychik, R. (October 10, 2015). "'Palestinian' Linda Sarsour Trashes Israel; 'Million Man March'"; 10-10-2015." *YouTube*. Retrieved February 9, 2016 from https://www.youtube.com/watch?v=igwtMJ_rqOw.

[326] Sarsour, L. (October 10, 2015). "Linda Sarsour - #JusticeOrElse Speech" *Facebook.com*. Retrieved February 9, 2016 from https://www.facebook.com/UmmahWide/videos/vb.330399110372183/964761970269224/?type=2&theater

[327] "Be the Change". (April 6, 2009). "Be the change: Support our young leaders campaign." *Muslim Public Affairs Council*. Retrieved February 9, 2016 from http://www.mpac.org/events/be-the-change-support-our-young-leaders-programs.php.

[328] Napolitano, J. (April 24, 2009). "Statement by Secretary Napolitano on President Obama's Intent to Nominate David Heyman as Assistant Secretary for Policy and her Appointment of Arif Alikhan as Assistant Secretary for Policy Development.". Department of Homeland Security Office of the Press Secretary. Retrieved February 9, 2016 from http://www.dhs.gov/news/2009/04/24/secretary-makes-personnel-announcements.

[329] "Be the Change". (April 6, 2009). "Be the change: Support our young leaders campaign." *Muslim Public Affairs Council*. Retrieved February 9, 2016 from http://www.mpac.org/events/be-the-change-support-our-young-leaders-programs.php

[330] MPAC Press Release (November 16, 2007). "Muslims Welcome the Removal of LAPD's Mapping Program." (2007, November 16). *Muslim Public Affairs Council*. Retrieved February 9, 2016 from http://www.mpac.org/issues/civil-rights/muslims-welcome-removal-of-lapds-mapping-program.php.

[331] Schwartz, S. (June 4, 2009). " Islamic Shura Council Celebration." *The Muslim Observer*. Retrieved February 9, 2016 from http://muslimobserver.com/islamic-shura-council-celebration/.

[332] "Homepage." (n.d.). "Homepage of the Islamic Shura Council of Southern California". *Islamic Shura Council of Southern California*. Retrieved February 9, 2016 from http://shuracouncil.org/about.html.

[333] "Decision of the United States Court of Appeals 9th District Court" (July 31, 2013). *Islamic Shura Council of Southern California et al. vs. Federal Bureau of Investigation.*" Retrieved February 9, 2016 from http://caselaw.findlaw.com/us-9th-circuit/1640531.html.

[334] ISCSC, (December 12, 2009) " Profile of Islamic Shura Council of Southern California." *Islamic Finder*. Retrieved February 9, 2016 from http://www.islamicfinder.org/getitWorld.php?id=33768&lang=.

[335] "Islamic Shura Council". (n.d.). "Organizations of the Muslim Brotherhood: Islamic Shura Council of Southern California" *Unmasking the Muslim Brotherhood in America*. Retrieved February 9, 2016 from http://www.brotherhoodunmasked.net/organizations-connected-to-the-muslim-brotherhood/islamic-shura-council-of-southern-california.

[336] IPT News (March 31, 2011). "Court: FBI can keep surveillance data secret." *Investigative Project on Terrorism*. Retrieved February 9, 2016 from http://www.investigativeproject.org/2732/court-fbi-can-keep-surveillance-data-secret.

[337] "CVE Working Group" (2010) "Recommendations of the DHS Countering Violent Extremism Working Group." *Homeland Security Advisory Council*. Retrieved February 9, 2016 from http://www.dhs.gov/xlibrary/assets/hsac_cve_working_group_recommendations.pdf

[338] IPT News (n.d.) "An IPT Investigative Report: Dawud Walid- Executive Director, Cair-Michigan." (n.d.). *The Investigative Project on Terrorism*. Retrieved February 9, 2016 from http://www.investigativeproject.org/documents/misc/454.pdf.

[339] GSN News (May 5, 2011). "DHS to investigate CBP's interviews of Muslims." (2011, May 5). *GSN: Government Security News*. Retrieved February 9, 2016 from http://gsnmagazine.com/article/23202/dhs_investigate_cbp%E2%80%99s_interviews_muslims.

[340] "Memorandum and Order Granting in Part and Denying in Part Official-Capacity Defendants' Motion to Dismiss (Doc. 32)" (N.D) *AbdulRahman Cherri, et al., s. Robert S Mueller III, et al*. Retrieved February 9, 2016 from https://www.cair.com/images/pdf/order-on-MTD.pdf

[341] Al Arabiya News. (November 15, 2014). "UAE Blacklists 82 groups as 'terrorist'." *Al Arabiya News*. Retrieved February 9, 2016 from http://english.alarabiya.net/en/News/middle-east/2014/11/15/UAE-formally-blacklists-82-groups-as-terrorist-.html.
[342] Russia Today. (December 6, 2013). "Tighter Rules of Engagement Contributed to US Casualty Rate in Afghanistan- report." *Russia Today*. Retrieved from https://www.rt.com/usa/battlefield-deaths-rules-engagement-change-862/.

[343] "Commander's Initial Assessment" (September 21, 2009). "Commander's Initial Assessment, The International Security Assistance Force, (Unclassified) -- Searchable Document." The Washington Post. Retrieved from http://www.washingtonpost.com/wp-dyn/content/article/2009/09/21/AR2009092100110.html

[344] West, D. (September 27, 2009). "Gen. McChrystal, meet Abu Qatada." *Diana West*. Retrieved from http://dianawest.net/Home/tabid/36/EntryId/1040/Gen-McChrystal-Meet-Abu-Qatada.aspx.

[345] Vandiver, J. (July 8, 2010). "Petraeus to clarify, not alter, war fighting rules in Afghanistan." *Stars and Stripes*. Retrieved from http://www.stripes.com/news/petraeus-to-clarify-not-alter-warfighting-rules-in-afghanistan-1.110376.

[346] "Cultural Cards" (September, 28, 2008). "Cultural Cards: Afghanistan and Islamic Culture *Maneuver Center of Excellence, Department of the Army*. Retrieved from http://fas.org/irp/doddir/army/culture.pdf.

[347] Scarborough, R. (December 5, 2013). "Shades of Vietnam: Spike in U.S. troops deaths tied to stricter rules of engagement." *The Washington Times*. Retrieved from http://www.washingtontimes.com/news/2013/dec/5/increase-in-battlefield-deaths-linked-to-new-rules/?page=all.

[348] West, A. (February 13, 2014). "U.S. military deaths in Afghanistan have skyrocketed under Obama." *Allen B. West: Steadfast and Loyal*. Retrieved from http://www.allenbwest.com/2014/02/us-military-deaths-afghanistan-skyrocket-obama/.

[349] Kaplan, R. (September 10, 2014). ""Full Speed Ahead" on fight against ISIS, John Kerry says." *CBS News*. Retrieved from http://www.cbsnews.com/news/full-speed-ahead-on-fight-against-isis-john-kerry-says/.

[350] Yousafzai, S. (September 29, 2015). " The Taliban Take a Major City, Stunning Washington and Kabul." *The Daily Beast*. Retrieved from http://www.thedailybeast.com/articles/2015/09/29/the-taliban-take-a-major-city-stunning-washington-and-kabul.html.

[351] Tapper, J. (December 19, 2011). "Vice President Biden Says That, "The Taliban, per se, is not Our Enemy." *ABC News*. Retrieved February 9, 2016 from http://abcnews.go.com/blogs/politics/2011/12/vp-biden-says-that-the-taliban-per-se-is-not-our-enemy/.

[352] Londono, E. (June 1, 2014). "Taliban-held U.S. soldier sold in exchange for Afghan detainees." *The Washington Post*. Retrieved February 9, 2016 from https://www.washingtonpost.com/world/national-security/taliban-held-us-soldier-released-in-exchange-for-afghan-detainees/2014/05/31/8b764dac-e8db-11e3-a86b-362fd5443d19_story.html?hpid=z1.

[353] Fox News (n.d.) "Detainees Released from Guantanamo Bay." *Fox News*. Retrieved February 9, 2016 from http://a57.foxnews.com/global.fncstatic.com/static/managed/img/fn2/video/863/485/REPORTER_HERRIDGE_060214.jpg?ve=1&tl=1.

[354] "Closure of Guantanamo Detention Facilities." (January 22, 2009). "Executive Order- Review and Disposition of Individuals Detained At the Guantánamo Bay Naval Base and Closure of Detention Facilities". *The White House*. Retrieved February 9, 2016 from https://www.whitehouse.gov/the-press-office/closure-guantanamo-detention-facilities.

[355] Obama, B. "Remarks by the President to the UN General Assembly." (September 25, 2012). *The White House Office of the Press Secretary*. Retrieved February 9, 2016 from https://www.whitehouse.gov/the-press-office/2012/09/25/remarks-president-un-general-assembly.

[356] Urbanski, D. (September 11, 2015). "Three Years After the Benghazi Terror Attacks, Victims' Families Say the Wait for Answers 'Feels Like Decades'." *The Blaze*. Retrieved February 9, 2016 from http://www.theblaze.com/stories/2015/09/11/three-years-after-benghazi-terror-attacks-victims-families-say-the-wait-for-answers-feels-like-a-decade/.

[357] Kralev, N. (November 15, 2007). "U.S. engages Muslim Brotherhood despite Rice" *Washington Times*. Retrieved February 9, 2016 from http://www.ikhwanweb.com/article.php?id=14621

[358] Clinton, H. (July 15, 2011). "Remarks at the Organization of the Islamic Conference (OIC) High-Level Meeting on Combating Religious Intolerance". *Department of State*. Retrieved February 9, 2016 from http://www.state.gov/secretary/20092013clinton/rm/2011/07/168636.htm

[359] Fox News (February 11, 2011). "Obama's Intel Chief: Muslim Brotherhood Nonviolent, "Secular" Group." *Fox News: Nation*. Retrieved February 9, 2016 from http://nation.foxnews.com/culture/2011/02/10/obamas-intel-chief-muslim-brotherhood-non-violent-secular-group.

[360] Tapper, J. (February 10, 2011). "Office of the Director of National Intelligence "Clarifies" Remarks on Muslim Brotherhood." *ABC News*. Retrieved February 9, 2016 from http://blogs.abcnews.com/politicalpunch/2011/02/office-of-the-director-of-national-intelligence-clarifies-remarks-on-muslim-brotherhood.html.

[361] Charpentier, W. (n.d.). "What does a CIA Protective Agent do?" *The Houston Chronicle*. Retrieved February 9, 2016 from http://work.chron.com/cia-protective-agent-do-14612.html.

[362] MWCOG, (n.d). "Homepage: Metropolitan Washington Council of Governments." *Metropolitan Washington Council of Governments*. Retrieved February 9, 2016 from http://www.mwcog.org/.

[363] Gertz, B. (October 5, 2011). "Inside the Ring: Anti-terror Trainer Blocked" *Washington Times*. Retrieved February 9, 2016 from http://www.washingtontimes.com/news/2011/oct/5/inside-the-ring-295822498/?page=all.

[364] "National Strategy for Counterterrorism." (June 28, 2011). *The White House Office of the President*. Retrieved February 9, 2016 from https://www.whitehouse.gov/sites/default/files/counterterrorism_strategy.pdf.

[365] "Stephen C. Coughlin." (n.d.). "ISAC Scholars: Stephen C. Coughlin, Esq." *International Assessment and Strategy Center*. Retrieved February 9, 2016 from http://www.strategycenter.net/scholars/scholarID.18/scholar_detail.asp.

[366] "Steve Emerson." (n.d.). "Homepage of Steve Emerson," *Steve Emerson*. Retrieved February 9, 2016 from http://www.steveemerson.com/.

[367] Gertz, B. (October 5, 2011). "Inside the Ring: Anti-terror Trainer Blocked" *Washington Times*. Retrieved February 9, 2016 from http://www.washingtontimes.com/news/2011/oct/5/inside-the-ring-295822498/?page=all.

[368] Ibid.

[369] Ibid.

[370] "David G. Major." (n.d.). "CI Centre President David G. Major." *CI Centre*. Retrieved February 9, 2016 from http://www.cicentre.com/?page=bio_dgm.

[371] Orwell, G. (1949). "Chapter 1." *1984*. Secker & Warburg (London). Retrieved February 9, 2016 from http://www.george-orwell.org/1984/0.html.

[372] Orwell, G. (1949). "Appendix: Principles of Newspeak." *1984*. Secker & Warburg (London). Retrieved February 9, 2016 from http://www.george-orwell.org/1984/0.html. http://orwell.ru/library/novels/1984/english/en_app.

[373] Holder, E. (June 4, 2009). "Attorney General Eric Holder on Department of Justice's Outreach and Enforcement Efforts to Protect American Muslims." The United States Department of Justice. Retrieved February 9, 2016 from http://www.justice.gov/opa/speech/attorney-general-eric-holder-department-justice-s-outreach-and-enforcement-efforts.

[374] Obama, B. (June 4, 2009). "Text: Obama's Speech in Cairo." *The New York Times: Politics Section.* Retrieved February 9, 2016 from http://www.nytimes.com/2009/06/04/us/politics/04obama.text.html?_r=3.

[375] "DOJ Backgrounder". (June 4, 2009). "Department of Justice Backgrounder on Outreach and Enforcement Efforts to Protect American Muslims." *Mainjustice.com.* Retrieved February 9, 2016 from http://www.mainjustice.com/files/2009/06/backgrounder-on-efforts-to-protect-american-muslims1.pdf.

[376] "UN.Res. 16/18". (April 12, 2011). "UN Resolution 16/18 Adopted by the Human Rights Council." *United Nations Human Rights Council.* Retrieved February 9, 2016 from http://www.ifex.org/international/2011/11/15/un_resolution_16_18.pdf.

[377] "SB 1038." (May 23, 2013). "Senate Bill 1038- End Racial Profiling Act." *Senate Judiciary Committee.* Retrieved February 9, 2016 from https://www.congress.gov/bill/113th-congress/senate-bill/1038/text.

[378] "DOJ Guidance" (December 8, 2014.) "Guidance or Federal Law Enforcement Agencies Regarding the Use of Race, Ethnicity, Gender, National Origin, Religion, Sexual Orientation, or Gender Identity." *U.S. Department of Justice.* Retrieved February 9, 2016 from http://www.justice.gov/sites/default/files/ag/pages/attachments/2014/12/08/use-of-race-policy.pdf.

[379] "H.R. Bill 2899" (June 25, 2015). "House of Representatives Bill No. 2899 to Amend the Homeland Security Act of 2002 to authorize the Office of Countering Violent Extremism." *The House of Representatives.* Retrieved February 9, 2016 from https://www.congress.gov/114/bills/hr2899/BILLS-114hr2899ih.pdf.

[380] "H.R. Bill 560". (December 17, 2015). "House of Representatives Bill No. 560 Condemning violence, bigotry, and hateful rhetoric towards Muslims in the United States." *The House of Representatives.* Retrieved February 9, 2016 from https://www.congress.gov/bill/114th-congress/house-resolution/569/text

[381] IPT News, (November 24, 2008). "HLF Officials Convicted on All Counts." *The Investigative Project on Terrorism.* Retrieved February 9, 2016 from http://www.investigativeproject.org/865/hlf-officials-convicted-on-all-counts.

[382] Karnitschnig, M., Solomon, D., Pleven, L., and Jon E. Hilsenrath. (September 16, 2008). "U.S. to Takeover AIG in $85 Billion Bailout; Central Banks Inject Cash as Credit Dries Up." *The Wall Street Journal.* Retrieved February 9, 2016 from http://www.wsj.com/articles/SB122156561931242905.

[383] "AIG". (n.d.). "Homepage: American International Group." *AIG.* Retrieved February 9, 2016 from http://www.aig.com/_3171_411330.html?cmpid=KNC-Bing-aig.

[384] "Islamic Finance 101." (November 6, 2008). "Islamic Finance 101: Seminar at the US Department of the Treasury." *The United States Department of the Treasury.* Retrieved February 9, 2016 from http://www.saneworks.us/uploads/news/applications/7.pdf.

[385] Schilling, C. (November 5, 2008). "U.S. Treasury Teaches "Islamic Finance 101." *World Net Daily.* Retrieved February 9, 2016 from http://www.wnd.com/2008/11/80003/.

[386] Flatten, M. (May 22, 2013). "Newly released docs show inconsistencies in FBI training manual censorship." *The Washington Examiner.* Retrieved February 9, 2016 from http://www.washingtonexaminer.com/newly-released-docs-show-inconsistencies-in-fbi-training-manual-censorship/article/2530247.

[387] Judicial Watch. (June 3, 2013). "Documents Obtained By Judicial Watch Reveal FBI Training Curricula Purged of Material Deemed "Offensive" to Muslims." *Judicial Watch.* Retrieved February 9,

2016 from http://www.judicialwatch.org/press-room/press-releases/documents-obtained-by-judicial-watch-reveal-fbi-training-curricula-purged-of-material-deemed-offensive-to-muslims/.

[388] West, D. (2013). *American Betrayal: The Secret Assault on Our Nation's Character.* United States: Macmillan.

[389] "Transcript for Lou Dobbs Tonight." (2005, December 1). *CNN.* Retrieved February 9, 2016 from http://transcripts.cnn.com/TRANSCRIPTS/0512/01/ldt.01.html.

[390] "Words that Work." (March 14,2008). "Words the Work and Words that Don't: A Guide for Counterterrorism Communication." *Counterterrorism Communication Center.* Retrieved February 9, 2016 from http://www.investigativeproject.org/documents/misc/127.pdf.

[391] NCTC (n.d.). "National Counterterrorism Center Homepage." *National Counterterrorism Center.* Retrieved February 9, 2016 from http://www.nctc.gov/.

[392] NCTC (July 22, 2011). "Behavioral Indicators Offer Insights for Spotting Extremists Mobilizing for Violence." *National Counterterrorism Center.* Retrieved February 9, 2016 from https://info.publicintelligence.net/NCTC-SpottingHVEs.pdf.

[393] Ackerman, S. (July 27, 2011.). "FBI "Islam 101" Guide Depicted Muslims as 7th-Century Simpletons." *Wired.* Retrieved February 9, 2016 from http://www.wired.com/2011/07/fbi-islam-101-guide/.

[394] "CTC Homepage." (n.d.). "Homepage of the Combating Terrorism Center at West Point." *Combating Terrorism Center.* Retrieved February 9, 2016 from https://www.ctc.usma.edu/.

[395] "Ackerman, S. (September 14, 2011). "FBI Teaches Agents: Mainstream Muslims are Violent, Radical." *Wired.* Retrieved February 9, 2016 from http://www.wired.com/2011/09/fbi-muslims-radical/.

[396] Ackerman, S. and Noah Shachtman. (September 20, 2011). "William Gawthrop, FBI Counterterrorism Trainer: Fight Against Al Qaeda A 'Waste,' Real Threat Is Islam." The Huffington Post. Retrieved February 9, 2016 from http://www.huffingtonpost.com/2011/09/20/william-gawthrop-fbi-counterterrorism-islam_n_971447.html.

[397] Muslim Advocates (September 15, 2011). "Letter to Inspector General Schnedar." (2011, September 15). *Muslim Advocates.* Retrieved February 9, 2016 from http://www.muslimadvocates.org/files/FBI-DOJ-biased-training-materials-muslim-advocates.pdf.

[398] "Farhana Khera." (n.d.). "Biography: Farhana Khera." *Islamic Society of North America.* Retrieved February 9, 2016 from http://www.isna.net/farhana-khera.html.

[399] "Homepage." (n.d.). "Muslim Advocates Homepage." *Muslim Advocates.* Retrieved February 9, 2016 from https://www.muslimadvocates.org/.

[400] Ramonas, A. (October 22, 2009). "Holder Honors Hundreds at Justice Department 'Oscars'." *Main Justice.* Retrieved February 9, 2016 from http://www.mainjustice.com/tag/cynthia-a-schnedar/.

[401] Winter, M. (2011, September 15). "FBI halts training lecture critical of Muslims." *USA Today.* Retrieved February 9, 2016 from http://content.usatoday.com/communities/ondeadline/post/2011/09/fbi-drops-anti-islam-lecture-from-agents-training/1#.VpgVlsArKCR.

[402] "Homepage." (n.d.) "Naval Criminal Investigative Service." *Naval Criminal Investigative Service, Department of the Navy.* Retrieved February 9, 2016 from http://www.ncis.navy.mil/Pages/publicdefault.aspx.

[403] MPAC Press Release (October 5, 2011). "MPAC Co-signs Letter to FBI Demanding Reformation in Flawed, Anti-Muslim training." *Muslim Public Affairs Council.* Retrieved February 9, 2016 from http://www.mpac.org/programs/government-relations/mpac-co-signs-letter-to-fbi-demanding-reformation-in-flawed-anti-muslim-training.php.

[404] "ACLU letter." (October 4, 2011). "American Civil Liberties Union letter to Director Mueller." *American Civil Liberties Union.* Retrieved February 9, 2016 from https://www.aclu.org/files/assets/sign_on_letter_to_dir_mueller_re_radicalization_report_10_4_11.pdf.

[405] FBI Counterterrorism Division (May 10, 2006.) "The Radicalization Process: From Conversion to Jihad." *FBI.* Retrieved February 9, 2016 from http://media.cygnus.com/files/cygnus/document/OFCR/2012/JAN/theradicalizationprocessfromco_10619306.pdf.

[406] Waterman, S. (October 6, 2011). "Islam content spurs FBI review of anti-terror training. *The Washington Times.* Retrieved February 9, 2016 from http://www.washingtontimes.com/news/2011/oct/6/islam-content-spurs-fbi-review-of-anti-terror-trai/.

[407] "About DoD" (n.d.)"Office of the Secretary of Defense." *U.S. Department of Defense.* Retrieved February 9, 2016 from http://www.defense.gov/About-DoD/Office-of-the-Secretary-of-Defense.

[408] "Screening Process". (October 17, 2011). "Screening Process for Countering Violent Extremism (CVE) Trainers and Speakers" *Department of Defense.* Retrieved February 9, 2016 from http://dailycaller.com/wp-content/uploads/2011/11/Joint-Staff-Action-Trainers.pdf.

[409] Rozen, L. (2010, January 4). "Introducing the National Security Staff." *Politico.* Retrieved February 9, 2016 from http://www.politico.com/blogs/laurarozen/0110/Introducing_the_National_Security_Staff.html.

[410] Clinton, H. (July 15, 2011). "Hilary Clinton Inaugural Address at OIC." *Department of State.* Retrieved February 9, 2016 from http://www.state.gov/secretary/20092013clinton/rm/2011/07/168636.htm.

[411] Shideler, K. (May 10, 2013). "The Istanbul Process, the Missing Piece of the Filmmaker Puzzle." *Center for Security Policy.* Retrieved February 9, 2016 from http://www.centerforsecuritypolicy.org/2013/05/10/the-istanbul-process-the-missing-piece-of-the-filmmaker-puzzle/.

[412] Cook, S. (December 12, 2011). "Remarks for Istanbul Process Conference." *Department of State.* Retrieved February 9, 2016 from http://www.state.gov/j/drl/rls/rm/2011/178640.htm.

[413] Al-Marayati, S. (October 19, 2011). "The wrong way to fight terrorism." *Los Angeles Time: Op-ed.* Retrieved February 9, 2016 from http://articles.latimes.com/2011/oct/19/opinion/la-oe-almarayati-fbi-20111019.

[414] Munro, N. (October 21, 2011). "Progressives, Islamists huddle at Justice Department." *The Daily Caller.* Retrieved February 9, 2016 from http://dailycaller.com/2011/10/21/progressives-islamists-huddle-at-justice-department/?print=1.

[415] "ACLU letter." (October 4, 2011). "American Civil Liberties Union letter to Director Mueller." *American Civil Liberties Union.* Retrieved February 9, 2016 from https://www.aclu.org/files/assets/sign_on_letter_to_dir_mueller_re_radicalization_report_10_4_11.pdf.

[416] Munro, N. (2011, October 21). "Progressives, Islamists huddle at Justice Department." *The Daily Caller.* Retrieved February 9, 2016 from http://dailycaller.com/2011/10/21/progressives-islamists-huddle-at-justice-department/?print=1.

[417] "Tomas E. Perez" (n.d.). "Secretary of Labor Tomas E. Perez." *United States Department of Labor: Office of the Secretary.* Retrieved February 9, 2016 from http://www.dol.gov/agencies/osec.

[418] Munro, N. (October 21, 2011). "Progressives, Islamists huddle at Justice Department." *The Daily Caller.* Retrieved February 9, 2016 from http://dailycaller.com/2011/10/21/progressives-islamists-huddle-at-justice-department/?print=1.

[419] Reilly, R. (October 6, 2011). "Mueller: FBI Training that Smears all Muslims has been Isolated." *Talking Points Memo.* Retrieved February 9, 2016 from http://talkingpointsmemo.com/muckraker/mueller-fbi-training-that-smears-all-muslims-has-been-isolated-video.

[420] Reilly, R. (October 19, 2011). "DOJ Official: Holder Firmly Committed to Eliminating Anti-Muslim Training." *Talking Point Memo.* Retrieved February 9, 2016 from http://talkingpointsmemo.com/muckraker/doj-official-holder-firmly-committed-to-eliminating-anti-muslim-training.

[421] TPM. (October 3, 2011). "The Five Most Bizarre Terror Plots Hatched Under the FBI's Watch." *Talking Point Memo.* Retrieved February 9, 2016 from http://talkingpointsmemo.com/muckraker/the-five-most-bizarre-terror-plots-hatched-under-the-fbi-s-watch.

[422] Ackerman, S. (September 14, 2011). "FBI Teaches Agents: Mainstream Muslims are Violent, Radical." *Wired.* Retrieved February 9, 2016 from http://www.wired.com/2011/09/fbi-muslims-radical/.

[423] DHS CRCL (October 19, 2011). "Countering Violent Extremism (CVE): Do's and Don'ts." *DHS: Office of Civil Rights and Civil Liberties.* Retrieved February 9, 2016 from http://www.training.fema.gov/emiweb/docs/shared/cve%20do%20and%20dont.pdf.

[424] Cultural Cards" (September, 28, 2008). "Cultural Cards: Afghanistan and Islamic Culture *Maneuver Center of Excellence, Department of the Army.* Retrieved from http://fas.org/irp/doddir/army/culture.pdf.

[425] Beutel, A. (April 11, 2010). "Building Bridges." *Muslim Public Affairs Council.* Retrieved February 9, 2016 from http://www.mpac.org/assets/docs/publications/building-bridges/MPAC-Building-Bridges--Complete_Unabridged_Paper.pdf.

[426] Blight, G., Sheila Pulham, and Torpey, P. (January 5, 2012). "Arab Spring: Interactive Timeline." *The Guardian.* Retrieved February 9, 2016 from http://www.theguardian.com/world/interactive/2011/mar/22/middle-east-protest-interactive-timeline.

[427] ISCSC (October 19, 2011). "Joint Islamic Organization letter to John Brennan." *Islamic Shura Council of Southern California.* Retrieved February 9, 2016 from http://www.shuracouncil.org/Shura/Community_letter_to_Brennan_re_FBI_trainings_10-19-11.pdf.

[428] "MAS-ICNA" (n.d.) "14th Annual MAS-ICNA Convention Confirmed Speakers". *MAS-ICNA Annual Convention.* Retrieved February 9, 2016 from http://www.masconvention.org/speakers.html.

[429] IRUSA, (n.d.). "Homepage of Islamic Relief USA" *Islamic Relief USA.* Retrieved February 9, 2016 from http://irusa.org/.

[430] "ACLU letter." (October 4, 2011). "American Civil Liberties Union letter to Director Mueller." *American Civil Liberties Union.* Retrieved February 9, 2016 from https://www.aclu.org/files/assets/sign_on_letter_to_dir_mueller_re_radicalization_report_10_4_11.pdf.

[431] "Advisory Council." (n.d.). "Anti-terrorism Advisory Council." *U.S. Attorney's Office District of Colorado, U.S. Department of Justice.* Retrieved February 9, 2016 from http://www.justice.gov/usao-co/anti-terrorism-advisory-council.

[432] "Schlanger letter" (October 24, 2011). "CAIR Letter to Margo Schlanger." *CAIR*. Retrieved February 9, 2016 from http://www.cair.com/images/pdf/Letter-to-DHS-CRCL-re-See-Something-Say-Something.pdf.

[433] "About the Campaign" (n.d.) "See Something, Say Something: About the Campaign" *Department of Homeland Security*. Retrieved February 9, 2016 from http://www.dhs.gov/see-something-say-something/about-campaign.

[434] Judicial Watch, (January 8, 2013). "FBI Internal Directive Memo" *Scribd*. Retrieved February 9, 2016 from http://www.scribd.com/doc/142625630/Tracking-System-No-2-JW1367-1787#page=360.

[435] Munro, N. (November 10, 2011). "Eric Holder's Stereotyping of Muslims irresponsible, say critics." *The Daily Caller*. Retrieved February 9, 2016 from http://dailycaller.com/2011/11/10/eric-holders-stereotyping-of-muslims-irresponsible-say-critics/.

[436] Cloherty, J. and Pierre, T. (December 21, 2010). "Attorney General's Blunt Warning on Terrorism." *ABC News*. Retrieved February 9, 2016 from http://abcnews.go.com/Politics/attorney-general-eric-holders-blunt-warning-terror-attacks/story?id=12444727.

[437] IPT News, (November 17, 2011.) "Audio Excerpt from 'Islamic Radicalization: Myth or Reality'." *The Investigative Project on Terrorism*. Retrieved February 9, 2016 from http://www.investigativeproject.org/3404/excerpt-from-islamist-radicalization-myth-or.

[438] "Media Advisory" (November 16, 2011). "Media Advisory: Islamic Radicalization: Myth or Reality" *Committee on Homeland Security Press Center*. Retrieved February 9, 2016 from http://hsc-democrats.house.gov/press/index.asp?ID=689.

[439] CAP. (n.d.) "Center for American Progress Homepage." *Center For American Progress*. Retrieved February 9, 2016 from https://www.americanprogress.org/.

[440] Brennan Center. (n.d.). "Expert: Faiza Patel." *Brennan Center for Justice*. Retrieved February 9, 2016 from http://www.brennancenter.org/expert/faiza-patel.

[441] Brennan Center (n.d.). "Liberty and National Security." *Brennan Center for Justice*. Retrieved February 9, 2016 from http://www.brennancenter.org/issues/liberty-national-security.

[442] Gertz, B. (October 5, 2011). "Inside the Ring: Anti-terror Trainer Blocked" *Washington Times*. Retrieved February 9, 2016 from http://www.washingtontimes.com/news/2011/oct/5/inside-the-ring-295822498/?page=all

[443] Mauro, R. (September 2, 2011.). "Allen West Hosts "Islamaphobic" Anti-Ground Zero Mosque." *Islamist Watch*. Retrieved February 9, 2016 from http://www.islamist-watch.org/7874/allen-west-hosts-islamophobic-anti-ground-zero.

[444] Goode, E. (September 16, 2011.). "FBI Chided for Training That Was Critical of Islam." *The New York Times*. Retrieved February 9, 2016 from http://www.nytimes.com/2011/09/17/us/fbi-chided-for-training-that-was-critical-of-islam.html?_r=2.

[445] CAIR Press Release. (March 11, 2015) "CAIR Calls for Reforms of FBI's Training on Islam, Muslims." *CAIR*. Retrieved February 9, 2016 from http://www.cair.com/press-center/press-releases/3636-cair-calls-for-reform-of-fbi-s-training-on-islam-muslims.html.

[446] Fox News. (October 25, 2011). "Nashville Hotel Cancels Anti-Shariah Conference." *Fox News*. Retrieved February 9, 2016 from http://www.foxnews.com/us/2011/10/25/nashville-hotel-cancels-anti-sharia-conference.html.

[447] Shibley, H. (October 29, 2011). "Extremists must not hijack our political discourse." *Tampa Bay Online*. Retrieved February 9, 2016 from https://web.archive.org/web/20111102234932/http://www2.tbo.com/news/opinion/2011/oct/28/meopino2-extremists-must-not-hijack-our-political--ar-298695

[448] Burnes, B. (November 17, 2011). "Some dislike speaker's message at Independence prayer breakfast." *The Kansas City Star*. Retrieved February 9, 2016 from http://www.kansascity.com/news/local/article299743/Some-dislike-speaker%E2%80%99s-message-at-Independence-prayer-breakfast.html.

[449] CAIR Press Release (March 23, 2012). "CAIR Seeks Probe of Anti-Islam Bias in Military Training." *PR Newswire*. Retrieved February 9, 2016 from http://www.prnewswire.com/news-releases/cair-seeks-probe-of-anti-islam-bias-in-military-training-88935352.html.

[450] Markoe, L. (March 27, 2012.). "Muslims call new religious freedom appointee a "puppet" for Islam foes." *The Washington Post*. Retrieved February 9, 2016 from https://www.washingtonpost.com/national/on-faith/muslims-call-new-religious-freedom-appointee-a-puppet-for-islam-foes/2012/03/27/gIQAdH6meS_story.html.

[451] Eckholm, E. (January 30, 2012). "General Withdraws From West Point Talk." *The New York Times*. Retrieved February 9, 2016 from http://www.nytimes.com/2012/01/31/us/lt-gen-william-boykin-known-for-anti-muslim-remarks-cancels-west-point-talk.html?_r=0.

[452] Starnes, T. (n.d.). "Muslims, Atheists Pressure Military to Remove Christian Speaker." *Fox News*. Retrieved February 9, 2016 from http://radio.foxnews.com/toddstarnes/top-stories/muslims-atheists-pressure-military-to-remove-christian-speaker.html.

[453] CAIR Press Release. (January 30, 2012). "CAIR Welcomes Withdraw of Anti-Islam Speaker from West Point Event." *PR Newswire*. Retrieved February 9, 2016 from http://www.prnewswire.com/news-releases/cair-welcomes-withdrawal-of-anti-islam-speaker-from-west-point-event-138368604.html.

[454] West, D. (February 3, 2012.). "The Battle over Boykin at West Point." *Diana West*. Retrieved February 9, 2016 from http://dianawest.net/Home/tabid/36/EntryId/2020/The-Battle-over-Boykin-at-West-Point.aspx.

[455] Eckholm, E. (January 30, 2012.) "General Withdraws From West Point Talk." *The New York Times*. Retrieved February 9, 2016 from http://www.nytimes.com/2012/01/31/us/lt-gen-william-boykin-known-for-anti-muslim-remarks-cancels-west-point-talk.html?_r=0.

[456] "Home." (n.d.). "Homepage of VoteVets.org" *VoteVets.org*. Retrieved February 9, 2016 from http://www.votevets.org/.

[457] IPT News. (n.d.). "Profile: Nihad Awad." *Investigative Project on Terrorism*. Retrieved February 9, 2016 from http://www.investigativeproject.org/profile/113/nihad-awad.

[458] Eckholm, E. (January 30, 2012). "General Withdraws From West Point Talk." *The New York Times*. Retrieved February 9, 2016 from http://www.nytimes.com/2012/01/31/us/lt-gen-william-boykin-known-for-anti-muslim-remarks-cancels-west-point-talk.html?_r=0.

[459] "Home." (n.d.). "Homepage: People for the American Way". *People for the American Way*. Retrieved February 9, 2016 from http://www.pfaw.org/.

[460] Yanover, Y. (February 21, 2012.). "Mueller Appeased Arab Groups on 1000 "Offensive" FBI Documents." *The Jewish Press*. Retrieved February 9, 2016 from http://www.jewishpress.com/news/us-news/mueller-appeased-arab-groups-on-1000-offensive-fbi-documents/2012/02/21/.

⁴⁶¹ "CTC Homepage." (n.d.). "Homepage of the Combating Terrorism Center at West Point." *Combating Terrorism Center*. Retrieved February 9, 2016 from https://www.ctc.usma.edu/.

⁴⁶² Detroit Free Press. (February 20, 2012.) "FBI Ditches Training Materials Criticized As Anti-Muslim." *WUSA 9*. Retrieved February 9, 2016 from http://archive.wusa9.com/news/article/191909/158/FBI-Ditches-Training-Materials-Criticized-As-Anti-Muslim.

⁴⁶³ MPAC Press Release. (February 15, 2012). "MPAC & Interfaith Leaders Meet with FBI Director Mueller to Address Concerns Regarding Training Materials." *MPAC*. Retrieved February 9, 2016 from http://www.mpac.org/programs/government-relations/mpac-interfaith-leaders-meet-with-fbi-director-mueller-to-address-concerns-regarding-training-materials.php#.Um6wLpGG71o.

⁴⁶⁴ FBI. (n.d.) "Working with the Office of Public Affairs." *FBI Washington Field Office*. Retrieved February 9, 2016 from https://www.fbi.gov/washingtondc/news-and-outreach/press-room/office-of-public-affairs.

⁴⁶⁵ IPT News. (n.d.). "Profile: Salam al- Marayati." *Investigative Project on Terrorism*. Retrieved February 9, 2016 from http://www.investigativeproject.org/profile/114/salam-al-marayati.

⁴⁶⁶ Warikoo, N. (February 20, 2012.). "FBI ditches training materials criticized as anti-Muslim." *USA Today*. Retrieved February 9, 2016 from http://usatoday30.usatoday.com/news/nation/story/2012-02-20/fbi-anti-muslim-training/53168966/1.

⁴⁶⁷ Detroit Free Press. (February 20, 2012.) "FBI Ditches Training Materials Criticized As Anti-Muslim." *WUSA 9*. Retrieved February 9, 2016 from http://archive.wusa9.com/news/article/191909/158/FBI-Ditches-Training-Materials-Criticized-As-Anti-Muslim.

⁴⁶⁸ Mueller. R. (March 16, 2012). "Director Mueller's Prepared Statement." *FBI: Testimony*. Retrieved February 9, 2016 from https://www.fbi.gov/news/testimony/oversight-of-the-federal-bureau-of-investigation.

⁴⁶⁹ Ibid

⁴⁷⁰ Cole, J. (March 20, 2012.). "Memorandum for Heads of Components and United States Attorneys." *U.S. Department of Justice*. Retrieved February 9, 2016 from http://www.justice.gov/sites/default/files/dag/legacy/2012/03/20/training-guiding-principles.pdf.

⁴⁷¹ Apuzzo, M. (January 30, 2014.). "Justice Department Starts Quest for Inmates to Be Freed." *The New York Times*. Retrieved February 9, 2016 from http://www.nytimes.com/2014/01/31/us/politics/white-house-seeks-drug-clemency-candidates.html.

⁴⁷² "Guiding Principles". (2012). "The FBI's Guiding Principles: Touchstone Document on Training." *FBI*. Retrieved February 9, 2016 from https://www.fbi.gov/about-us/training/guiding-principles.

⁴⁷³ Mueller, R. (May 9, 2012). "Second Prepared Statement by Mueller." *FBI: Testimony*. Retrieved February 9, 2016 from https://www.fbi.gov/news/testimony/oversight-of-the-federal-bureau-of-investigation-3.

⁴⁷⁴ "About NSB." (n.d.). "About the National Security Branch, Federal Bureau of Investigation". *FBI: National Security Branch*. Retrieved February 9, 2016 from https://www.fbi.gov/about-us/nsb/nsb.

⁴⁷⁵ "JW v. FBI & DOJ 7/18." (July 18, 2012). "Judicial Watch vs. The Federal Bureau of Investigation, Department of Justice." *Scribd*. Retrieved February 9, 2016 from http://www.scribd.com/doc/100829633/JW-v-FBI-DOJ-7-18.

[476] "Judicial Watch Special Report: U.S. Government Purges of Law Enforcement Training Material Deemed "Offensive" to Muslims." (2013, December 5). *Judicial Watch*. Retrieved February 9, 2016 from http://www.judicialwatch.org/document-archive/judicial-watch-special-report-u-s-government-purges-of-law-enforcement-training-material-deemed-offensive-to-muslims/.

[477] Gill, K. (n.d.). "Oaths of Office For Federal Officials." *About News*. Retrieved February 9, 2016 from http://uspolitics.about.com/od/usgovernment/a/oaths_of_office_4.htm.

[478] Vicinanzo, A. and Kimery, A. (December 10, 2014.). "Survey: Low Morale Among DHS Workers; "Unacceptable," Lawmakers say." *Homeland Security Today*. Retrieved February 9, 2016 from http://www.hstoday.us/single-article/survey-low-morale-among-dhs-workers-unacceptable-lawmakers-say/708243e841fc9921d7e6cb9346fae151.html.

[479] "Agency Report". (n.d.) "Agency Report: Department of Homeland Security is 19/19 out of Agencies to work for". *The Best Places to Work in the Federal Government*. Retrieved February 9, 2016 from http://bestplacestowork.org/BPTW/rankings/detail/HS00.

[480] Kimery, A. (February 23, 2015.). "DHS Continues to Study, Suffer From Morale Problem." *Homeland Security Today*. Retrieved February 9, 2016 from http://www.hstoday.us/single-article/dhs-continues-to-study-suffer-from-morale-problems/091a91916c1455b32944f33897d437ab.html.

[481] Johnson, J. (April 29, 2015.). "Written testimony of DHS Secretary Jeh Johnson for a Senate Committee on Appropriations, Subcommittee on Homeland Security hearing to review the Fiscal Year of 2016 funding request and budget justification for the U.S. Department of Homeland Security." *Department of Homeland Security*. Retrieved February 9, 2016 from http://www.dhs.gov/news/2015/04/29/written-testimony-dhs-secretary-jeh-johnson-senate-appropriations-subcommittee.

[482] MIIS. (n.d.). "Faculty: Jeffery M. Bale." *Middlebury Institute of International Studies at Monterey*. Retrieved February 9, 2016 from http://www.miis.edu/academics/faculty/jbale.

[483] Bale, J. (October, 2013.). "Denying the Link between Islamist Ideology and Jihadist Terrorism: "Political Correctness" and the Undermining of Counterterrorism." *Perspectives on Terrorism*. Retrieved February 9, 2016 from http://www.investigativeproject.org/documents/testimony/395.pdf.

[484] IPT News (February 10, 2011). "FBI Chief: Muslim Brotherhood Supports Terrorism." *Investigative Project on Terrorism*. Retrieved February 9, 2016 from http://www.investigativeproject.org/2581/fbi-chief-muslim-brotherhood-supports-terrorism.

[485] Fox News (February 11, 2011). "Obama's Intel Chief: Muslim Brotherhood Nonviolent "Secular" Group." *Fox News*. Retrieved February 9, 2016 from http://nation.foxnews.com/culture/2011/02/10/obamas-intel-chief-muslim-brotherhood-non-violent-secular-group.

[486] "DHS I&A"(n.d.). "DHS Office of Intelligence and Analysis." *DHS Office of Intelligence and Analysis*. Retrieved February 9, 2016 from http://www.dhs.gov/office-intelligence-and-analysis.

[487] "Thomas A. Ferguson". (n.d.) "Biography: Thomas A. Ferguson." *National Conference Services Inc*. Retrieved February 9, 2016 from https://www.ncsi.com/dodiis12/bios/ferguson.html

[488] "BIR" (n.d.) "Bureau of Intelligence and Research." *Bureau of Intelligence and Research, U.S. Department of State*. Retrieved February 9, 2016 from http://www.state.gov/s/inr/.

[489] Al Jazeera (February 11, 2011). "Hosni Mubarak Resigns as President." *Aljazeera*. Retrieved February 9, 2016 from http://www.aljazeera.com/news/middleeast/2011/02/201121125158705862.html.

[490] Khomami, N. (May 16, 2015). " Mohamed Morsi Sentenced to Death by Egyptian Court." *The Guardian*. Retrieved February 9, 2016 from http://www.theguardian.com/world/2015/may/16/mohammed-morsi-sentenced-death-egyptian-court-former-president.

[491] BBC News. (May 16, 2015). "Mohammed Morsi, Egypt's ex-Leader, Sentenced to Death." *BBC News*. Retrieved February 9, 2016 from http://www.bbc.com/news/world-middle-east-32763215.

[492] Ambinder, M. (June 3, 2009) "'Brotherhood' Invited to Obama Speech." *The Atlantic*. Retrieved February 9, 2016 from http://www.theatlantic.com/politics/archive/2009/06/-brotherhood-invited-to-obama-speech-by-us/18693

[493] Beauprez, B. (January 17, 2013.). "Muslim Brotherhood in the White House." *Townhall.com*. Retrieved February 9, 2016 from http://finance.townhall.com/columnists/bobbeauprez/2013/01/17/muslim-brotherhood-in-the-white-house-n1490354/page/full.

[494] "Home." (n.d.). "Homepage of the U.S. Copts Association." *U.S. Copts Association*. Retrieved February 9, 2016 from http://www.copts.com/english/.

[495] Meunier, M. (December 21, 2012.). "Obama Gives Cold Shoulder to Egyptian Secular Democrats." *The Investigative Project on Terrorism*. Retrieved February 9, 2016 from http://www.investigativeproject.org/3862/obama-gives-cold-shoulder-to-egyptian-secular.

[496] Rogin, J. and Lake, E. (July 10, 2013.). "Ambassador Anne Patterson, the Controversial Face of America's Egypt Policy." *The Daily Beast*. Retrieved February 9, 2016 from http://www.thedailybeast.com/articles/2013/07/10/ambassador-anne-patterson-the-controversial-face-of-america-s-egypt-policy.html.

[497] "Salafi Islam." (n.d.). "Introduction: Salafi Islam". *Global Security*. Retrieved February 9, 2016 from http://www.globalsecurity.org/military/intro/islam-salafi.htm.

[498] "MB Petition" (July 7, 2013). "Petition: Declare the Muslim Brotherhood a Terrorist Organization." *The White House*. Retrieved February 9, 2016 from https://petitions.whitehouse.gov/petition/declare-muslim-brotherhood-organization-terrorist-group.

[499] "Milestones" (n.d.). "Sayyid Qutb's Ma'alim fi-l-Tariq." *What are They Reading: An Analysis of Seven Texts Advocating Violent Jihad Found in American Mosque*s Retrieved February 9, 2016 from http://mappingsharia.com/?page_id=99.

500 Munro, N. (January 16, 2013). "White House now requires 'We the People' petitions to have 100,000 signatures for official response." *The Daily Caller*. Retrieved February 9, 2016 from http://dailycaller.com/2013/01/16/white-house-now-requires-we-the-people-petitions-to-have-100000-signatures-for-official-response/.

[501] Taylor, S. (December 1, 2014.). "White House Shoots Down Petition to Declare Muslim Brotherhood a Terrorist Organization." *The Washington Free Beacon*. Retrieved February 9, 2016 from http://freebeacon.com/national-security/white-house-shoots-down-petition-to-declare-muslim-brotherhood-a-terrorist-organization/.

[502] Klein, J. (February 3, 2015.). "Obama Bolsters the Brotherhood." *Front Page*. Retrieved February 9, 2016 from http://www.frontpagemag.com/fpm/250740/obama-bolsters-brotherhood-joseph-klein.

[503] Jones, S. (October 10, 2013.). "General Al-Sisi's Popularity Soars as U.S. aid Cut-off to Egypt." *The Daily Beast*. Retrieved February 9, 2016 from http://www.thedailybeast.com/articles/2013/10/10/general-al-sisi-s-popularity-soars-after-u-s-aid-cut-off-to-egypt.html.

[504] Al Jazeera, (June 8, 2014). "Profile: Abdel Fattah el-Sisi." *Aljazeera*. Retrieved February 9, 2016 from http://www.aljazeera.com/news/middleeast/2013/07/201373112752442652.html

[505] Weymouth, L. (August 3, 2013.). "Rare interview with Gen. Abdel Fatah el-Sisi." *The Washington Times*. Retrieved February 9, 2016 from https://www.washingtonpost.com/world/middle_east/rare-interview-with-egyptian-gen-abdel-fatah-al-sissi/2013/08/03/a77eb37c-fbc4-11e2-a369-d1954abcb7e3_story.html.

[506] Hamid, S. (January 12, 2014.). "Hey General, It's Me, Chuck. Again." *Politico Magazine*. Retrieved February 9, 2016 from http://www.politico.com/magazine/story/2014/01/chuck-hagel-al-sissi-egypt-102068.

[507] Beutel, A. (August, 2010). "Building Bridges to Strengthen America." *Muslim Public Affairs Council*. Retrieved February 9, 2016 from http://www.mpac.org/assets/docs/publications/building-bridges/MPAC-Building-Bridges--Complete_Unabridged_Paper.pdf.

[508] Ibrahim, R. (February 4, 2014). "Exposed: The Muslim Brotherhood/Al-Qaeda Connection." Published by CBS News Available at http://www.meforum.org/3739/muslim-brotherhood-al-qaeda-connection.

[509] Quoted by Rubin, M. (October 19, 2006.). ""Mr. Erdogan's Turkey", *The Wall Street Journal*, Retrieved February 9, 2016 from http://www.wsj.com/articles/SB116121690776497100

[510] Ibrahim, R. (February 4, 2014.). "Exposed: The Muslim Brotherhood/Al-Qaeda Connection." Published by CBS News Available at http://www.meforum.org/3739/muslim-brotherhood-al-qaeda-connection.

511 Michael, M. (August 17, 2013.). "Mohammed Al-Zawahiri Arrested: Brother Of Al-Qaeda Chief Ayman Al-Zawahiri Reportedly Detained In Egypt." *The Huffington Post*. Retrieved February 9, 2016 from http://www.huffingtonpost.com/2013/08/17/mohammed-al-zawahiri-arrested_n_3772315.html.

[512] Bajoria, J. and Lee Hudson Teslik. (July 14, 2011.). "Ayman al-Zawahiri." *Council on Foreign Relations*. Retrieved February 9, 2016 from http://www.cfr.org/terrorist-leaders/profile-ayman-al-zawahiri/p9750.

[513] Munro, N. (July 27, 2012.). "DOJ Official Refuses to Denounce Demands for Saudi-style Blasphemy Law." *The Daily Caller*. Retrieved February 9, 2016 from http://dailycaller.com/2012/07/27/doj-official-refuses-to-denounce-demands-for-saudi-style-blasphemy-law/.

[514] "Thomas Perez." (n.d.) "Meet the Assistant District Attorney." *The United States Department of Justice*. Retrieved February 9, 2016 from http://www.justice.gov/crt/meet-aag-banner.

[515] "Civil Rights Division." (n.d.) "The Civil Rights Division: About the Division". *United States Department of Justice*. Retrieved February 9, 2016 from http://www.justice.gov/crt.

[516] "The Subcommittee" (n.d.) "Judiciary Committee: Subcommittee on the Constitution and Civil Justice." *U.S. House of Representative Judiciary Committee*. Retrieved February 9, 2016 from http://judiciary.house.gov/index.cfm/subcommittee-on-the-constitution-and-civil-justice.

[517] Hunter, M. (July 26, 2012). "DOJ Official Won't Say Whether Justice Department Would "Criminalize Speech Against any Religion."" *CNS News*. Retrieved February 9, 2016 from http://cnsnews.com/news/article/doj-official-won-t-say-whether-justice-department-would-criminalize-speech-against-any.

[518] Munro, N. (October 21, 2011). "Progressives, Islamists Huddle at Justice Department." *The Daily Caller*. Retrieved February 9, 2016 from http://dailycaller.com/2011/10/21/progressives-islamists-huddle-at-justice-department/.

[519] "Challenges and Opportunities" (October 19, 2011). "Confronting Discrimination in the Post 9/11 Era: Challenges and Opportunities Ten Years Later." *U.S. Department of Justice*. Retrieved February 9, 2016 from http://www.justice.gov/sites/default/files/crt/legacy/2012/04/16/post911summit_report_2012-04.pdf.

[520] "James Cole". (n.d.) " Meet the Deputy Attorney General: James Cole". *U.S. Department of Justice*. Retrieved February 9, 2016 from http://www.justice.gov/dag/meet-deputy-attorney-general-0.

[521] Munro, N. (2011, October 21). "Progressives, Islamists Huddle at Justice Department." *The Daily Caller*. Retrieved February 9, 2016 from http://dailycaller.com/2011/10/21/progressives-islamists-huddle-at-justice-department/.

[522] "Sahar F. Aziz, Associate Professor of Law." (n.d.). *Texas A&M School of Law*. Retrieved February 9, 2016 from http://law.tamu.edu/faculty-staff/find-people/faculty-profiles/sahar-aziz.

[523] Limon, M., Ghanea, N. and Power, H. (n.d.). "Combating global religious intolerance: the implementation of Human Rights Council resolution 16/18." *Universal Rights Group*. Retrieved at http://www.universal-rights.org/urg-policy-reports/combatting-global-religious-intolerance-the-implementation-of-human-rights-council-resolution-1618/.

[524] "Benghazi Watch." (September 11, 2012). *CBS News*. Retrieved February 9, 2016 from http://www.cbsnews.com/feature/us-consulate-attack-in-benghazi/.

[525] Boston Globe. (April 15 2013). "Terror at the Marathon." *The Boston Globe*. Retrieved February 9, 2016 from http://www.bostonglobe.com/metro/specials/boston-marathon-explosions.

[526] Rosenthal, J. (May 2, 2013.). "Newsmax Exclusive: U.S. Hired al-Qaeda-Linked Group to Defend Benghazi Mission." *Newsmax*. Retrieved February 9, 2016 from http://www.newsmax.com/Newsfront/benghazi-consulate-protected-alqaida/2013/05/02/id/502565/.

[527] Jeffrey, T. (May 1, 2013.). "Militia Hired by State Dept. Warned it Wouldn't Protect Stevens' Movements in Benghazi." *CNS News*. Retrieved February 9, 2016 from http://www.cnsnews.com/news/article/militia-hired-state-dept-warned-it-wouldn-t-protect-stevens-movements-benghazi.

[528] Lister, J. and Cruickshank, P. (November 16, 2012). "What is Ansar al-Sharia and was it behind the consulate attack in Benghazi?" *Cable News Network*. Retrieved February 9, 2016 from http://www.cnn.com/2012/11/16/politics/benghazi-ansar-al-sharia/index.html.

[529] Cafarella, J. (n.d.). "Jabhat al-Nusra in Syria." *Institute for the Study of War*. Retrieved February 9, 2016 from http://www.understandingwar.org/report/jabhat-al-nusra-syria.

[530] "Global Al Qaeda" (n.d.) "Map of Jihadist Groups: Global Al Qaeda." *Stanford University*. Retrieved February 9, 2016 from http://web.stanford.edu/group/mappingmilitants/cgi-bin/maps/view/alqaeda.

[531] Fletcher, H. (May 30, 2008). "Jamaat Islamiyya." *Council on Foreign Relations*. Retrieved February 9, 2016 from http://www.cfr.org/egypt/jamaat-al-islamiyya/p9156.

[532] MEM. (May 31, 2014.). "Egypt's Al-Jamaa Al-Islamiya: Al-Sisi is waging a war against Islam." *Middle East Monitor*. Retrieved February 9, 2016 from https://www.middleeastmonitor.com/news/africa/11783-egypts-al-jamaa-al-islamiya-al-sisi-is-waging-a-war-against-islam.

[533] "FTO List". (October 8, 1997) "Foreign Terrorist Organizations". *U.S. Department of State*. Retrieved February 9, 2016, from http://www.state.gov/j/ct/rls/other/des/123085.htm

[534] "Logo." (n.d.). "Al-Gama Al-Islamiyya." *Wikipedia*. Retrieved February 9, 2016 from https://en.wikipedia.org/wiki/Al-Gama%27a_al-Islamiyya#/media/File:Al-Gama%27a_al-Islamiyya_logo.jpg.

[535] Itani, F. (February 15, 2012.) "Al-Jamaa Al-Islamiyya: Is the Future Theirs?" *Al-Akhbar*. Retrieved February 9, 2016 from http://english.al-akhbar.com/node/4234.

[536] "Dereliction of Duty" (n.d.) "Dereliction of duty Law & Legal Definition." *U.S. Legal*. Retrieved February 9, 2016 from http://definitions.uslegal.com/d/dereliction-of-duty/.

[537] Roach Yeats, M. (1979). "Abrogation of the Contributory Negligence Bar in Cases of Disparate Risks." *Louisiana Law Review*. Retrieved February 9, 2016 from http://digitalcommons.law.lsu.edu/cgi/viewcontent.cgi?article=4407&context=lalrev.

[538] Fitton, T. (May 29, 2015.). "Judicial Watch Unravels Benghazi Scandal with new Documents." *Breitbart*. Retrieved February 9, 2016 from http://www.breitbart.com/national-security/2015/05/29/judicial-watch-unravels-benghazi-scandal-with-new-documents/.

[539] Judicial Watch. (June 5, 2014.) "Judicial Watch Sues Departments of Defense and State for Records about Benghazi Briefings of Congressional Leaders." *Judicial Watch*. Retrieved February 9, 2016 from http://www.judicialwatch.org/press-room/press-releases/judicial-watch-sues-departments-defense-state-records-benghazi-briefings-congressional-leaders/.

[540] Herridge, C. (May 18, 2015.). "Military intel predicted the rise of ISIS in 2012, detailed arms shipments from Benghazi to Syria." *Fox News*. Retrieved February 9, 2016 from http://www.foxnews.com/politics/2015/05/18/military-intel-predicted-rise-isis-in-2012-detailed-arms-shipments.html.

[541] NRCC Communications (May 8, 2013). "Susan Rice: Attack on Benghazi was Direct Response to Video." *Youtube*. Retrieved February 9, 2016 from https://www.youtube.com/watch?v=hGXy_yhOfNg&feature=youtu.be.

[542] Ingersoll, G. and Kelley, M. (Dec. 9, 2012.). "REPORT: The U.S. Is Openly Sending Heavy Weapons From Libya To Syrian Rebels," *Business Insider*, Retrieved February 9, 2016 from http://www.businessinsider.com/obama-admin-admits-to-covertly-sending-heavy-weapons-to-syrian-rebels-2012-12

[543] See for example, Anjarini, S. (May 22, 2014.) "Harakat Hazm: America's new favorite jihadist group," *Al-Akhbar*. Retrieved February 9, 2016 from http://english.al-akhbar.com/content/harakat-hazm-america%E2%80%99s-new-favorite-jihadist-group

[544] Judicial Watch. (April 12, 2012)."Pgs. 287-293 (291) JW vs. DOD and State 14-812." *Judicial Watch*. Retrieved February 9, 2016 from http://www.judicialwatch.org/document-archive/pgs-287-293-291-jw-v-dod-and-state-14-812-2/.

[545] Lewis, J. (September, 2013). "Al-Qaeda in Iraq Resurgent." *Understanding War*. Retrieved February 9, 2016 from http://www.understandingwar.org/sites/default/files/AQI-Resurgent-10Sept_0.pdf.

[546] Lee, T. (September 12, 2012). "Al-Qaeda Catches Obama White House Flat-Footed During Egypt, Libya Attack" Breitbart News. Retrieved February 9, 2016 from http://www.breitbart.com/national-security/2012/09/12/al-qaeda-catches-obama-white-house-flat-footed-during-egypt-libya-attacks/

547 Obama, B. (September 25, 2012). "Remarks by the President to the UN General Assembly." *The White House Office of the Press Secretary.* Retrieved February 9, 2016 from https://www.whitehouse.gov/the-press-office/2012/09/25/remarks-president-un-general-assembly.

548 Mitchell, A. (September 11, 2012). "American Killed in Libya During Protests about Prophet Muhammad Video." *NBC News.* Retrieved at http://worldnews.nbcnews.com/_news/2012/09/11/13807579-american-killed-in-libya-during-protests-about-prophet-muhammad-video?lite.

549 Lebl, L. (2013). "The EU, the Muslim Brotherhood and the Organization of Islamic Cooperation." *Foreign Policy Research Institute.* Retrieved February 9, 2016 from http://www.leslielebl.com/files/Orbis_Winter_2013_article.pdf.

550 "UN. Res. 67/178" (March 28, 2013.) "U.N Resolution 67/178: Combating intolerance, negative stereotyping, stigmatization, discrimination, incitement to violence and violence against persons, based on religion or belief." *The United Nations General Assembly.* Retrieved February 9, 2016 from http://www.un.org/en/ga/search/view_doc.asp?symbol=A/RES/67/178.

551 Limon, M., Ghanea, N. and Power, H. (n.d.). "Combating global religious intolerance: the implementation of Human Rights Council resolution 16/18." *Universal Rights Group.* Retrieved at http://www.universal-rights.org/urg-policy-reports/combatting-global-religious-intolerance-the-implementation-of-human-rights-council-resolution-1618/.

552 Goodenough, P. (December 22, 2010.) "U.N. Passes Religious "Defamation" Resolution Sponsored by Islamic Nations, but Support Dwindles." *CNS News.* Retrieved http://www.cnsnews.com/news/article/un-passes-religious-defamation-resolution-sponsored-islamic-nations-support-dwindles.

553 Parfitt, T. (April 28, 2013). "Boston bombs: the Canadian boxer and the terror recruiter who 'led Tsarnaev on path to jihad'" *Telegraph UK.* Retrieved February 9, 2016 from http://www.telegraph.co.uk/news/worldnews/europe/russia/10024185/Boston-bombs-the-Canadian-boxer-and-the-terror-recruiter-who-led-Tsarnaev-on-path-to-jihad.html

554 Henze, P. (n.d.). "Islam in the North Caucus: The Example of Chechnya." *Circassian World.* Retrieved February 9, 2016 from http://aheku.net/datas/users/1-henze_islam_northcaucasus.pdf.

555 "Imarat Kavkaz." (n.d.). "Paramilitary Groups: Imarat Kavkaz." *Global Security.* Retrieved February 9, 2016 from http://www.globalsecurity.org/military/world/para/ik.htm.

556 Johnson, J. (September 10, 2014.) "Remarks by Secretary of Homeland Security Jeh Johnson at the Council on foreign Relations - as Delivered." *Department of Homeland Security.* Retrieved February 9, 2016 from http://www.dhs.gov/news/2014/09/10/remarks-secretary-homeland-security-jeh-johnson-council-foreign-relations-%E2%80%93.

557 "Empowering Local Partners" (August 8, 2011). "Empowering Local Partners to Prevent Violent Extremism in the United States." *The White House.* Retrieved February 9, 2016 from https://www.whitehouse.gov/sites/default/files/empowering_local_partners.pdf.

558 Ibid

559 MPAC Press Release. (October 5, 2011). "MPAC Co-Signs Letter to FBI Demanding Reformation in Flawed, Anti-Muslim Training." *Muslim Public Affairs Council.* Retrieved February 9, 2016 from http://www.mpac.org/programs/government-relations/mpac-co-signs-letter-to-fbi-demanding-reformation-in-flawed-anti-muslim-training.php.

560 "DeBlasio Letter". (September 21, 2015). "Letter from CAIR and ACLU et al. to New York City Mayor Bill DeBlasio." *Politico New York.* Retrieved February 9, 2016 from

http://www.capitalnewyork.com/sites/default/files/092115%20Coalition%20Letter%20to%20Mayor%20Re%20CVE.pdf.

[561] "LA Groups Question CVE" (November 13, 2014). "Los Angeles Based Groups Serving American Muslim Communities Question Federal Government's "Countering Violent Extremism" Program as Ill-Conceived, Ineffective, and Stigmatizing." *Asian American Advancing Justice.* Retrieved February 9, 2016 from http://www.advancingjustice-la.org/sites/default/files/20141113%20-%20MR%20-%20CVE%20Statement.pdf.

[562] Holder, E. (September 15, 2014.) **"Attorney General Holder Announces Pilot Projects to Counter Violent Extremism in Communities Nationwide."** U.S. *Department of Justice.* Retrieved February 9, 2016 from http://www.justice.gov/opa/video/countering-violent-extremism.

[563] CBS News (November 13, 2014.) "Homeland Security Secretary Visits San Gabriel Valley Islamic Center." *CBS News Los Angeles.* Retrieved February 9, 2016 from http://losangeles.cbslocal.com/2014/11/13/homeland-security-secretary-to-visit-san-gabriel-valley-islamic-center/.

[564] "CAIR Facebook Post." (November 13, 2014.) "Muslim, Civil Rights Leaders to Comment on Meeting with DHS Director." *Facebook.* Retrieved February 9, 2016 from https://www.facebook.com/CAIRNational/posts/10152531879812695.

[565] IPT News. (n.d.). "Hussam Ayloush." *The Investigative Project on Terrorism.* Retrieved February 9, 2016 from http://www.investigativeproject.org/documents/misc/709.pdf.

[566] WAM. (November 15, 2014.) "UAE Cabinet approves list of designated terrorist organizations, groups." *Emirates News Agency.* Retrieved February 9, 2016 from http://www.wam.ae/en/news/emirates-international/1395272478814.html.

[567] Ibrahim, A. (November 18, 2014.) "U.S. rejects UAE terrorist designation of American groups." *Middle East Eye.* Retrieved February 9, 2016 from http://www.middleeasteye.net/news/us-rejects-uae-terrorist-designation-american-groups-555861953.

[568] Office of the Press Secretary, (February 4, 2015.) "Readout of the President's Meeting with American Muslim Leaders." *The White House Office of the Press Secretary.* Retrieved February 9, 2016 from https://www.whitehouse.gov/the-press-office/2015/02/04/readout-president-s-meeting-american-muslim-leaders.

[569] Boyer, D. (February 6, 2015). *The Washington Times.* Retrieved February 9, 2016 from http://www.washingtontimes.com/news/2015/feb/6/wh-gives-names-muslim-leaders-who-met-obama/.

[570] ISNA (n.d.). "ISNA President: Azhar Azeez." *Islamic Society of North America.* Retrieved February 9, 2016 from http://www.isna.net/azhar-azeez.html.

[571] ISNA (n.d.). "Mohamed Magid." *Islamic Society of North America.* Retrieved February 9, 2016 from http://www.isna.net/mohamed-magid1.html.

[572] Friedland, E. (February 8, 2015). "Who Are the Muslim Brotherhood-Linked Leaders Obama Met?" *The Clarion Project.* Retrieved February 9, 2016 from http://www.clarionproject.org/analysis/obama-meets-us-muslim-brotherhood-leaders.

[573] "Hoda Hawa." (n.d.). *Muslim Public Affairs Council.* Retrieved February 9, 2016 from http://www.mpac.org/about/staff-board/hoda-hawa.php.

[574] Rice, S. (February 6, 2015.) "Remarks by National Security Advisor Susan Rice on the 2015 National Security Strategy." *The White House Office of the Press Secretary,* Retrieved February 9, 2016 from

https://www.whitehouse.gov/the-press-office/2015/02/06/remarks-national-security-advisor-susan-rice-2015-national-security-stra.

[575] "National Security Strategy." (February, 2015,). "2015 National Security Strategy of the United States." *The White House.* Retrieved February 9, 2016 from https://www.whitehouse.gov/sites/default/files/docs/2015_national_security_strategy_2.pdf.

[576] Richter, G. (February 8, 2015.) "Homeland Security Chief: Terrorist Sleeper Cells in U.S., Poised to Attack." *Fox News.* Retrieved February 9, 2016 from http://nation.foxnews.com/2015/02/08/homeland-security-chief-terrorist-sleeper-cells-us-poised-attack.

[577] USCMO Press Release (November 14, 2015.) "USCMO hold Press Conference to Strongly Condemn the Terror Attacks in Paris." *U.S. Council of Muslim Organizations.* Retrieved February 9, 2016 from http://www.uscmo.org/council-news.

[578] "LA Groups Question CVE" (November 13, 2014). "Los Angeles Based Groups Serving American Muslim Communities Question Federal Government's "Countering Violent Extremism" Program as Ill-Conceived, Ineffective, and Stigmatizing." *Asian American Advancing Justice.* Retrieved February 9, 2016 from http://www.advancingjustice-la.org/sites/default/files/20141113%20-%20MR%20-%20CVE%20Statement.pdf.

[579] Ibid

[580] "Executive Team." (n.d.). "Executive Team & Board Members of the U.S. Council of Muslim Organizations." *U.S. Council of Muslim Organizations.* Retrieved February 9, 2016 from http://www.uscmo.org/board-members.

[581] Khan, F. (February 17, 2015.) "Muslim Advocates Express Extraordinary Disappointment Over White House CVE Summit." *Muslim Advocates.* Retrieved February 9, 2016 from https://www.muslimadvocates.org/muslim-advocates-expresses-extraordinary-disappointment-over-white-house-cve-summit/.

[582] Muslim Advocates (n.d.). "Homepage." *Muslim Advocates.* Retrieved February 9, 2016 from https://www.muslimadvocates.org.

[583] IPT News. (n.d.). "Farhana Khera & Muslim Advocates." *The Investigative Project on Terrorism.* Retrieved February 9, 2016 from http://www.investigativeproject.org/documents/misc/633.pdf.

[584] ADC. (n.d.). "ADC Homepage." *Arab American Anti-Discrimination Committee* Retrieved February 9, 2016 from http://www.adc.org/.

[585] ADC. (May 14, 2008.) "American Muslim and Arab-American Organizations: Senate Homeland Security Committee Report Lacks Substantive Analysis, Contradicts Own Recommendations." *Arab American Anti-Discrimination Committee.* Retrieved February 9, 2016 from http://www.adc.org/2008/05/american-muslim-and-arab-american-organizations-senate-homeland-security-committee-report-lacks-substantive-analysis-contradicts-own-recommendations/.

[586] Lieberman, J. and Collins, S. (May 8, 2008.) "Violent Islamist Extremism, the Internet, and the Homegrown Terrorist Threat." *United states Committee on Homeland Security and Governmental Affairs.* Retrieved February 9, 2016 from http://www.hsgac.senate.gov/imo/media/doc/IslamistReport.pdf?attempt=2.

[587] CAIR-MN, (February 17, 2015.) "Press Conference Stigmatizing and Ineffective CVE Program." *Youtube.* Retrieved February 9, 2016 from https://www.youtube.com/watch?v=VbV9Xnp9Dcs.

[588] WBUR (May 9, 2013.) "Should Muslims Monitor Muslims?" *Here and Now: WBUR.* Retrieved February 9, 2016 from http://hereandnow.wbur.org/2013/05/09/boston-mosque-imam.

[589] Bender, B. (February 18, 2015.) "Islamic leader says U.S. officials unfairly target Muslims." *The Boston Globe.* Retrieved February 9, 2016 from http://www.bostonglobe.com/news/nation/2015/02/18/islamic-leader-boston-says-justice-department-effort-identify-homegrown-terrorists-unfairly-targeting-muslim-community/uqzG0M3czJeuVH8HhSDtRN/story.html#comments.

[590] Hanson, J. (May 13, 2015.) "The Dirty Dozen- President Obama's Model Mosque." *The Center for Security Policy.* Retrieved February 9, 2016 from http://www.centerforsecuritypolicy.org/2015/05/13/the-dirty-dozen-president-obamas-model-mosque/.

[591] McCauley, L. (February 18, 2015.) "At Extremist Summit, Rep. Ellison Says Bigotry Against Muslims Breeds Hate." *Common Dreams.* Retrieved February 9, 2016 from http://www.commondreams.org/news/2015/02/18/extremism-summit-rep-ellison-says-bigotry-against-muslims-breeds-hate.

[592] Ahmad Ibn Naqib al-Misri. (July 1, 1997). "Book R- Holding One's Tongue" from *Reliance of the Traveler: The Classic Manual of Islamic Law.* Trans. Nu Ha Mim Keller. *Amana Publications.* Retrieved February 9, 2016 from http://shariahthethreat.org/wp-content/uploads/2011/04/reliance_of_the_traveller.pdf

[593] "Slander: How it is Used and Abused Under Shariah." (n.d.). *Shariah the Threat to America.* Retrieved February 9, 2016 from http://shariahthethreat.org/a-short-course-1-what-is-shariah/a-short-course-6-slander/.

[594] "Book 43, Hadith 102" (n.d.) "Sunan Abi Dawud 4874, Book 43, Hadith 102," *Sunnah.* Retrieved February 9, 2016 from http://sunnah.com/abudawud/43#102.

[595] "Fitnah" (n.d.) "Fitnah: definition." *Corpus Quran.* Retrieved February 9, 2016 from http://corpus.quran.com/qurandictionary.jsp?q=ftn#(2:191:8).

[596] CVE Fact Sheet (February 18, 2015.) "Fact Sheet: The White House Summit on Countering Violent Extremism." *The White House Office of the Press Secretary.* Retrieved February 9, 2016 from https://www.whitehouse.gov/the-press-office/2015/02/18/fact-sheet-white-house-summit-countering-violent-extremism.

[597] Bender, B. (February 18, 2015.). "Islamic leader says U.S. officials unfairly target Muslims." *The Boston Globe.* Retrieved February 9, 2016 from http://www.bostonglobe.com/news/nation/2015/02/18/islamic-leader-boston-says-justice-department-effort-identify-homegrown-terrorists-unfairly-targeting-muslim-community/uqzG0M3czJeuVH8HhSDtRN/story.html#comments.

[598] "A Framework" (February, 2015.) "A Framework for Prevention and Intervention Strategies: Incorporating Countering Violent Extremism into Violence Prevention Efforts." *U.S. Department of Justice.* Retrieved February 9, 2016 from http://www.justice.gov/sites/default/files/usao-ma/pages/attachments/2015/02/18/framework.pdf.

[599] Dorell, O. (April 25, 2013.). "Mosque that Boston suspects attended has radical ties." *USA Today.* Retrieved February 9, 2016 from http://www.usatoday.com/story/news/nation/2013/04/23/boston-mosque-radicals/2101411/.

[600] CBS News. (April 23, 2013.) "Dzhokhar and Tamerlan: A Profile of the Tsarnaev Brothers.". *Forty Eight Hours.* Retrieved February 9, 2016 from http://www.cbsnews.com/news/dzhokhar-and-tamerlan-a-profile-of-the-tsarnaev-brothers/.

[601] McPhee, M. (July 3, 2014.). "Before Boston Attack, Alleged Bomber Posed with Black Flag of Jihad at Local Mosque." *ABC News.* Retrieved February 9, 2016 from http://abcnews.go.com/Blotter/boston-attack-alleged-bomber-posed-black-flag-jihad/story?id=24399566.

[602] Qutb, S. (1964) *Milestones*. Kazi Publications. Retrieved February 9, 2016 from http://majalla.org/books/2005/qutb-nilestone.pdf.

[603] Inam, S. (November 11, 2015.) "Fighting for Social Justice – Two Sides to the Same Coin." *Patheos*. Retrieved February 9, 2016 from http://www.patheos.com/blogs/altmuslim/2015/11/fighting-for-social-justice-two-sides-of-the-same-coin/.

[604] "Saif Inam." (n.d.). "Board and Staff: Saif Inam" *Muslim Public Affairs Council*. Retrieved February 9, 2016 from http://www.mpac.org/about/staff-board/saif-inam.php.

[605] Solway, D. (April, 12, 2010.). "The Return of Tariq Ramadan." *Front Page*. Retrieved February 9, 2016 from https://web.archive.org/web/20120121024459/http://frontpagemag.com/2010/04/12/the-return-of-tariq-ramadan/.

[606] Johnson, B. (February 18, 2015.) "DHS Secretary: Administration Should Give Voice to Plight of Muslims Living in this Country." *PJ Media*. Retrieved February 9, 2016 from https://pjmedia.com/blog/dhs-secretary-administration-should-give-voice-to-plight-of-muslims-living-in-this-country.

[607] Ricciuti, J. (December, 2014.). *Groupthink: A Significant Threat to the Homeland Security of the United States*. United States: Naval Postgraduate School.

[608] Holder, E. (September 15, 2014.) "Attorney General Holder Announces Pilot Projects to Counter Violent Extremism in Communities Nationwide." U.S. *Department of Justice*. Retrieved February 9, 2016 from http://www.justice.gov/opa/video/countering-violent-extremism.

[609] Sperry, P. (September 7, 2014.). "Boston bombers' mosque tied to ISIS." *The New York Post*. Retrieved February 9, 2016 from http://nypost.com/2014/09/07/jihadi-behind-beheading-videos-linked-to-notorious-us-mosque/.

[610] Mauro, R. (December 10, 2013.) "Islamic Society of Boston." *The Clarion Project*. Retrieved February 9, 2016 from http://www.clarionproject.org/analysis/islamic-society-boston.

[611] MSA West (February 21, 2015). "Muslim Student Associations Across CA Against Federal Government's Countering Violent Extremism Programs." *MSA West*. Retrieved February 9, 2016 from http://us4.campaign-archive2.com/?u=30d739eaae2442c8d20aad278&id=25a5c44b43&e=%5bUNIQID.

[612] Espinoza, A. (May 13, 2010.) "St. Cloud school officials say harassment complaints not valid." *MPR News*. Retrieved February 9, 2016 from http://www.mprnews.org/story/2010/05/13/st-cloud-harassment-complaints.

[613] IPT News (n.d.). "Cherri, Abdulrahman, et al. v. Mueller, Robert, et al." *The Investigative Project on Terrorism*. Retrieved February 9, 2016 from http://www.investigativeproject.org/case/623/cherri-et-al-v-mueller-et-al.

[614] GSN News (May 5, 2011). "DHS to investigate CBP's interviews of Muslims." (2011, May 5). *GSN: Government Security News*. Retrieved February 9, 2016 from http://gsnmagazine.com/article/23202/dhs_investigate_cbp%E2%80%99s_interviews_muslims.

[615] "Insan al-Kamil, al-." (n.d.)."Definition of Insan al-Kamil, al-." *Oxford Islamic Studies*. Retrieved February 9, 2016 from http://www.oxfordislamicstudies.com/article/opr/t125/e1040.

[616] Levy, J. (April 11, 2010.) " Eternal Islamic Enmity toward the Jews." *American Thinker*. Retrieved February 9, 2016 from http://www.americanthinker.com/articles/2010/04/eternal_islamic_enmity_toward.html.

[617] "DeBlasio Letter". (September 21, 2015). "Letter from CAIR and ACLU Et Al. to New York City Mayor Bill DeBlasio." *Politico New York*. Retrieved February 9, 2016 from http://www.capitalnewyork.com/sites/default/files/092115%20Coalition%20Letter%20to%20Mayor%20Re%20CVE.pdf.

[618] Paybarah, A. (September 24, 2015,). "Activists urge DeBlasio to avoid federal counterterrorism program." *Politico New York*. Retrieved February 9, 2016 from http://www.capitalnewyork.com/article/city-hall/2015/09/8577559/activists-urge-de-blasio-avoid-federal-counterterrorism-program.

[619] "NYPD Counterterrorism Units." (n.d.). "NYPD Counterterrorism Units: Mission Statement" *New York Police Department, New York City*. Retrieved February 9, 2016 from http://www.nyc.gov/html/nypd/html/administration/counterterrorism_units.shtml.

[620] ACLU. (January 7, 2016). "Raza v. City of New York- Legal Challenge to NYPD Muslim Surveillance Program." *American Civil Liberties Union*. Retrieved February 9, 2016 from https://www.aclu.org/cases/raza-v-city-new-york-legal-challenge-nypd-muslim-surveillance-program.

[621] Patel, F. (March 8, 2011.). "Rethinking Radicalization." *Brennan Center for Justice*. Retrieved February 9, 2016 from https://www.brennancenter.org/publication/rethinking-radicalization.

[622] Ellison, K. (July 18, 2012.). "Ellison Response to Michelle Bachman Letter." *Minnesota State Government Website*. Retrieved February 9, 2016 from from https://ellison.house.gov/media-center/press-releases/ellison-response-to-michele-bachmanns-letter

[623] MacEoin, D. (Summer , 2010). "Keith Ellison's Stealth Jihad." *The Middle East Quarterly*. Retrieved February 9, 2016 from http://www.meforum.org/2756/keith-ellison-stealth-jihad

[624] IPT News. (April 22, 2012.) "Keith Ellison's Muslim Brotherhood Support." *The Investigative Project on Terrorism*. Retrieved February 9, 2016 from http://www.investigativeproject.org/1913/keith-ellisons-mb-support

[625] Miller, S. (July 18, 2012.). "McCain Defends Clinton Aide Huma Abedin Against Bachmann Accusation About Muslim Brotherhood." *ABC News*. Retrieved February 9, 2016 from http://abcnews.go.com/blogs/politics/2012/07/mccain-defends-clinton-aide-huma-abedin-against-house-gop-charges-of-muslim-brotherhood-scheme/

[626] McCarthy, A. (July 27, 2012.). "Huma Abedin's Brotherhood Ties Are Not Just A Family Affair." *PJ Media*. Retrieved February 9, 2016 from from https://pjmedia.com/andrewmccarthy/2012/07/27/huma-abedins-brotherhood-ties-are-not-just-a-family-affair/

[627] Lee, K. (July 19, 2012.) "Speaker Boehner is the Latest Republican to Defend Huma Abedin." *New York Daily News*. Retrieved February 9, 2016 from http://www.nydailynews.com/news/national/speaker-boehner-latest-top-republican-defend-huma-abedin-article-1.1117806

[628] Davs, S. (2012, July 20). "House Intel Leaders Disavow Bachmann Allegations." *USA Today*. Retrieved February 9, 2016 from http://content.usatoday.com/communities/onpolitics/post/2012/07/michele-bachmann-huma-abedin-rogers-ruppersberger/1#.Vp_nPrNRHcs

[629] Condon, S. (2012, July 19). "Bachmann Under Fire From More Republicans." *CBS News*. Retrieved February 9, 2016 from http://www.cbsnews.com/news/bachmann-under-fire-from-more-republicans/

[630] "H.R. 2899." (June 25, 2015.) "House Bill 2899: To amend the Homeland Security Act of 2002 to authorize the Office for Countering Violent Extremism." *U.S. House of Representatives*. Retrieved February 9, 2016 from https://www.congress.gov/114/bills/hr2899/BILLS-114hr2899ih.pdf

[631] Horowitz, D. (2015, July 20). "Why Won't GOP Chairman Mention Islamic Terror in New Bill?" *Conservative Review*. Retrieved February 9, 2016 from https://www.conservativereview.com/commentary/2015/07/why-wont-gop-chairman-mention-islamic-terror-in-new-bill

[632] Homeland Security Committee Press Release. (July 9, 2015.). "McCaul Leads Government Efforts to Counter Violent Extremism." *Homeland Security House Committee*. Retrieved February 9, 2016 from https://homeland.house.gov/press/mccaul-leads-government-efforts-counter-violent-extremism/

[633] "The Rise of Radicalization." (July 20, 2015.) "Hearing: The Rise of Radicalization: Is the U.S. Government Failing to Counter International and Domestic Terrorism?" *House Homeland Security Committee*. Retrieved February 9, 2016 from from https://homeland.house.gov/hearing/rise-radicalization-us-government-failing-counter-international-and-domestic-terrorism/

[634] Hughes, S. (July 15, 2015.) "Testimony of Seamus Hughes: The Rise of Radicalization: Is the U.S. Government Failing To Counter International and Domestic Terrorism?" *House Homeland Security Committee*. Retrieved February 9, 2016 from http://docs.house.gov/meetings/HM/HM00/20150715/103739/HHRG-114-HM00-Wstate-HughesS-20150715.pdf

[635] Pandith, F. (July 15, 2015). "Testimony of Farah Pandith: The Rise of Radicalization: Is the United States Government Failing to Counter International and Domestic Terrorism." *House Homeland Security Committee*. Retrieved February 9, 2016 from http://docs.house.gov/meetings/HM/HM00/20150715/103739/HHRG-114-HM00-Wstate-PandithF-20150715.pdf

[636] Cohen, R. (July 15, 2015.) "Testimony of Richard Cohen: The Rise of Radicalization: Is the U.S. Government Failing to Counter International and Domestic Terrorism. *House Homeland Security Committee*. Retrieved February 9, 2016 from http://docs.house.gov/meetings/HM/HM00/20150715/103739/HHRG-114-HM00-Wstate-CohenJ-20150715.pdf

[637] "Seamus Hughes" (n.d.) "Background of Seamus Hughes", *George Washington University: Center for Cyber and Homeland Security*. Retrieved February 9, 2016 from https://cchs.gwu.edu/seamus-hughes

[638] Pandith, F. (July 1, 2009.) "Special Briefing by Farah Pandith, Special Representative to Muslim Communities." *U.S. Department of State*. Retrieved February 9, 2016 from http://www.state.gov/r/pa/prs/ps/2009/july/125561.htm

[639] "Farah Pandith." (n.d.) "Biography: Farah Pandith." *Harvard University Kennedy School of Government*. Retrieved February 9, 2016 from http://www.iop.harvard.edu/farah-pandith

[640] "Farah Pandith Appointed." (n.d.) "Farah Pandith Appointed as Special Representative to Muslim Communities." *United States Department of State*. Retrieved February 9, 2016 from http://m.state.gov/md125492.htm

[641] Harvard University. The Prince Alwaleed Bin Talal Islamic Studies Program. *Harvard University*. Retrieved February 9, 2016 from http://www.islamicstudies.harvard.edu/

[642] "Islamic Studies Speakers" (n.d.). "Harvard University: The Prince Alwaleed Bin Talal Islamic Studies Program. Biography: Farah Pandith." *Harvard University*. Retrieved February 9, 2016 from http://www.islamicstudies.harvard.edu/conference/speakers/farah-pandith/

[643] SPLC (n.d.) "Biography: Richard Cohen, President of Southern Poverty Law Center." *Southern Poverty Law Center*. Retrieved February 9, 2016 from https://www.splcenter.org/about/staff/richard-cohen

[644] SPLC (n.d.) "Southern Poverty Law Center: Intelligence Report." *Southern Poverty Law Center Media*. Retrieved February 9, 2016 from https://www.splcenter.org/intelligence-report

[645] SPLC (n.d.) "Fighting Hate." *Southern Poverty Law Center*. Retrieved February 9, 2016 from https://www.splcenter.org/fighting-hate

[646] SPLC (n.d.) "Hate Watch." *Southern Poverty Law Center*. Retrieved February 9, 2016 from https://www.splcenter.org/hatewatch

[647] Steinback, R & Hermanson, B. (June 7, 2011). "The Anti-Muslim Inner Circle." *Southern Poverty Law Center*. Retrieved February 9, 2016 from https://www.splcenter.org/fighting-hate/intelligence-report/2011/anti-muslim-inner-circle

[648] MPAC. "Not Qualified: Exposing The Deception Behind America's Top 25 Pseudo Experts on Islam." (December 13, 2012.). Muslim Public Affairs Council. Retrieved February 9, 2016 from http://www.mpac.org/assets/docs/publications/MPAC-25-Pseudo-Experts-On-Islam.pdf

[649] Steinback, R. & Victore, J. (June 17, 2011.) "Jihad Against Islam." Southern Poverty Law Center. Retrieved February 9, 2016 from https://www.splcenter.org/fighting-hate/intelligence-report/2011/jihad-against-islam

[650] Stolberg, S. & Goodstein, L. (March 11, 2011.) "Domestic Terrorism Hearings Open With Contrasting Views on Danger." *New York Times*. Retrieved February 9, 2016 from http://www.nytimes.com/2011/03/11/us/politics/11king.html?_r=0

[651] Homeland Security Committee Press Release. (July 16, 2015.) "Bipartisan Support in Congress to Counter Terrorism." *House Homeland Security Committee*. Retrieved February 9, 2016 f from https://homeland.house.gov/press/bipartisan-support-congress-counter-violent-extremism/

[652] Horowitz, D. (July 20, 2015.) "Why Won't GOP Chairman Mention Islamic Terror in New Bill?" *Conservative Review*. Retrieved February 9, 2016 from https://www.conservativereview.com/commentary/2015/07/why-wont-gop-chairman-mention-islamic-terror-in-new-bill

[653] Howerton, J. (June 7, 2012.). "Eric Holder Duck's Congresses' Questions About Massive Terrorism Financing Trial." *The Blaze*. Retrieved February 9, 2016 from from http://www.theblaze.com/stories/2012/06/07/eric-holder-ducks-congresss-questions-about-massive-terrorism-financing-trial/

[654] Clinton, H. (2010). "Special Order Note." *Exercise of Discretionary Authority under Section 212(d)(3)(B)(i) of the Immigration and Nationality Act*. Retrieved February 9, 2016 from http://graphics8.nytimes.com/packages/pdf/world/clinton_statedeptorder_ramadanhabib.pdf.

[655] Judicial Watch. (January 21, 2010.) "Hillary Clinton Welcome Banned Islamic Radicals." *Judicial Watch*. Retrieved February 9, 2016 from http://www.judicialwatch.org/blog/2010/01/clinton-welcomes-banned-islamic-radicals/.

[656] IPT News. (n.d.). "Tariq Ramadan." *The Investigative Project on Terrorism*. Retrieved February 9, 2016 from http://www.investigativeproject.org/profile/111/tariq-ramadan.

[657] Le Quesne, N. (December 11, 2000.) "Trying to Bridge a Great Divide." *Time Magazine*. Retrieved February 9, 2016 from http://content.time.com/time/magazine/article/0,9171,998765,00.html.

[658] "ACLU. (n.d.). "Biography of Adam Habib." *American Civil Liberties Union*. Retrieved February 9, 2016 from https://www.aclu.org/biography-adam-habib.

[659] Lyall, S. (January 20, 2010.) "In Shifts, U.S. Lifts Visa Curbs on Professor." *The New York Times*. Retrieved February 9, 2016 from http://www.nytimes.com/2010/01/21/world/europe/21london.html.

[660] Swiss Info. (January 20, 2010.) "Clinton end US visa ban on Tariq Ramadan." *Swissinfo*. Retrieved February 9, 2016 from http://www.swissinfo.ch/eng/clinton-ends-us-visa-ban-on-tariq-ramadan/8131190.

[661] Rothschild, M. (June 26, 2006.) "Tariq Ramadan Wins One." *The Progressive*. Retrieved February 9, 2016 from http://www.progressive.org/mag_mc062606.

[662] "Attachment A" (n.d.) "Attachment A: List of Unindicted Co-Conspirators and/or Joint Venturers." *United States vs. Holy Land Foundation et al*. Retrieved February 9, 2016 from https://www.investigativeproject.org/documents/case_docs/423.pdf

[663] IQRA (January 20, 2010.) "U.S. Government Lifts Ban on Tariq Ramadan." *IQRA*. Retrieved February 9, 2016 from http://iqra.ca/2010/us-government-lifts-ban-on-tariq-ramadan/.

[664] ACLU (n.d.). "National Security Project." *American Civil Liberties Union*. Retrieved February 9, 2016 from https://www.aclu.org/issues/national-security.

[665] Shephard, M. (January 15, 2013.). "How a lawyer from Canada became a leading critic of U.S. national security policies." *The Star*. Retrieved February 9, 2016 from http://www.thestar.com/news/world/2013/01/15/how_a_lawyer_from_canada_became_a_leading_critic_of_us_national_security_policies.html.

[666] MAS-PACE. (n.d.). "Home." *Muslim American Society Public Affairs and Civic Engagement*. Retrieved February 9, 2016 from http://www.maspace.org/.

[667] MAS-PACE. (n.d.). "Biography: Congressman Andre Carson." *Muslim American Society Public Affairs and Civic Engagement*. Retrieved February 9, 2016 from http://www.maspace.org/speakers-bios.html.

[668] ADL (September 17, 2014.) "Profile: American Muslims for Palestine." *Anti-Defamation League*. Retrieved February 9, 2016 from http://www.adl.org/israel-international/anti-israel-activity/profile-american-muslims-for.html.

[669] AMP. (n.d.) "Home" *American Muslims for Palestine*. Retrieved February 9, 2016 from http://www.ampalestine.org/.

[670] Johnson, J. and Kerry, J. (February 5, 2014.) "Exercise of Authority Under Section 212(d)(3)(B)(i) of the Immigration and Nationality Act." *Federal Register*. Retrieved February 9, 2016 from https://www.federalregister.gov/articles/2014/02/05/2014-02357/exercise-of-authority-under-section-212d3bi-of-the-immigration-and-nationality-act.

[671] "8 U.S.C. 1182." (n.d.). *U.S. Code Title 8 Chapter 12.II.III Sec 1182*. Retrieved February 9, 2016 from https://www.gpo.gov/fdsys/pkg/USCODE-2014-title8/html/USCODE-2014-title8-chap12-subchapII-partII-sec1182.htm.

[672] Ibid.

[673] Ibid.

[674] Ibid.

[675] Ibid.

[676] Ghazali, A. (n.d.) "American Muslims six years after 9/11." *Islamic Research Foundation International, Inc.* Retrieved February 9, 2016 from http://www.irfi.org/articles/articles_1401_1450/american_muslims_six_years_after.htm.

[677] "Indictment"(July 26, 2004.) *U.S. v. Holy Land Foundation et al.* Retrieved February 9, 2016 from http://www.investigativeproject.org/documents/case_docs/74.pdf.

[678] MPAC Press Release (July 15, 2009). "Calling on Treasury Dept. to Address Zakat-Giving Challenges Ahead of Ramadan." *Muslim Public Affairs Council.* Retrieved February 9, 2016 from http://www.mpac.org/issues/civil-rights/calling-on-treasury-dept.-to-address-zakat-giving-challenges-ahead-of-ramadan.php.

[679] Shariah Finance Watch. (August 28, 2012). "How Zakat Funds Jihad." *Center for Security Policy.* Retrieved February 9, 2016from http://www.shariahfinancewatch.org/blog/2012/08/28/how-zakat-funds-jihad/

[680] Pavlich, K. (September 11, 2015.). "Homeland Security Chairman Warns U.S. Doesn't Have Proper Vetting System for 10,000 Syrian Refugees." *Town Hall.* Retrieved February 9, 2016 from http://townhall.com/tipsheet/katiepavlich/2015/09/11/house-homeland-security-chairman-warns-us-doesnt-have-proper-vetting-system-for-10000-syrian-refugees-n2050931?utm_source=thdailypm&utm_medium=email&utm_campaign=nl_pm&newsletterad=http://www.bustle.com/.

[681] Hohmann, L. (October 1, 2015.) "Feds Admit: "We Have No Outside Dats " on Syrian Refugees." *WND.* Retrieved February 9, 2016 from http://www.wnd.com/2015/10/feds-admit-we-have-no-outside-data-on-syrian-refugees/.

[682] Emrich, M and Strack, B. (October 1, 2015.) "Hearing on 'Refugee Admissions, Fiscal Year 2016' before the Senate Committee on the Judiciary." *U.S. Citizenship and Immigration Services.* Retrieved February 9, 2016 from http://www.uscis.gov/tools/resources/hearing-refugee-admissions-fiscal-year-2016-senate-committee-judiciary-october-1-2015-chief-refugee-affairs-division-barbara-l-strack-and-acting-associate-director-matthew-d-emrich.

[683] USCIS. (n.d.) "Home." *U.S. Citizenship and Immigration Services.* Retrieved February 9, 2016 from https://www.us-immigration.com/.

[684] ILW. (October 2, 2015.) "News: USCIS Senate Hearing Testimony on FY2016 Refugee Admissions." *ILW.* Retrieved February 9, 2016 from http://discuss.ilw.com/content.php?5111-News-USCIS-Senate-Hearing-Testimony-on-FY2016-Refugee-Admissions.

[685] Steinbach, M. (February 11, 2015.) "Statement Before the House Committee on Homeland Security." *FBI.* Retrieved February 9, 2016 from https://www.fbi.gov/news/testimony/the-urgent-threat-of-foreign-fighters-and-homegrown-terror.

[686] AFP. (February 11, 2015.) "US lacks intel to vet Syrian refugees." *Yahoo News.* Retrieved February 9, 2016 from http://news.yahoo.com/us-lacks-intel-vet-syrian-045246525.html.

[687] Strack, B. (December 4, 2012). "Written testimony of U.S. Citizenship and Immigration Services, Refugee, Asylum & International Operations Directorate Refugee Affairs Division Chief Barbara Strack for a House Committee on Homeland Security, Subcommittee on Counterterrorism and Intelligence hearing titled 'Terrorist Exploitation of Refugee Programs'." *U.S. Department of Homeland Security.* Retrieved February 9, 2016 from http://www.dhs.gov/news/2012/12/04/written-testimony-uscis-house-homeland-security-subcommittee-counterterrorism-and.

[688] NDU. (n.d.). "Home." *Joint Forces Staff College, National Defense University.* Retrieved February 9, 2016 from http://jfsc.ndu.edu/.

[689] Shachtman, N. and Ackerman, S. (May 10, 2012.). "U.S. Military Taught Officers: Use "Hiroshima" Tactics for "Total War" on Islam." *Wired.* Retrieved February 9, 2016 from http://www.wired.com/2012/05/total-war-islam/.

[690] Ackerman, S. (May 10, 2012.) "Top U.S. Officer: Stop This Total War On Islam Talk." Retrieved http://www.wired.com/2012/05/dempsey-islam-irresponsible/.

[691] Shachtman, N. and Spencer Ackerman. (May 10, 2012.). "U.S. Military Taught Officers: Use "Hiroshima" Tactics for "Total War" on Islam." *Wired.* Retrieved February 9, 2016 from http://www.wired.com/2012/05/total-war-islam/.

[692] Ackerman, S. (April 24, 2012.) "Exclusive: Senior U.S. General Orders Top-To-Bottom Review of Military's Islam Training." *Wired.* Retrieved February 9, 2016 from http://www.wired.com/2012/04/military-islam-training/.

[693] Ackerman, S. (November 29, 2011.) "Obama Orders Government to Clean Up Terror Training." *Wired.* Retrieved http://www.wired.com/2011/11/obama-islamophobia-review/.

[694] "Ackerman, S. (September 14, 2011.). "FBI Teaches Agents: Mainstream Muslims are Violent, Radical." *Wired.* Retrieved February 9, 2016 from http://www.wired.com/2011/09/fbi-muslims-radical/.

[695] Ackerman, S. (2012, March 28). "FBI Taught Agents They Could "Bend or Suspend the Law."" *Wired.* Retrieved http://www.wired.com/2012/03/fbi-bend-suspend-law/.

[696] Ackerman, S. (July 27, 2011.). "FBI 'Islam 101' Guide Depicted Muslims as 7th-Century Simpletons." *Wired.* Retrieved February 9, 2016 from http://www.wired.com/2011/07/fbi-islam-101-guide/.

[697] Burki, S. (2015). *The Politics of State Intervention: Gender politics in Pakistan, Afghanistan, and Iran.* United States: Lexington Books.

[698] Trifkovic, S. (2007). *The Sword of the Prophet: Islam; History, Theology, Impact on the World.* United States: Regina Orthodox Press.

[699] CAIR Press Release (May 10, 2012.) "CAIR Asks Pentagon to Dismiss Officer Who Taught "Total War" on Islam." *PR Newswire.* Retrieved February 9, 2016 from http://www.prnewswire.com/news-releases/cair-asks-pentagon-to-dismiss-officer-who-taught-total-war-on-islam-150986605.html.

[700] ISCSC. (October 19, 2011.) "Community Letter to John Brennan Re: FBI Training" *Shura Council.* Retrieved February 9, 2016 from http://www.shuracouncil.org/Shura/Community_letter_to_Brennan_re_FBI_trainings_10-19-11.pdf.

[701] Alexander, D. (June 20, 2012.). "Military instructor suspended over Islam course." *Reuters.* Retrieved February 9, 2016 from http://www.reuters.com/article/us-usa-defense-islam-idUSBRE85J0XJ20120620.

[702] Shachtman, N. and Spencer Ackerman. (2012, May 10). "U.S. Military Taught Officers: Use Hiroshima Tactics for Total War on Islam." *Wired.* Retrieved February 9, 2016 from http://www.wired.com/2012/05/total-war-islam/.

[703] Thomas More Law Center (December , 2011.) "Bombshell- Pentagon Buries the Truth- Newly Revealed Document Vindicated Army Lt. Colonel Matthew Dooley in Anti-Islam Controversy." *Thomas More Law Center.* Retrieved February 9, 2016 from https://www.thomasmore.org/news/bombshell-pentagon-buries-the-truth-newly-revealed-document-vindicates-army-lt-colonel-matthew-dooley-in-anti-islam-controversy/.

[704] Thomas More Law Center. (December 2, 2011.) Thomas More Law Center "NDU's Response to Joint Staff Action Request." (December 2, 2011.) *Thomas More Law Center.* Retrieved February 9, 2016

from https://web.archive.org/web/20140720090043/http://www.thomasmore.org/sites/default/files/files/NDU%20Response%20to%20Screening%20Process%20for%20CVE%20Trainers%20and%20Speakers(2).pdf.

[705] Thomas More Law Center (December, 2011.) "Bombshell- Pentagon Buries the Truth- Newly Revealed Document Vindicated Army Lt. Colonel Matthew Dooley in Anti-Islam Controversy." *Thomas More Law Center.* Retrieved February 9, 2016 from https://www.thomasmore.org/news/bombshell-pentagon-buries-the-truth-newly-revealed-document-vindicates-army-lt-colonel-matthew-dooley-in-anti-islam-controversy/.

[706] LA Times. (December 9, 2015.) "San Bernardino shooting updates." *Los Angeles Times.* Retrieved February 9, 2016 from http://www.latimes.com/local/lanow/la-me-ln-san-bernardino-shooting-live-updates-htmlstory.html

[707] Diamond, J. (December 2, 2015). "Obama calls for gun reforms in wake of San Bernardino shooting," *Cable News Network.* http://www.cnn.com/2015/12/02/politics/san-bernardino-shooting-obama/index.html

[708] Pollack, J. (December 2, 2015.) "Updated: San Bernardino Shooting Day Three: Confirmed Terror." *Breitbart.com.* Retrieved February 9, 2016 from http://www.breitbart.com/big-government/2015/12/02/san-bernadino-mass-shooting/

[709] Stanton, J. (December 3, 2015.) "Loretta Lynch: "Actions Predicated On Violent Talk" Toward Muslims Will Be Prosecuted," *Buzzfeed.com* Retrieved February 9, 2016 from http://www.buzzfeed.com/johnstanton/loretta-lynch-actions-predicated-on-violent-talk-toward-musl#.qcErEBrxg

[710] C-SPAN. (December 3, 2015.) "Attorney General Loretta Lynch at Muslim Advocates Dinner." *C-SPAN.org.* Retrieved February 9, 2016 from http://www.c-span.org/video/?401446-1/attorney-general-loretta-lynch-remarks-muslim-advocates

[711] Thomas, D. (December 8, 2015.) "Analysis: Why Muslims should not have to apologize for San Bernardino shooting." *Los Angeles Times.* Retrieved February 9, 2016 from http://www.latimes.com/local/lanow/la-me-muslims-apologize-san-bernardino-20151205-story.html

[712] Fox News. (December 4, 2015.) "Muslim leader from CAIR tells CNN America bears some blame for terror attacks." *Fox News.com* Retrieved February 9, 2016, from http://www.foxnews.com/us/2015/12/04/muslim-leader-from-cair-tells-cnn-america-bears-some-blame-for-terror-attacks.html?intcmp=hpbt2

[713] Obama, B. (December 5, 2015). "Remarks of President Barack Obama." *White House.gov* Retrieved February 9, 2016 from https://www.whitehouse.gov/the-press-office/2015/12/05/weekly-address-we-will-not-be-terrorized

[714] White House. (December 5, 2015). "Readout of the President's Update on the Investigation into the San Bernardino Shootings." *White House.gov.* Retrieved February 9, 2016 from https://www.whitehouse.gov/the-press-office/2015/12/05/readout-presidents-update-investigation-san-bernardino-shootings

[715] Johnson, J. (December 7, 2015). "Remarks By Secretary Of Homeland Security Jeh C. Johnson At The Adams Center - As Prepared For Delivery." *U.S. Department of Homeland Security.* http://www.dhs.gov/news/2015/12/07/remarks-secretary-homeland-security-jeh-c-johnson-adams-center-prepared-delivery

[716] Munro, N. (October 21, 2011). "Progressives, Islamists huddle at Justice Department." *The Daily Caller.* Retrieved February 9, 2016 from http://dailycaller.com/2011/10/21/progressives-islamists-huddle-at-justice-department/?print=1.

[717] Fox News (December 12.) "Whistleblower: DHS Pulled Plug on Surveillance That Could've ID'ed CA Terrorists." *Fox News.com.* Retrieved February 9, 2016 from http://insider.foxnews.com/2015/12/10/whistleblower-says-he-could-have-prevented-ca-attack-if-government-didnt-cut-funding.

[718] Haney, P (February 5, 2016). "DHS ordered me to scrub records of Muslims with terror ties," The Hill.com Retrieved February 9, 2016 from http://thehill.com/blogs/congress-blog/homeland-security/268282-dhs-ordered-me-to-scrub-records-of-muslims-with-terror

[719] Haney, P. (December 16, 2015). "Administration nixed probe into Southern California jihadists," *The Hill.com* Retrieved from http://thehill.com/blogs/congress-blog/homeland-security/263284-administration-nixed-probe-into-southern-california

[720] Haney, P (February 5, 2016). "DHS ordered me to scrub records of Muslims with terror ties," The Hill.com Retrieved February 9, 2016 from http://thehill.com/blogs/congress-blog/homeland-security/268282-dhs-ordered-me-to-scrub-records-of-muslims-with-terror

[721] Haney, P (February 5, 2016). "DHS ordered me to scrub records of Muslims with terror ties," The Hill.com Retrieved February 9, 2016 from http://thehill.com/blogs/congress-blog/homeland-security/268282-dhs-ordered-me-to-scrub-records-of-muslims-with-terror

[722] Lehrer, J. (2010, January 5). "Obama: U.S. Failed to Connect the Dots in Bomb Plot." *PBS.* Retrieved from http://www.pbs.org/newshour/bb/terrorism-jan-june10-obama1_01-05/.

[723] Haney, P (February 5, 2016). "DHS ordered me to scrub records of Muslims with terror ties," The Hill.com Retrieved February 9, 2016 from http://thehill.com/blogs/congress-blog/homeland-security/268282-dhs-ordered-me-to-scrub-records-of-muslims-with-terror

[724] Rossamondo, J. (December 28, 2015). "Obama White House Turns To Islamists Who Demonize Terror Investigations) *The Investigative Project on Terrorism.* Retrieved February 9, 2016 from http://www.investigativeproject.org/5107/obama-white-house-turns-to-islamists-who-demonize

[725] Obama, B. (December 6, 2015). "Address to the Nation by the President." *The White House.gov.* Retrieved February 9, 2016 from https://www.whitehouse.gov/the-press-office/2015/12/06/address-nation-president

[726] Rossamondo, J. (December 28, 2015). "Obama White House Turns To Islamists Who Demonize Terror Investigations) *The Investigative Project on Terrorism.* Retrieved February 9, 2016 from http://www.investigativeproject.org/5107/obama-white-house-turns-to-islamists-who-demonize

[727] Rossamondo, J. (December 28, 2015). "Obama White House Turns To Islamists Who Demonize Terror Investigations) *The Investigative Project on Terrorism.* Retrieved February 9, 2016 from http://www.investigativeproject.org/5107/obama-white-house-turns-to-islamists-who-demonize

[728] "H.R. Bill 560". (December 17, 2015). "House of Representatives Bill No. 560 Condemning violence, bigotry, and hateful rhetoric towards Muslims in the United States." *The House of Representatives.* Retrieved February 9, 2016 from https://www.congress.gov/bill/114th-congress/house-resolution/569/text

[729] "UN.Res. 16/18". (April 12, 2011). "UN Resolution 16/18 Adopted by the Human Rights Council." *United Nations Human Rights Council.* Retrieved February 9, 2016 from http://www.ifex.org/international/2011/11/15/un_resolution_16_18.pdf.

[730] Nakashima, E. (January 7, 2016). "Obama's top national security officials to meet with Silicon Valley CEOs" *Washington Post*. Retrieved February 9, 2016 from https://www.washingtonpost.com/world/national-security/obamas-top-national-security-officials-to-meet-with-silicon-valley-ceos/2016/01/07/178d95ca-b586-11e5-a842-0feb51d1d124_story.html

[731] USG. (January 8, 2016). "U.S. Government Meeting with Technology Executives on Counterterrorism" *Washington Post*. Retrieved February 9, 2016 from http://apps.washingtonpost.com/g/documents/politics/us-government-meeting-with-technology-executives-on-counterterrorism/1842/

[732] State Department Press Release, "Fact Sheet: A New Center for Global Engagement." *U.S. Department of State*. Retrieved February 9, 2016 from "http://www.state.gov/r/pa/prs/ps/2016/01/251066.htm

[733] Rita Katz, (September 16, 2014). "The State Department's Twitter War with ISIS is Embarassing." *Time Magazine*. Retrieved February 9, 2016 from http://time.com/3387065/isis-twitter-war-state-department/

[734] McCarthy, A. (January 4, 2016). "Islam v. Free Speech: Twitter Surrenders." *National Review Online*. Retrieved February 9, 2016 from http://www.nationalreview.com/article/429190/islam-twitter-and-free-speech

[735] Cartes, P. (February 9, 2016). "Announcing the Twitter Trust & Safety Council." *Twitter.com* Retrieved February 9, 2016 from https://blog.twitter.com/2016/announcing-the-twitter-trust-safety-council

[736] ACLU. (January 7, 2016). "Raza v. City of New York- Legal Challenge to NYPD Muslim Surveillance Program." *American Civil Liberties Union*. Retrieved February 9, 2016 from https://www.aclu.org/cases/raza-v-city-new-york-legal-challenge-nypd-muslim-surveillance-program.

[737] Silber M and Bhatt, (August 13, 2007). "Radicalization in the West: The Homegrown Threat." *NYPD Intelligence Division*. Retrieved February 9, 2016 from http://www.judicialwatch.org/wp-content/uploads/2016/01/NYPD_Report-Radicalization_in_the_West.pdf

Made in the USA
Middletown, DE
06 March 2016